Bartholomew Sastrow
Being The Memoirs Of
A German Burgomaster

by

Bartholomäus Sastrow

Bartholomew Sastrow
Being The Memoirs Of
A German Burgomaster
by Bartholomäus Sastrow

ISBN: 978-93-60462-50-5

Published by

DOUBLE 9 BOOKS

2/13-B, Ansari Road
Daryaganj, New Delhi – 110002
info@double9books.com
www.double9books.com
Tel. 011-40042856

ABOUT THE AUTHOR

Bartholomäus Sastrow, also known as Bartholomew, was a German official, notary, and mayor of Stralsund who lived from August 21, 1520, until February 7, 1603. Written in 1595 at the age of seventy-five, he left behind an autobiography that is significant both historically and culturally. At Greifswald's Lange Straße 54, there is a plaque designating the location of his birth. The son of merchant Nicolaus Sastrow (born 1488) and his wife Anna Schmiterlow, a niece of Stralsund mayor Nikolaus Smiterlow, Bartholomäus Sastrow was born in Greifswald. Prior to relocating to Greifswald in 1487, his grandfather Hans Sastrow (murdered in 1494) worked as a tenant farmer in Quilow. Three of eight children, Sastrow's mother and four younger sisters perished in an epidemic in 1549–1550. The only other long-living family members were him, his oldest sister Anna (1516–1594), who was married to Greifswald Mayor Peter Frubose, and their brother Karsten, also known as Christian (1530–1580). At the age of 29 or 30, Johannes, his older brother, passed away. He went on to become a lawyer, provost, and poet. About 1523, his father Nicolaus was compelled to leave Greifswald after killing a well-respected man in a dispute.

CONTENTS

INTRODUCTION

If we wish to understand the pedestrian side of German life in the sixteenth century, I know of no better document than the autobiography of Bartholomew Sastrow. This hard-headed, plain-spoken Pomeranian notary cannot indeed be classed among the great and companionable writers of memoirs. Here are no genial portraits, no sweet-tempered and mellow confidings of the heart such as comfortable men and women are wont to distil in a comfortable age. The times were fierce, and passion ran high and deep. One might as well expect to extract amiability from the rough granite of an Icelandic saga. There is no delicacy, no charm, no elevation of tone in these memoirs. Everything is seen through plain glass, but seen distinctly in hard and fine outlines, and reported with an objectivity which would be consistently scientific, were it not for some quick touches of caustic humour, and the stored hatreds of an active, unpopular and struggling life. Nobody very readily sympathizes with bitter or with prosperous men, and when this old gentleman took up his pen to write, he had become both prosperous and bitter. He had always been a hard hitter, and at the age of seventy-five set himself down to compose a fighting apologia. If the ethics are those of Mr. Tulliver, senior, we must not be surprised. Is not the blood-feud one of the oldest of Teutonic institutions?

I frankly confess that I do not find Mr. Bartholomew Sastrow very congenial company, though I am ready to acknowledge that he had some conspicuous merits. Many good men have been naughty boys at school, and it is possible that even distinguished philanthropists have tippled brandy while Orbilius was nodding. If so, an episode detailed in these memoirs may be passed over by the lenient reader, all the more readily since the Sastrovian oats do not appear to have been very wildly or copiously sown. It is clear that the young man fought poverty with pluck and tenacity. He certainly had a full measure of Teutonic industry, and it argues no little character in a man past thirty years of age to attend the lectures of university professors in order to repair the defects of an early education. I also suspect that any litigant who retained Sastrow's services would have been more than satisfied with this swift and able transactor of business, who appears to have had all the combativeness of Bishop Burnet, with none of his indiscretion.

He was just the kind of man who always rows his full weight and more than his weight in a boat. But, save for his vigorous hates, he was a prosaic fellow, given to self-gratulation, who never knew romance, and married his housemaid at the age of seventy-eight.

A modern German writer is much melted by Sastrow's Protestantism, and apparently finds it quite a touching spectacle. Sastrow was of course a Lutheran, and believed in devils as fervently as his great master. He also conceived it to be part of the general scheme of things that the Sastrows and their kinsmen, the Smiterlows, should wax fat and prosper, while all the plagues of Egypt and all the afflictions of Job should visit those fiends incarnate, the Horns, the Brusers and the Lorbeers. For some reason, which to me is inscrutable, but which was as plain as sunlight to Sastrow, a superhuman apparition goes out of its way to help a young Pomeranian scribe, who upon his own showing is anything but a saint, while the innocent maidservant of a miser is blown up with six other persons no less blameless than herself, to enforce the desirability of being free with one's money. This, however, is the usual way in which an egoist digests the popular religion.

Bartholomew Sastrow was born at Greifswald, a prosperous Hanseatic town, in 1520. The year of his birth is famous in the history of German Protestantism, for it witnessed the publication of Luther's three great Reformation tracts--the *Appeal to the Christian Nobility of the German Nation*, the *Babylonish Captivity*, and the *Freedom of a Christian Man*. It seemed in that year as if the whole of Germany might be brought to make common cause against the Pope. The clergy, the nobility, the towns, the peasants all had their separate cause of quarrel with the old régime, and to each of these classes in turn Luther addressed his powerful appeal. For a moment puritan and humanist were at one, and the printing presses of Germany turned out a stream of literature against the abuses of the papal system. The movement spread so swiftly, especially in the north, that it seemed a single spontaneous popular outburst. But the harmony was soon broken. The rifts in the political and social organization of Germany were too deep to be spanned by any appeal to merely moral considerations. The Emperor Charles V, himself half-Spanish, set his face against a movement which was directly antagonistic to the Imperial tradition. The peasants revolted, committed excesses, and were ruthlessly crushed, and the violence of anabaptists and ignorant men threw discredit on the Lutheran cause. Then, too, dogmatic differences began to reveal themselves within the circle of the reformers themselves. There were disputes as to the exact significance and philosophic explanation of the Lord's Supper. A conference was held at Marburg, in 1529, under the auspices of Philip of Hesse, with a view to adjusting the differences between the divines of Saxony and Switzerland, but Luther and Zwingli failed to arrive at a compromise. The Lutheran and the Reformed Churches now definitely separated, and the divisions of the Protestants were the opportunity of the Catholic Church. The emperor tried in vain to reconcile Germany to the old faith. Rival theologians met, disputed, formulated creeds in the presence of temporal princes and their armed retainers. In 1530 the Diet of Augsburg forbade Protestant teaching and ordered the restoration of church property. Then a Protestant league was signed at Smalkald by John of Saxony, by Hesse, Brunswick-Luneberg, Anhalt, and several towns, and the emperor was defied. This was in 1531. It was the beginning of the religious wars of Germany, the beginning of that tremendous duel which lasted till the peace of Westphalia in 1648, the duel between the League of Smalkald and Charles V, between Gustavus Adolphus and Wallenstein, between the Protestant North and the Catholic South.

In the initial stage of this combat the great military event was the rout of the Smalkaldic allies at Muhlberg, in April, 1547, where Charles captured John Frederic of Saxony, transferred his dominions--save only a few scattered territories in Thuringia--to his ally, Maurice, and reduced all north Germany save the city of Magdeburg. It seemed for a moment as if this battle might decide the contest. Charles summoned a Diet at Augsburg in 1548, and carried all his proposals without opposition. He strengthened his political position by the reconstitution of the Imperial Chamber, by the organization of the Netherlands into a circle of the empire, and by the formation of a new military treasury. He obtained the consent of the Diet to a religious compromise called the Interim which, while insisting on the seven sacraments in the Catholic sense, vaguely agreed to the Lutheran doctrine of justification by faith, and declared that the two questions of the Communion in both kinds and the celibacy of clergy were to be left till the summoning of a free Christian council. The strict Lutheran party--and Pomerania was a stronghold of strict Lutheranism--regarded the Interim as a base betrayal of Protestant interests. Their pamphleteers called it the *Interitum*, or the death-blow, and the conversion of a prince like Joachim of Brandenburg to such a scheme was regarded as an ominous sign for the future.

In reality, however, the success of the emperor rested upon the most brittle foundations. That he was chilly, reserved, un-German, and therefore unpopular was something, but not nearly all. The princes of Germany had conquered practical independence in the thirteenth century, and were jealous of their prerogatives. The Hanseatic towns formed a republican confederacy in the north, corresponding to the Swiss confederacy in the south. There was no adequate central machinery, and the Jesuit order was only just preparing to enter upon its career of German victories. The

Spanish troops made themselves detestable, outraging women--a dire offence in a nation so domestic as Germany--and there was standing feud between the famous Castilian infantry and the German lansquenets. The popes did not like the emperor's favourite remedy of a council, and busily thwarted his ecclesiastical schemes. Henry II of France was on the watch for German allies against a powerful rival. The allies were ready. A great spiritual movement can never be stifled by the issue of one battle. For good or evil, men had taken sides; interests intellectual, moral, and material had already been invested either in the one cause or the other; there had been brutal iconoclasm; there had been ardent preaching, so simple and moving that ignorant women understood and wept; there had been close and stubborn dogmatic controversy; there had been the shedding of blood, and the upheavals in towns, and the building of a new church system, and the growth of a new religious literature. Almost a whole generation had now been consumed in this controversy, a controversy which touched all lives, and cemented or divided families. The children were reading Luther's Bible, and singing Luther's hymns, and learning Luther's short catechism. Could it be expected that such a river should suddenly lose itself in the sand? Nevertheless there is something surprising in the quick revolution of the story. In 1550 Maurice of Saxony intrigues with the Protestants, and in the following year definitely goes over to their side. In 1552 the emperor has to flee for his life, and the Peace of Passau seals the victory of the Protestant cause.

One of the first provinces to be conquered for Lutheranism was the duchy of Pomerania. John Bugenhagen, himself a Pomeranian and the historian of Pomerania, was the chief apostle of this northern region, and those who visit the Baltic churches will often see his sable portrait hanging side by side with Huss and Luther on the whitewashed walls. Sastrow gives us an excellent picture of the various forces which co-operated with the teaching of Bugenhagen to effect the change. In Eastern Pomerania there was the violent propaganda of Dr. Amandus, who wanted a clean sweep of images, princes, and established powers. There was the democratic movement in Stralsund, led by the turbulent Rolof Moller, who, accusing the council of malversation, revolutionized the constitution of his city. There was the mob of workmen who were only too glad of an excuse to plunder the priests and break the altars. But side by side with greed and violence there was the moral revolt against "the fables, the absurdities, and the impious lies" of the pulpit, and against the vices of priest and monk. The recollection of the early days of Puritan enthusiasm, when the fathers of the Protestant movement preached the gospel to large crowds in the open air, as, for instance, under "St. George's churchyard elm" at Stralsund, remained graven on many a lowly calendar. Even the texts of these sermons were remembered as epochs in spiritual life. Sastrow records how, ceding to the request of a great number of burgesses, Mr. Ketelhot (being detained in the port of Stralsund by contrary winds), preached upon Matthew xi. 28: "Come unto Me, all ye that labour and are heavy laden, and I will give you rest"; and then upon John xvi. 23: "Verily, verily, I say unto you, Whatsoever ye shall ask the Father in My name, He will give it you"; and, finally: "Go ye therefore and teach all nations." The general pride in civic monuments proved to be stronger than the iconoclastic mood. Certainly the high altar in the Nicolai Kirche at Stralsund--probably the most elaborate specimen of late fifteenth-century wood carving which still survives in Germany--would have received a short shrift from Cromwell's Ironsides.

It was Burgomaster Nicholas Smiterlow, of Stralsund, who brought Protestantism into the Sastrow family. He had seen Luther in 1523, had heard him preach at Wittenberg, and became a convert to the "true gospel." Smiterlow's daughter Anna married Nicholas Sastrow, a prosperous brewer and cornfactor of Greifswald, and Nicholas deserted the mass for the sermon. Their eldest son, John, was sent to study at Wittenberg, where he made the acquaintance of Luther and Melanchthon. He became something, of a scholar, wrote in praise of the English divine, Robert Barns, and was crowned poet laureate by Charles V in 1544. The second son was Bartholomew, author of these memoirs. Three years after his arrival the family life at Greifswald was rudely disturbed. Bartholomew's father had the misfortune to commit manslaughter (uncharitable people called it murder), and Greifswald was made too hot to hold the peccant cornfactor. The father of our chronicler lived in banishment for several years, while his wife brought up the children at Greifswald, and carried on the family business. It happened that Bartholomew's great-uncle, Burgomaster Nicholas Smiterlow the second, of Stralsund, was at that time residing at Greifswald. He possessed the avuncular virtues, had his great-nephew taught Latin, and earned his eternal gratitude. In time the heirs of the slain man were appeased and 1,000 marks of blood-money enabled the elder Sastrow to return to his native city. He did not, however, remain long in Greifswald, but sold his house and settled in the neighbouring city of Stralsund, the home of his wife's relations. Bartholomew received his early education at Greifswald and Stralsund, but in 1538 was sent to Rostock (a university had been founded in this town in 1415), where he studied under two well-known pupils of Luther and Melanchthon, Burenius and Heinrich Welfius (Wulf). The teaching combined the chief elements of Humanism and of Protestant theology, the works of Cicero and Terence on the one hand, and the De Anima of Melanchthon on the other.

Meanwhile (1534-37) there were great disturbances in Stralsund. An ambitious demagogue of Lubeck, George Wullenweber, had involved the Hanseatic League in a Danish war. Smiterlow and Nicolas Sastrow thought that the war was wrong and foolish, and that it would endanger the interests of Stralsund. But a democracy, when once bitten by the war frenzy, is hard to curb, and regards moderation in the light of treason. Stralsund rose against its conservative council, forced Smiterlow to resign and compelled the elder Sastrow to remain a prisoner in his house for the period of a year. Father and son never forgot or forgave these years of plebeian uproar. For them the art of statesmanship was to avoid revolution and to keep the people under. "I recommend to my children submission to authority, no matter whether Pilate or Caiaphas governs." This was the last word of Bartholomew's political philosophy.

In 1535-6 the forces of the Hanse were defeated both by land and sea, and the war party saw the error of its ways. Sastrow was released, and his uncle-in-law was restored to office to die two years later, in 1539. But meanwhile things had gone ill with the Sastrow finances. Some skilful but dishonest ladies had purchased large consignments of cloth, not to speak of borrowing considerable sums of money from Nicholas Sastrow, and declined to pay their bill. During his imprisonment Nicholas had been unable to sell the stock of salt which he had laid in with a view to the Schonen herring season. A certain Mrs. Bruser, wife of a big draper, with a hardy conscience, had bought 1,725 florins' worth of the Sastrow cloth of the dishonest ladies. The Sastrows determined to get the money out of the Brusers. Bruser first avowed the debt, and then repudiated it, taking a mean advantage of the civic troubles of Stralsund and the decline of the Smiterlow-Sastrow interest. Thereupon began litigation which was not to cease for thirty-four years. The case was heard before the town court of Stralsund, then before the council of Stralsund, then before the *oberhof* or appellate court of Lubeck, and finally before the Imperial court of Spires. Bartholomew accompanied his father on the Lubeck journey, obtained his first insight into legal chicanery, and was, no doubt, effectually inoculated with the anti-Bruser virus. In 1541 the elder Sastrow obtained permission to return to Greifswald, and Bartholomew attended for a year the lectures of the Greifswald professors. The family circumstances, however (there were by this time five daughters and three sons), were too straitened to support the youth in idleness. Accordingly, in June, 1542, the two eldest sons left their home, partly to seek their fortunes, but more especially to watch the great Bruser case, which was winding its slow and slippery course through the reticulations of the Imperial Court at Spires.

There is no need to anticipate the lively narrative of Bartholomew's experiences in this home of litigation long-drawn-out. The reader will, however, note that he was lucky enough to come in for a Diet, and has an excellent story to tell of how the emperor was inadvertently horsewhipped by a Swabian carter. On May 19, 1544, Sastrow received the diploma of Imperial notary, and a month later he left Spires and entered the chancellerie of Margrave Ernest of Baden, at Pforzheim. This, however, was destined to prove but a brief interlude. In the summer of 1545 Sastrow is in the service of a receiver of the Order of St. John, Christopher von Löwenstein, who, after his Turkish wars, was living a frolicsome old age among his Frisian stallions, his huntsmen and his hounds. The picture of this frivolous old person, with his dwarf, his mistress, and his chaplain, is drawn with some spirit. Sastrow, who had so long felt the pinch of poverty, was now luxuriating in good fare and fine raiment. He has little to do, plenty to eat and drink, and his festivity was untempered by moral considerations. "Do not think to become a doctor in my house," said the genial host, and it must be confessed that the surroundings were not propitious to the study of the Institutes.

The news of John Sastrow's death put an end to this jollity. The poet laureate had been crossed in love, and sought oblivion in Italy. The panegyrist of Barns entered the service of a cardinal, and died at Acquapendente, without explaining theological inconsistencies, pardonable perhaps in lovelorn poets. Bartholomew determined to recover the property of his deceased brother, and set out for Italy on April 8, 1546. He walked to Venice over the Brenner, thence took ship to Ancona, and then travelled over the Apennines to Rome, by way of Loretto. The council was sitting at Trent, but theological gossip does not interest our traveller so much as the alto voices in the church choirs, and "the tomb of the infant Simeon, the innocent victim of the Jews." Nor is he qualified to play the rôle of intelligent tourist among the antiquities and art treasures of Italy. He was not a Benvenuto Cellini, still less a Nathaniel Hawthorne, bent on instructing the Philistine in the art of cultured enthusiasm. "A magnificent palace, a church all of marble, variously tinted and assorted with perfect art, twelve lions and lionesses, two tigers and an eagle that is all I remember of Florence."

Many modern tourists may not remember as much without Sastrow's excuses. Italy was by this time by no means a safe place for a German. Paul III was recruiting mercenaries to help the emperor to fight the League of Smalkald, and the Spanish Inquisition was industriously raging in Rome.

It was sufficient to be a German to be suspected of heresy, and for the heretic, the pyre and the gibbet were ready prepared. It would be difficult to conceive a moment less propitious for aesthetic enjoyment. "Not a week without a hanging," says Sastrow, who was apparently careful to attend these lugubrious ceremonies. The excellence of the Roman wine increased the risk of an indiscretion, and by July Sastrow had determined that it would be well to extricate himself from the perils of Rome.

His reminiscences of the papal capital are vivid and curious. We seem to see the cardinal sweating in his shirt sleeves under the hot Italian sun, while his floor is being watered. Heavy-eyed oxen of the Campagna are dragging stone and marble through the streets to build the Farnese palace and splendid houses for the cardinals; the whole town is a tumult of building and unbuilding. Streets are destroyed to improve a view. If one of the effects of a celibate clergy is to promote immorality, another is to improve the cuisine of the taverns. Upon both topics Sastrow is eloquent, and there are too many confirmations from other quarters to permit us to doubt the substantial accuracy of his indictment.

By August 29, 1546, Sastrow was back at Stralsund. Through the good offices of Dr. Knipstrow, the general superintendent, he secured a post in the ducal chancellerie at Wolgast. His acuteness and industry obtained the respect of the Pomeranian chancellor, James Citzewitz, and he was given the most important business to transact. On March 10, 1547, he accompanied the ducal chancellors in the character of notary on a mission to the emperor. Ten years before the Dukes of Pomerania had joined the League of Smalkald, and they were now thoroughly alarmed at the Imperial victory at Muhlberg, and anxious to make their peace with Charles. The journey of the envoys is full of historical interest. Sastrow had to cross the field of Muhlberg and received ocular assurance of the horrors of the war and of the barbarities practised by the Spanish troops. He was a spectator of the humiliation of the Landgrave Philip of Hesse, at Halle, and to his narrative alone we owe the knowledge of the ironical laugh of the prince, and the angry threat of the emperor. From Halle the Pomeranian envoys followed Charles to Augsburg, having the good fortune to fall in with the drunken but scriptural Duke Frederick III of Liegnitz, of whose wild doings Sastrow can tell some surprising tales.

It must have been an astonishing experience, this life at Augsburg, while the Diet was sitting. The gravest theological and political problems, problems affecting the destiny of the Empire, were being handled in an atmosphere of unabashed debauchery and barbarism. Every one, layman and clerk, let himself go. Joachim of Brandenburg consented to the Interim for a bribe, and the Cardinal Granvelle, like Talleyrand afterwards, was able to build up an enormous fortune out of "the sins of Germany." In the midst of the coarse revels of the town the horrid work of the executioner was everywhere manifest. And, meanwhile, the grim emperor dines silently in public, seeming to convey a sullen rebuke to the garrulous hospitality of his brother Ferdinand, and to the loose morals of the princes.

The cause of the Pomeranian mission did not much prosper at Augsburg, and Sastrow and his friends pursued the emperor to Brussels, where they were at last able to effect the desired reconciliation. For the services rendered on this occasion Sastrow was made the Pomeranian solicitor at the court of Spires. The second Spires residence was clearly a period of honourable and not ungainful activity. Sastrow is busy with ducal cases; he makes another journey to the Netherlands in order to present Cardinal Granvelle with some golden flagons, and has occasion to admire the treasures of the great Flemish cities. The seagirt Stralsund, with its thin gusty streets, high gables, red Gothic gateways and tall austere whitewashed churches could not, of course, show the ample splendours of Brussels or Antwerp. Then, too, upon this Flemish voyage he saw King Philip and was impressed by the young man's stupid face and stiff Spanish formality. Such a contrast to his father Charles! Again he was sent on a mission to Basle, carrying information about Pomerania to Sebastian Munster, the "German Strabo," as he loved to hear himself called, that it might be incorporated in that learned scholar's universal cosmography. In 1550, however, Sastrow became aware that his position was being undermined by the councillors at Stettin. He accordingly gave up his ducal appointment, and determined to confine himself to private practice. He marries a wife (January 5, 1551), settles at Greifswald, and builds up a prosperous business, and from this date his memoirs are mostly concerned with the cases in which he was engaged.

There is yet one more change of place and occupation to be noticed in this bustling life. In 1555 Sastrow was enticed to Stralsund by the offer of the post of secretary, and for the next eight-and-forty years, till his death in 1603, he lived in that town, battling in the full stream of municipal politics, councillor in 1562, burgomaster in 1578, and frequently chosen to represent the city on embassies and other ceremonial occasions. A *Rubricken Bock*, or collection of municipal diplomata testifies to another branch of his useful activities. Enemies were as plentiful as gooseberries, and he never wanted for litigation. His second marriage created a scandal, and furnished an occasion for the foeman to scoff. But the choleric old gentleman was fully capable of taking care of himself. "At Stralsund," he says, "I fell full into the infernal caldron, and I have roasted there for forty years." But he took good heed that the enemy should roast likewise, and at the age of seventy-five began to lay the fire. The first two parts of the memoirs were composed in 1595, the third at the end of 1597, doubtless on the basis of some previous diary. They were composed for the benefit of his children, that they might enjoy the roasting. We too now can look on while the flames crackle.

HERBERT A. L. FISHER.

New College,
Oxford.

PART I

CHAPTER I

My father was born in 1488, in the village of Rantzin, in the inn close to the cemetery, on the road to Anclam. Even before his marriage, my grandfather, Johannes Sastrow, exceeded by far in worldly goods, reputation, power and understanding, the Horns, a family established at Rantzin. Hence, those Horns, frantic with jealousy, constantly attacked him, not only with regard to his property, but also in the consideration he enjoyed among his fellowmen; they did not scruple to attempt his life. Not daring to act openly, they incited one of their labourers to go drinking to the inn, to pick a quarrel with its host, and to fall upon him. Their inheritance, in fact, was so small that they only needed one ploughmaster. What was the upshot? My grandfather, who was on his guard, got wind of the affair, and took the offensive. The emissary had such a cordial reception as to be compelled to beat a retreat "on all fours," and even this was not accomplished without difficulty.

The enmity of the Horns obliged my grandfather to look to his security. About the year 1487, in virtue of a friendly agreement with the old overlord Johannes Osten von Quilow, he redeemed his vassalage (lastage), and acquired the citizenship of Greifswald, where he bought a dwelling at the angle of the Butchers' Street. Thither he gradually transferred his household goods. Johannes Sastrow, therefore, left the Ostens and became a citizen before my father's birth.

The infamous attempt occurred in this way. In 1494, there was a christening not far from Rantzin, namely at Gribon, where there lived a Horn. In his capacity of a near relative my grandfather received an invitation, and as the distance was short, he took my father, who was then about seven, with him. The Horns took advantage of the opportunity; on the pretext of paying a visit to their cousin, they repaired to Gribon. They had come down in the world, and they no longer minded either the company or the fare of the peasantry; consequently, during the meal that followed they sat down at the same table with my grandfather. When they had drunk their fill towards nightfall, they all got up together to have a look at the stables. They fancied they were among themselves; as it happened one of our relatives was hiding in a corner, and heard them discuss matters. They intended to watch Sastrow's going, to gallop after him and intercept him on the road, and to kill him and his child. My grandfather, having been warned, immediately took the advice not to delay his departure for a moment. Taking his son by the hand, he started there and then. Alas, the atrocious murderers who were lying in wait for him in a clearing, trampled him under their horses' hoofs, inflicted ever so many wounds; then, their rage not being spent, they dragged him to a large stone on the road, and which may be seen unto this day, chopped off his right hand at the wrist, and left him for dead on the spot. The child had crept into some damp underwood, inaccessible to horses; the fast gathering darkness saved him from being pursued. The labourers on the Horn farm, driven by curiosity, had mounted their cattle; they picked up the victim, and pulled the child from his hiding place. One of them galloped to Rantzin, whence he returned with a cart on which they laid the wounded man, who scarcely gave a sign of life, and, in fact, breathed his last at the entrance to the village.

The nearest relatives realized the inheritance of the orphan, sold the house, the proceeds of the whole amounting to 2,000 florins.[1] Lords who allow their vassals to amass similar sums are rare nowadays. The child was brought up carefully; he was taught to read, to write and to cipher, afterwards he was sent to Antwerp and to Amsterdam to get a knowledge of business. When he was old enough to manage his own affairs, he bought the angle of Long Street and of Huns' Street, on the right, towards St. Nicholas' Church, that is, two dwelling houses and two shops in Huns' Street.[2] One of these houses he made his residence; the other he converted into a brewery, and on the site of the shops he built the present front entrance. All this cost a great deal of trouble and money. He was an attractive young fellow with an assured bit of bread, so he had no difficulty in obtaining the hand of the daughter of the late Bartholomäi Smiterlow, and the niece of Nicholas Smiterlow, the burgomaster of Stralsund.[3] Young and pretty, rather short than tall, but with exquisitely shaped limbs, amiable, clever, unpretending, an excellent managers, and exceedingly careful in her conduct, my mother unto her last hour was an honest and God-fearing woman. My father's register shows that the marriage took place in 1514, the Sunday after St. Catherine's Day; the husband, as I often heard him say, was still short of five and twenty.

At the fast just before Advent, in 1515, Providence granted the young couple a son who was named Johannes, after his paternal grandfather; he died in 1545, at Aquapendente, in Italy. In 1517, *in vigilia nativitatis Mariae*, my sister Anna was born; she died on August 16, 1594, at the age of seventy-seven; she was the widow of Peter Frobose, burgomaster of Greifswald.

On Tuesday, August 21, 1520, at six in the morning, I came into the world and was named Bartholomäi, after my maternal grandfather. I leave to my descendants the task of recording my demise, to which I am looking forward anxiously in my seventy-fifth winter.

The year 1523 witnessed the birth of my sister Catherine, a charming, handsome creature, amiable, loyal and pious. When my brother Johannes returned from the University of Wittemberg, she asked him what was the Latin for "This is certainly a good-looking girl?" "Profecto formosa puella," was the answer. "And how do they say, 'Yes, not bad?'" was the next question. "Sic satis," replied Johannes.

Some time after that, three students from Wittemberg, young fellows of good family, stopped for a short while in our town, and Christian Smiterlow asked his father, the burgomaster, to let them stay with him. The burgomaster, who had three grown-up daughters, invited my sister Catherine. Naturally, the young people talked to and chaffed each other, and the lads themselves made some remarks in Latin, which would, perhaps, have not sounded well in German to female ears. One of them happened to exclaim: "Profecto formosa puella!" "Sic satis!" retorted Catherine, and thereupon the students became afraid that she had understood the whole of their lively comments.

In 1544 Catherine married Christopher Meyer, an only son, but an illiterate, dissipated, lazy and drunken oaf, who spent all his substance, and ruined a servant girl while my sister was in childbed. God punished him for his misdeeds by bringing abject misery and a loathsome disease upon him, but Catherine died at twenty-six, weary of life.

My sister Magdalen was born in 1527; she died a single woman at twenty-two. These five children were born to my parents in Greifswald; the last three saw the light at Stralsund; namely, in 1529, Christian, who lived till he was sixty; in 1532, Barbara, who only reached eighteen; and in 1534, Gertrude.

From their very earliest age my sisters were taught by my mother the household and other work appropriate to their sex. One day while Gertrude, who was then about five, was plying her distaff--the spinning wheel was not known then--my brother Johannes announced the news that the Emperor, the King of the Romans, the electors, the princes and counts, in short all the great nobles, were to foregather at a diet. "What for?" asked Gertrude. "To look to the proper government of the world," was the answer. "Good Lord," sighed the child, "why don't they forbid little girls to spin."

The pest of 1549 took away my mother, Gertrude, Magdalen and Catherine. As her daughters were weeping bitterly my mother said: "Why do you weep? rather ask the Lord to shorten my sufferings." She died on

July 3. On the 16th it was Gertrude's turn. Magdalen was also dying; she left her bed to get her own shroud and that of Gertrude out of the linen press, and bade me be careful to fling only a little earth on her sister's grave, because she herself would soon be put into it; after which she returned to her bed and expired on July 18, the morning after Gertrude's burial. Magdalen was the tallest and most robust of my sisters, an accomplished manageress, hardworking, and her head screwed tightly on her shoulders. Catherine sent me all this news on September 9, two days before her own death of the plague. She did not try to disguise her approaching end; on the contrary, she prayed fervently for it, and bade me be resigned to it. She had had two children by her worthless husband; I undertook the care of the boy, Christopher Meyer, and my sister Frobose at Greifswald mothered the girl, who was but scantily provided for. Christopher gave me much trouble; neither remonstrance nor punishment proved of any avail; when he grew up he would not settle down, and practically followed in the footsteps of his father, yielding to dissipation, and indulging in all kinds of vice. Nevertheless, I made him contract a good marriage which gave him a kind of position. He left two sons; the elder was placed by his guardians at Dantzig, with most respectable people, who, however, declined to keep him. The younger remained with me for two years, going to school meanwhile, and causing me greater trouble than was consistent with my advanced age. But I had hoped to do some good with him; alas! he was so bent upon following his father's example as to make me rejoice getting rid of the cub.

My sister Barbara had been sent to Greifswald; when the plague abated, my father recalled her, for he was old, wretched and bowed down with care. Barbara was only fifteen, very pretty, amiable and hardworking. She married Bernard Classen, then a widower for the second time. My father did not like this son-in-law, against whom he had acted in the law courts for the other side; but Classen was not to be shaken off, and finally obtained my father's consent. The wedding took place on St. Martin's Day (November 11), 1549. On my return from Spires, I paid a visit to the young couple; my brother-in-law showed me the window of his study ornamented with my monogram and name, taking care to mention that he had paid a Stralsund mark to the glazier; I loosened my purse-strings and counted the sum to him, but the proceeding did not commend itself to me after the protestations of friendship my father had conveyed to me from Classen's part.[4]

In 1521, at the Diet of Worms, where Doctor Martin Luther so courageously made his confession of faith, Duke Bagislaw X, the grandfather of the two dukes at present reigning, received from His Imperial Majesty Charles V the solemn investiture under the open sky and with the standards unfurled, to the great displeasure of the Elector of Brandenburg. The imperial councillors were instructed to bring the two competitors to an agreement at Nuremberg, or to refer the matter further to His Majesty in case of the failure of negotiations.

In 1522 occurred the disturbances in connexion with Rolof Moller, a young man of about thirty, if that. His grandfather had been burgomaster, and in consequence he had detained in his possession a register of the revenues and privileges of the city. Having summoned a number of citizens to the monastery of St. John, he tried to prove by means of said register the enormous revenues of the city, and to accuse the council of malversation; after which he invaded the town hall, took the councillors to task, and treated them all like so many thieves, including one of his own relatives, Herr Schroeder, whom he reproached with being small in stature, but big in scoundrelism. Burgomaster Zabel Oseborn indignantly denied the accusation, and worked himself into such a state of excitement that he had to be conveyed home. In consequence of these slanders Moller constituted himself a following among the burghers; his numerous adherents chose forty-eight of their own (double the number of the members of the council), to exercise the chief power; the council saw its influence annulled, an act defining the limits of its competence and rules for its conduct was presented for signature to the councillors, and they were furthermore required to take the oath. Herr Nicholas Smiterlow alone resisted; hence, during the whole period of their domination, namely up to 1537, the Forty-Eight made him pay for his courage by unheard-of persecutions.

The primary cause of this agitation, so disastrous to the city, was the absence of a permanent record-office. The burgomasters, or the secretary, took the secret papers home with them[5] ; at the magistrate's death those documents passed to the children and grandchildren, then fell into the hands of strangers; and the natural result were indiscreet revelations hurtful to the public weal.

Johannes Bugenhagen, the Pomeranian, and rector of the school of Treptow on the Rega, converted several monks of the monastery of Belbuck to the pure faith. They left the monastery. Among them should be mentioned Herr Christian Ketelhot, Herr Johannes Kurcke, and Herr George von Ukermünde, whom the Stralsund people chose as their preacher. But when, after three sermons at St. Nicholas', he saw the citizens resolved to keep him, in spite of the council who forbade him the pulpit, when he saw the papist clergy increase their threats, and the dukes expel Ketelhot and Kurcke from Treptow, he was siezed with fear and went away in secret.[6]

Johannes Kurcke was about to set sail for Livonia, intending to engage in commerce there, when he was detained at Stralsund to preach, in the first place in the St. George's cemetery, then at the cloister of St. Catherine, and finally at St. Nicholas'. He died in 1527, and was buried at St. George's.

Ketelhot had been prior of the monastery of Belbuck during sixteen weeks. At the instigation of the Abbot Johannes Boldewan, the same who had given him the prior's hood, he left for the living of Stolpe, and preached the Gospel there for some time. The slanders of the priests induced the prince to prohibit him. In vain did he claim the right to justify himself by word of mouth and in writing before the sovereign, the prelates, the lords and the cities. He failed to obtain a hearing or even a safe-conduct. As a consequence he went to Mecklenburg, intending to adopt a trade; but unable to find a suitable master, he came to Stralsund determined to take ship for Livonia. Contrary winds kept him for several weeks in port; this gave him the opportunity of hearing the fables, absurdities and impious lies delivered from the pulpit; he beheld the misconduct of the priests, their debauchery, drunkenness, gluttony, fornication, adultery and worse. Acceding to the wish of a great number of burghers, and the Church of St. George's being too small to hold the crowd, he preached on the Sunday before Ascension Day under the great lime tree of the cemetery. He first took for his text Matthew xi. 28: "Come unto me, all ye that labour and are heavy laden, and I will give you rest"; then John xvi. 23: "Verily, verily, I say unto you, Whatsoever ye shall ask the Father in My name, He will give it you"; and finally: "Go ye therefore and teach all nations." In spite of the opposition of the council, which felt inclined to yield to the frantic protestation of the clergy, the burghers practically forced Ketelhot to come into the city, and made him preach at St. Nicholas'.

In 1523, Duke Bogislaw, accompanied by four hundred horsemen, proceeded to Nuremberg to settle his disagreement with the Elector of Brandenburg. Among his suite were Burgomaster Nicholas Smiterlow and his son Christian. The lad, lively and strong for his age, made his horse curvet and prance, so that it threw him and crushed him with all its weight. Young Smiterlow was deformed all his life; but when it became evident that there was no remedy, his father sent him to the University of Wittemberg; but for the accident he would have placed him in business at Lubeck.

On his way home Duke Bogislaw stopped at Wittemberg to see Luther, the turbulent monk. Before they had exchanged many words, the prince in a jocular tone said: "Master Doctor, you had better let me confess to you." Luther, however, replied very quickly: "No, no, gracious lord! Your Highness is too exalted a penitent, and I am too lowly to give him absolution." Luther was thinking of the august birth of his interlocutor, who, moreover, was exceedingly tall of stature, but the Duke took the reply as an allusion to the gravity of his backslidings, and dismissed Luther without inviting him to his table.

During the absence of Duke Bogislaw, the images were destroyed at Stralsund as I am going to narrate. On Monday of Holy Week, 1523, Frau Schermer sent her servant to St. Nicholas' for a box containing relics which she wished to have repaired.[7] Some workmen, noticing that a sacred object was being taken away, began to knock down everything; their constantly increasing numbers ran riot in the churches and in the convents; the altars were overtoppled, and the images thrown to the four winds. With the exception of the custodian of St. John's, monks and priests fled from the city. Thereupon the council issued an order that everybody had to bring back his loot on the following Wednesday to the old market. The burghers only obeyed reluctantly; they only restored the wooden images, but the more valuable ones were not to be found. Two women were brought before the council; the woman Bandelwitz deliberately defied the burgomaster, looked him straight into the face and addressed him as follows: "What dost thou want with me, Johannes Heye? Why hast thou summoned me before thee? What crime have I committed?"

"Thou shalt know very soon," replied the burgomaster, and had her put under lock and key. The same fate befell the other woman. In the market place the partisans of the old doctrines had taken to arms and were much excited, while the evangelists loudly expressed their indignation at this double incarceration. Bailiff (or sheriff) Schroeder made his appearance on horseback, and showed with a kind of affectation a communion cup he had confiscated, and swore to "do" for all the evangelicals. Leaping on to a fishmonger's bench, L. Vischer cried in a thundering voice: "Rally to me all those who wish to live and die for the Gospel."[8] The greater number rallied to his side. From the windows of the Town House the councillors had been watching the scene, and they began to fear for their personal safety when they should wish to go home. Rolof Moller went upstairs to make the situation clear to them; the two women were discharged after an imprisonment of less than an hour, and the Council asked the burghers to let the matter rest there, professing their goodwill towards them; but the crowd, slow to abate its anger, occupied the place up to four o'clock, after which the councillors could make their way without danger.

When Duke Bogislaw returned, the Stralsund council endeavoured to persuade His Highness that the destruction of the images had taken place in spite of them. In his great anger the prince would not hear of any justification; he accused the people of Stralsund of having failed in their duty towards religion as well as against the sovereign who was the patron of the city's churches. He added that the devil would bring them to account for it. The duke died on September 29 of the same year at Stettin, leaving two sons, George and Barnim.[9]

The disturbances, nevertheless, continued, for the burghers saw with displeasure that the council, following the example of Princes George and Barnim, persisted in popish practices, thereby delaying the progress of Evangelism. On the Monday of St. John, 1524, Rolof Moller, at the head of a big troop of men, made his appearance in the old market place and, mounted also on a fishmonger's stall, began addressing the people, who applauded him. The dissensions between the magistrates and the burghers became more accentuated every day, and plainly foretold the ruin of public business. Moller observed no measure in his attacks on the council. He was just about thirty, clever, and, with an attractive personality, he might count upon being sooner or later elected burgomaster. It was only a question of time. His presumption blinded him to the reality; intoxicated with popular favour, he allowed himself certain excesses against the council, took his flight before his wings had grown, and dragged a number of people down with him in his fall. The city itself did not recover from the effects of all this for close upon a century.

Burgomaster Nicholas Smiterlow, a personage of great consideration, a clever spokesman, and of a firm and generous disposition, was a member of the council for seventeen years. Duke Bogislaw, who fully appreciated his work, took him to the conference at Nuremberg. The journey enabled the burgomaster to hear the gospel preached in its purity, and to become aware of the fatal error of papism. At Wittemberg he heard Luther preach. As a consequence, he was the first to proclaim the wholesome doctrine in open council, though the opposition of that body prevented him from supporting the propagators of the true faith when they kept within reasonable limits. He interposed between the council, the princes, and the exalted personages of the land, who were still wedded to papism, and Rolof Moller, the Forty-Eight, and their adherents who wished to carry things with too high a hand. Smiterlow told the council to show themselves less unbending with the burghers in all just and reasonable things. On the other hand, he exhorted the citizens to show more deference to the magistrates, giving the former the assurance that the preachers should not be molested, and that the gospel should not be hampered in its course. Unfortunately, his efforts failed on both sides.

Then the crisis occurred. The ringleaders--among the most turbulent, Franz Wessel, L. Vischer, Bartholomäi Buchow, Hermann Meyer and Nicholas Rode lifted Rolof Moller from his fishmonger's bench--took him to the Town House, and made him take his seat in the burgomaster's chair. [10] The council was compelled to accept Rolof and Christopher Lorbeer as burgomasters, and eight of the citizens as councillors. In order to save their heads, the magistrates found themselves compelled to share with their sworn enemies both the small bench of the four burgomasters and the larger bench of twenty-four councillors. As for Smiterlow, his was the fate of those who interfere between two contending parties, the peacemakers invariably coming to grief like the iron between the anvil and the hammer. When Rolof Moller entered the burgomaster's pew Smiterlow left it, and inasmuch as his consummate experience foretold him of his danger he came to Greifswald with his two sons to ask my mother's hospitality.[11]

The tolerance shown at this conjuncture by the young princes George and Barnim was due to two reasons. In the first place they expected to get the upper hand of the city without much trouble after it became worn out with domestic dissensions. Secondly, a band of zealots, with Dr. Johannes Amandus at their head, scoured the country, especially Eastern Pomerania, inciting the people to break the images, and preaching from the pulpit the sweeping away of all refuse, princes included. In the eyes of the papists, those people and the evangelicals were but one and the same set, and as their number happened to be imposing, the princes considered it prudent to lay low.

The flight of the priests and monks gave the magistrates the opportunity of listening to the preaching of Christian Ketelhot and his colleagues. In a short while the council's eyes were opened to the true light, and in accord with the Forty-Eight and the burghers themselves, they assigned the churches to the evangelical preachers; the monastery, that is, the supreme direction of all the ministers and servitors of the church being confided to Ketelhot, who exercised it for twenty-three years, in fact, up to the day of his death. Canons and vicars had taken the precaution to collect all the specie, valuables and title deeds, amounting to considerable sums; they entrusted to certain councillors of Greifswald chests and lockers filled with chalices, rich chasubles and various holy vessels. They occasionally converted these into money and handed to the debtors certain annuities at half-price. Consequently, the hospitals, churches, and pious foundations lost both their capital and their income. A long time after these events the sons of my relative, Christian Schwartz, dispatched to me for restitution to the council of Stralsund, a sailor's locker which had stood for forty years under their father's bed. It contained velvet chasubles embroidered with silver and pearls, in addition to a couple of silver crucifixes. Though their rules forbade the monks of St. John to touch coined metal, the father custodian did not scruple to carry away with him all that the convent held in clinking coin and precious objects.

Called to the ministry by a small group of citizens who had not given a thought to the question of his salary, Ketelhot had no other resource for his daily sustenance than the city "wine cellar" and *The King Arthur*.[12] He found hospitable board and good company, but the life was detrimental to his studies. A Jew with whom he flattered himself he was studying the *lingua sancta* induced him to announce from the pulpit the *error a Judaeo conceptus*. As a consequence the council promptly appointed Johannes Knipstro as superintendent at Stralsund. He was the first that bore the title there, and Ketelhot neither suffered in consideration, rank, nor benefices. He remained all his life *primarius pastor*, and his effigy at St. Nicholas, facing the pulpit, is inscribed with the words: *Repurgator ecclesiae Sundensis*. Appointed in 1524, Knipstro, by his talent and solicitude, succeeded in leading Ketelhot back to the right path, for he broke for ever with the *error*. The two ministers lived in the most brotherly understanding. Ketelhot was no more jealous of the superintendent than Knipstro, took umbrage at the title of *primarius pastor*. They were not vainglorious, as were later on Runge and Kruse. Gradually the dukes admitted that the evangelicals, far from making common cause with the zealots of Eastern Pomerania, energetically opposed them. The Stralsund preachers were henceforth left in peace; they were more firmly established in their functions, and neither the council nor the citizens were any longer molested for having called them.

I now beg to resume the story of my family from the year 1523. My parents started house-keeping in the midst of plenty; they had a mill and a brewery, sold their corn, butter, honey, wool and feathers, and were even blessed with the superfluous. Everything was so cheap that it seemed easy to make money. It seemed as if the golden age had returned. Nevertheless, prosperity had to make room for misfortune.

In the course of that year (1523), in fact, George Hartmann, the son-in-law of Doctor Stroïentin,[13] bought of my father a quantity of butter. A violent discussion having occurred between them, Hartmann, who was on his way to Burgomaster Peter Kirchschwanz with a short sword belonging to the latter, went instead to his mother-in-law to pour his grievances into her ears. This haughty and purse-proud woman, full of contempt for very humble folk because she happened to have married a doctor and a ducal counsellor (I omit for charity's sake some details which I shall tell my children by word of mouth), that woman, I say, presented her son-in-law with a hatchet, saying: "There, go to market with this piece of money, and buy a bit of courage." Emboldened by a safe-conduct of the prince, which Doctor Stroïentin had got for him, Hartmann fell in with my father at the top of the Sporenmacher Strasse. He was going to the public weigh-house to have a case of honey weighed, and he had not as much as a pocket knife wherewith to repel an assailant armed with a sword and a hatchet. He rushed into a spurmaker's shop, getting hold of a large pitchfork, but the bystanders wrenched it out of his hands; moreover, they prevented him taking refuge in the gallery. Thereupon my father snatched up a long stick with an iron prod standing against the wall, and going back into the street, shouted:

"Let the fellow who wants to take my life come out and show himself." At these words, Hartmann issued from an adjoining workshop. Not satisfied with his short sword and his hatchet, he had taken a hammer from the anvil and flung it at my father, who warded it with his stick, though only partly, for my father spat blood for several days. The hatchet went the same way, and just caught my father on the shoulder. The double exploit having imbued him with the idea that the game was won, the aggressor made a rush with his bare sword, but my father spitted him on his iron-prodded pole, and Hartmann dropped down dead. This is the true account of this deplorable accident. I am quite aware of the version invented by the ill-will of the others, which is to the effect that my father having found Hartmann altogether disarmed behind the stove in the spurmaker's room, straightway killed him on the spot. These are vain rumours, *nugae sunt, fabulae sunt*.

My father sought asylum with the "black" monks, to whom he was known. They hid him at the top of the church in a recess near the vault. In a little while Doctor Stroïentin, at the head of his servants and of a numerous group of followers, came to search every nook and corner of the convent. Naturally, he went into the church, and the fugitive, fancying it was all over with him, was going to speak in order to prove his innocence; fortunately Providence closed his lips and shut his enemies' eyes. In the middle of the night the monks smuggled him over the wall. Keeping to the high road, he succeeded in reaching Neuenkirchen, where a peasant's cart, sent by his father-in-law, was waiting for him. He managed to squeeze himself into a sack of fodder by the side of a sack of barley. Doctor Stroïentin stopped the vehicle on the road. The driver told him he was going to Stralsund. "What have you got there?" asked the doctor, beating the sacks with him. "Barley and my fodder," was the answer. "Have not you noticed any one going in a great hurry either on horseback or on foot?" "Yes; I saw a man galloping as hard as he could in the direction of Horst. I may have been mistaken, but I fancy it was Sastrow, of Greifswald, and I was wondering why he should be scouring the highway at that hour of night." Stroïentin wanted to hear no more. He turned his horse's head as fast as it would go in the direction of Horst.

My father reached Stralsund without further trouble; the council gave him a safe-conduct, which was only a broken reed in the way of a guarantee, for he had to deal with proud, rich and powerful enemies. Doctor Stroïentin, His Highness' counsellor, took particular advantage of the fact that Hartmann enjoyed the protection of Duke George. My father went from pillar to post in Denmark, at Lubeck, at Hamburg, and other spots; finally, he appeased his suzerain by paying him a considerable sum in cash; then, after long-drawn negotiations, his father-in-law succeeded in reconciling him with his adversaries. The expiatory fine was 1,000 marks, but Greifswald, where the family of the deceased resided, remained closed to him. Nor did the 1,000 marks prove any benefit to the son of Hartmann; the contrary has been the case. Misfortune pursued him without cessation in his health, his wealth, his wife and children.

At the gates of Stralsund stood the monastery of St. Brigitta; monks and nuns inhabited different parts. A wall divided the gardens. It was, however, by no means high enough to prove an obstacle to a nimble climber. It is the monks that did the cooking, and the dishes came to the nuns in a kind of lift large enough for one person. How the vow of chastity was observed was proved on the day of the invasion of the convent, when the skeletons, head and bones of new-born children were found everywhere.

At the period of the invasion of the churches and the monasteries, Franz Wessel, who at that time had discharged the functions of councillor for more than a twelvemonth, was charged with preventing at St. Catherine's the abstraction of precious objects. In order to cut short the idolatrous practices, he had a trench dug at the door of the garden of eighteen ells long, in which the images were buried. On the Holy Thursday, between four and six in the morning, the nuns whose retreat had been attacked were taken to St. Catherine's. Wessel received them courteously on the threshold of the cloister, took the abbess by the hand and intoned the popish hymn *Veni, sponsa salvatoris*, etc. The abbess begged of him to cease this joking, and rather to welcome her with some flagons of wine. Wessel objected that the hour was too early to begin drinking.

I have narrated the circumstances which compelled Burgomaster Nicholas Smiterlow to take refuge at my mother's with his two sons, Nicholas and Bertrand. The first-named, a doughty young man, good-looking and of independent character, had with great credit to himself terminated his studies. I have rarely seen such beautiful handwriting as his. Impatient to see the world, he felt himself cramped in Pomerania, and when he heard that Emperor Charles had an army in Italy, he induced his father to give him an outfit and to allow him to join it. Provided with a well-lined purse, he joined the Imperial troops, took part in the storming and sacking of Rome, got a great deal of loot, but fell ill and died.

Fate proved not more lenient to Doctor Zutfeld Wardenberg, also the son of a burgomaster. Berckmann and other writers have made him pass as a great prelate. Be this as it may; he certainly fancied himself a member of the Trinity which rules the universe. In his official functions he observed no law but his own sweet will. His own house contained a prison, and he behaved as if the council did not exist. In short, he wound up by setting the magistrates against him to such an extent that one night he judged it prudent to leave the city. His brother, Joachim, opened the gates to him without authority--a piece of daring which cost him ten weeks of imprisonment in the Blue Tower. At the sacking of Rome, Zutfeld Wardenberg tried to hide himself among the invalids of a hospital. He was soon discovered, killed, and everything taken away from him. In the church of St. Mary, at Stralsund, stands the handsome mausoleum he had prepared for himself, together with an epitaph setting forth his titles, but his body lies somewhere at Rome, no one knows where.

Burgomaster Smiterlow was as frank in his speech as he was open of heart. When he conversed in the street his strong and clear voice could be heard a couple of yards off. All his speeches began with "Yes, in the name of Jesus." One day, after dinner, he went into his stables where, as a rule, he had three horses; he saw one of his stablemen strike one of the animals with a pitchfork, saying, in imitation of himself, "In the name of Jesus." Smiterlow snatched the implement away from him, then stuck it between his shoulders so that he dropped down, and quietly remarked: "Now and again I cause people to cry 'In the name of all the devils.'"

According to the custom of the papists, my mother went at half-past twelve, especially during Lent, to recite a Pater Noster and an Ave Maria before each of the three altars of her ordinary church. She always took her little Bartholomäi with her. On one occasion I sat down on the steps of the first altar and began to relieve nature; when she passed on to the second, I followed her and continued the operation, which I finished on the third. When my mother perceived what had occurred she rushed home in hot haste and sent a servant with a broom to repair the mischief. Seeing how young she was when separated from her husband and left with four young children, it is not surprising that my mother had moments of sadness and discouragement. One day that she was cutting up some dry fish, a piece fell from the block. I picked it up. Without noticing my mother stooped at the same time, and as I was rising, the edge of the hatchet cut my forehead. The scar was never effaced. The Lord be praised, though, the accident had no further consequence.

Hartmann's family having received satisfaction, my father appointed to meet his wife and his children at the manse of Neuenkirchen. It was in the autumn and the pears were ripe. After having shaken down and eaten as many as they could, the children began to pelt each other with them. A big pear dropped under the hoofs of a couple of horses tied to a large pear tree. When I stooped to get hold of it, one of the animals dealt me a severe kick at the temple. There was general consternation, and the wound being seemingly dangerous, we came back immediately to town, and I was taken to the doctor.

The Dukes George and Barnim came to Stralsund with four hundred horsemen; they received homage and confirmed the privileges of the city. As for the claims of the priests, it was decided to refer them to the Imperial Chamber. Burgomasters, councillors, burghers, preachers (in all about threescore), were summoned to depose on oath before the Imperial Commissioners, sitting at Greifswald. The lawsuit cost the city a considerable sum; the clergy practically flung the money away, but the rector, Hippolytus Steinwer, began to perceive that the chances were turning against them, and one day he was found dead. It was believed he had strangled himself from vexation. That event put an end to the litigation. The priests returned one after another to Stralsund.

Gradually the sobered citizens began to open their eyes to the serious prejudice which was being done to public and private interests by the agitation of Moller. On the other hand, the princes had learned to know Smiterlow during the journey to Nuremberg; they were also aware of the esteem in which he had been held by their father. All those feelings showed themselves on the occasion of the rendering of homage. Rolof Moller was obliged to leave the city, and Burgomaster Smiterlow re-entered it on August 1, 1526. Moller, after a stay of several years at Stettin, received permission to come back to Stralsund, Smiterlow giving his consent; but scarcely a fortnight after his return had gone by when he died, it was said, of grief; and the assumption was sufficiently plausible.

Hence, Smiterlow spent the time of his exile at my mother's, at Greifswald, while his house at Stralsund sheltered my father. The wives of the two banished men went constantly and at all seasons from one town to another, through hail, snow, rain, frost and cold, and also to the great detriment of their purse and their health.

I have often been told afterwards I was a restless, energetic child. I often went up to the tower of St. Nicholas's, and on one occasion I made the round of it outside. My mother, standing on the threshold of her house, facing the church, was a witness of the feat, and dared scarcely breathe until her son came down safe and skin-whole. It would appear that little Bartholomäi had his reward at her hands.

While at Greifswald I had already been sent to school. Besides reading, I was taught declension, comparisons and conjugation, according to the grammar of Donat; after which we passed to Torrentinus. On Palm Sunday I was selected to intone the *Quantus*; the preceding years I had sung at first the short, then the long *Hic est*. What an honour for the child and for the parents! It was a real feast, for as a rule the sharpest boys are chosen those who, undeterred by the crowds of priests and laymen, bring out their clearest notes, especially for the *Quantus*. The continuation of this story will, however, soon show how, from being sanguine, my temperament became melancholy, and how my gaiety and recklessness vanished.

CHAPTER II

Having acquired the certainty that the Hartmanns would never consent to my father's return to Greifswald, my parents, like the conscientious married couple they were, desired to bear in common the domestic burdens. In the spring of 1528 my mother, after having let her dwelling at Greifswald, joined her husband at Stralsund, where he had the freeman's right and a tumble-down old house. My maternal grandfather, Christian Schwarz, at that time city treasurer, kept me with him in order to let me pursue my studies. I underwent the ceremonial of installation, a kind of burlesque function of initiation applied to novices. My tutor was George Normann, of the island of Rügen, who terminated his career in the service of the King of Sweden. I was the reverse of a studious boy and fonder of roving about with my relative in his journeys about Greifswald than of books. As a consequence my mental progress was in proportion to my efforts.

There was at Greifswald a burgomaster named Victor Bole, belonging to a notable family of the island of Rügen. Before he attained his civic honours he was a good evangelical and a zealous friend of the preachers, but his apostasy was thorough. As much as he had supported the ministry before his election, as much did he oppose them afterwards. I remember seeing him at the meetings of the corporation seated in the front place in virtue of his dual quality of eldest member and burgomaster, more or less in liquor, browbeating and talking everybody down (in High-German always). As he had taken part in several expeditions, fighting was the invariable theme of his discourses. He generally summoned the musicians, cymbal players and pipers before him. "Dost thou know a war cry?" he asked of a piper. "Yes, certainly," was the reply, while shrill notes rent the air. But the burgomaster was beaming. "This, at any rate, is a useful kind of fellow; while that Knipstro of Stralsund stammers in the pulpit about *pap, pap, pap,* I am sure he could play a war cry. Then what's the good of him?"

"Those who laugh last laugh loudest," says the proverb. That same year, 1528, the King of the May was Bertrand Smiterlow. I walked in front of him carrying his crown. Bole did Smiterlow the honour to prance by his side, being very pleased to parade his servants and his horses, of the latter of which he had four in his stable. If the skies had shown a little bit more clement we should have been very happy. But though it was the 1st May, there was not a bud nor a blade of grass to be seen. On the contrary, the snow powdered our procession with large flakes, both on coming and on going. As a consequence everybody was in a hurry to get back again. Odd to relate, the seed did not seem to suffer. After they had presented the crown to the May King in the city, everybody galloped back to his own roof tree. When the burgomaster reached his house he was taken with such violent colic that he had scarcely time to hand his horse to his servant before he dropped down dead. His neck was entirely twisted round, and his face was black. As a matter of course, people ascribed it to a visitation of God for having made fun of those who preached His Word.

In 1528 the States were called together at Stettin to ratify the pact of succession between the Elector of Brandenburg and the Dukes of Pomerania. The deputy of Greifswald, Burgomaster Gaspard Bunsaw, my mother's first cousin, took me with him as page, or rather as companion, and also to enable me to see something new. Our host had a magnificent garden; on the banks of a vast lake uprose a vast tower with an inside staircase, closed by a trap. One day that the company was amusing itself in watching the carps from that tower, I hauled myself up to the window out of curiosity, but I forgot the yawning trap door behind me, and was flung right to the bottom. It was a miracle that I did not break my neck, or, at any rate, my arms and my legs. Heaven preserved me by means of its angels, who frustrate the tricks of the Evil One.

At the age of five, Nicholas, the eldest son of Bertrand Smiterlow, was already much taller and stronger than I; this incarnate fiend worried all the children of the neighbourhood, and instead of reprimanding him, his father took no notice of the complaints against him. This indulgence bore such excellent fruit that in order to prevent disputes and perhaps personal violence between young Nicholas' father and the neighbours, Christian Schwarz considered it advisable to take Nicholas to live with him, and so we shared the same bed. One morning as we were dressing on the big locker at the foot of the bed, the youngster, without saying a word and out of sheer mischief, hit me right in the chest and made me tumble backward, a downright dangerous fall. The grandfather gave a dinner-party to his children and other people. Late in the evening the servants came with links to take their masters home. While they were waiting for that purpose, Nicholas began to play them tricks, which they endured from fear of the grandfather. Rendered bold by impunity, Nicholas struck some of the servants on the lips, but one of these retorted by a box on the ears which sent Nicholas whining to his grandfather. After the banquet the lanterns were lighted, and everybody was preparing to get home quietly when Bertrand

Smiterlow, drawing his knife, rushed at the offending servant, who was lighting his master on his way, and wounded him seriously in the shoulder. On account of all this Christian Schwarz preferred to send me back to Stralsund to leaving me to enjoy the risky society of Nicholas. The boy grew up and his faults with him, for they amused his father, who encouraged them while nobody dared to say a word in protest. Nicholas had reached the age of twenty-seven when travelling to Rostock, he stopped for the night at Roevershagen. Some travellers, knowing his quarrelsome character, preferred to take themselves and their conveyance to the inn opposite. One of these had a sporting dog, which, running about, found its way into the hostel where Smiterlow was staying. The latter tied up the animal, did not send it back, and next morning the rightful owner saw it being taken away on a leash. Naturally, the man claimed his dog. Smiterlow, instead of giving him a civil answer, takes aim at him; the other, more prompt, quickly fires a bullet into the thigh. Smiterlow, in his wounded condition, got as far as Rostock, had his wound attended to; nevertheless died a few days later in consequence. The merchant continued his route without troubling himself, and no one lodged a complaint. Bertrand Smiterlow contracted the itch in the back; father and son, therefore, had their just reward. Heaven preserve me from criticizing the descendants of Herr Smiterlow, to whom I am doubly related, but I trust that mine will bring up their children in a more severe discipline and in the respect of their fellow-men.

In 1529 the English pest which had already been spoken of during the previous year, carried away many people at Stralsund. My mother had two attacks, from both of which she fortunately recovered. Being *enceinte* with my brother Christian, she ordered, like the good housewife she was, a general cleaning before her confinement. It so happened that we had a servant-girl who was possessed. Nobody had the faintest suspicion of this. When, at the moment of cleaning the kitchener and cooking utensils, she began noisily to fling about saucepans, frying-pans, etc., crying at the top of her voice, "I want to get out, I want to get out." Her mother, who lived in the Zinngiesser Strasse (Pewterers' Street), had to take her back. The poor girl was taken several times in a sleigh to St. Nicholas's, and they exorcised her after the sermon. Her case, as far as the answers tended to show, was as follows: The mother had brought new cheese at the market. In her absence, the daughter had opened the cupboard and made a large breach in the cheese; the mother, on her return, had expressed the wish that the devil might take the perpetrator of this thing, and from that moment dated the "possession." The girl had, nevertheless, been to Communion since; how, then, could the Evil One have kept his position? The priest, interrogated on that point, had answered: "The scoundrel, who has hidden himself under a bridge, lets the honest man pass over his head"; in other words, during the sacramental act, the Evil One hid himself under the girl's tongue. The Evil One was excommunicated and exorcised by the faithful on their bended knees. The formula of exorcism was received with derision. When the priest summoned him to go, he exclaimed: "I am agreeable, but you do not expect me to go with empty hands. I want this, and that, and the other." If they refused him one thing he asked for something quite different; and inasmuch as one of the faithful had remained "covered" during prayers, the Evil One politely snatched up his hat, and if God had let him have his own way, hair and skin would have accompanied the headgear.

At about the same period I witnessed an analogous fact. Frau Kron, an honest and pious matron, was possessed by a demon; the minister was preparing to drive it out at all costs when Frau Wolff entered. She was a young woman who surpassed her sisters in the art of beautifying her face, arranging her cap, and posing before the looking glass. When the evil spirit caught sight of her, he shouted. "Ah, you are here, are you? Just wait a bit till I arrange your cap before the mirror. Your ears shall tingle, I can tell you."

To come back to our own servant. When the power of mischief noticed that the time for tormenting her had passed away, and that the Lord was granting the prayers of the faithful, the Evil One asked in a mocking tone a pane of the belfry's window, which request was no sooner accorded to him than the pane shivered into ever so many splinters. The girl, however, ceased to be possessed; she married in the village, and had several children.

My brother Johannes had for his first tutor Herr Aepinus, before the latter had his doctor's degree,[14] and afterwards Hermannus Bonus,[15] who would have been pleased to settle at Stralsund with fifty florins per annum, but the council of that particular period did not contain one member who had had a university training. Like the princes the council inclined towards papism, and looked askance at men of letters; hence, it rejected Bonnus' overtures. The latter soon afterwards became the tutor of the young King of Denmark, for whose use he composed his *Praecepta Grammaticae*, which was much more easy than the Donat Grammar, and prevails to the present day under the title of the *Grammatica Bonni*. At his return from Denmark, Bonnus was appointed superintendent at Lubeck, where he is interred *honorifice* behind the choir.

When my brother left the school at Lubeck, my parents made many heavy sacrifices to keep him at Wittemberg for several years, where, notwithstanding some *delicta juventutis*, he studied with advantage.

My tutor's name was Matthias Brassanus. At the outset of his career he had been a monk at the monastery of Camp, but at the suppression of the institution he had lived at Wittemberg at the cost of the prince, like Leonard Meisisch, the future court preacher and minister at Wolgast, and afterwards pastor at Altenkirchen--a downright Epicurean pig! Brassanus, on the other hand, was a small, polite, temperate, well-bred, evenly balanced man. After his stay at Wittemberg he became the preceptor of George and Johannes Smiterlow, and afterwards *rector scholae*. Their worships of Lubeck having prevailed upon the council of Stralsund to part with this able teacher, Brassanus devoted the whole of his life successfully directing the school of Lubeck.

I profited as much by the lessons as my natural restlessness of character permitted. There was a great deal of aptitude, but the application failed. In the winter time I ran amusing myself on the floating ice with my fellow-scholars of my own age. Johannes Gottschalk, our ringleader, always got scot-free, thanks to his long legs, while the rest of the gang (and I was invariably with them) took many enforced footbaths in order to get safely to the banks. My father, in crossing the bridge had occasion more than once to witness the prowess of his son, who received many a sound drubbing when he came to dry himself before the stove, for my father was a choleric gentleman. In summer I was in the habit of bathing with my chums behind Lorbeer's grange, which at present is my property. Burgomaster Smiterlow, having noticed me from his garden, told of me, and one day, while I was still asleep, my father planted himself in front of my bed, flourishing a big stick. He spoke very loudly while placing himself into position, and I was obliged to open my eyes. The sight of the club told me that my hour had come; I burst into tears and pleaded for mercy. "Very well, my good sir," said my father; when he called me "my good sir" it was a bad sign. "Very well, my good sir, you have been bathing; now allow me to rub you down." Saying which, he got hold of his weapon, pulled my shirt over my head, and did frightful execution.

My parents brought us up carefully. My father was somewhat hasty, and now and again his anger carried him beyond all bounds. I put him out of temper one day when he was in the stable and I at the door. He caught up a pitchfork and flung it at me. I had just time to get out of the way; the pitchfork stuck into a bath made of oak, and they had much trouble to get it out. In that way the Evil One was frustrated in all his designs against me by Providence. In a similar case, my mother, who was gentleness and tenderness itself, came running to the spot. "Strike harder," she said, "the wicked boy deserves all he gets." At the same time she slyly held back the arm of her husband, preventing the stick from coming down too heavily. Oh, my children, pray that the knowledge may be vouchsafed to you of bringing up your family in the way they should go. Correct them temperately, without compromising either their health or their intelligence, but at the same time do not imitate the apes who from excess of tenderness, smother their young.

Rector Brassanus insisted upon his pupils being present when he preached. Some were clever enough to get away on the sly; they went to buy pepper cakes, and repaired afterwards to the dram shop. The trick was done before there was time to look round. When the sermon drew to its close, every one was in his place again, and we went back to school as if nothing had happened. One day, however, we drank so much brandy that I felt horribly sick and vomited violently, and found it impossible either to keep on my legs or to articulate a syllable. The strongest of my schoolfellows took me home. My parents were under the impression that I was seriously ill; had they suspected the real cause of my malady, their treatment would have been less tender. When, at last, I avowed the truth, the fear of punishment had long ago vanished. The adventure was productive of some good. It inspired me with a thorough disgust for brandy, so that I could not even bear the smell of it.

My daily playmate was George Smiterlow, for we were neighbours, nearly relatives, and of about the same age, I being but a year older than he. One day he cut me with his knife between the index and the thumb, and I still bear the scar.

As I was whittling a piece of wood, my sister Anna snatched it away from me, and in trying to get it back again, I drove the chisel into my right thigh up to the handle. Master Joachim Gelhaar, an excellent *chirurgus*, renowned far and wide, began by probing the wound, and by getting the bad blood out of it; after which he dressed it with a cabbage leaf which was constantly kept moist. I was just recovering the use of my leg again when I took it into my head to go to the wood with my schoolfellows, for it was always difficult for me to keep still. The fatigue thus incurred caused a relapse. Next morning I dragged myself as far as the surgeon, who suspected my excursion, and swore at seeing a month of his efforts wasted. I should have been in a nice predicament if he had complained to my father.

In 1531, on the Monday before St. Bartholomew, they burned at Stralsund, Bischof, a tailor who had outraged his own daughter, aged twelve. The fellow was so strong that he jumped from the pyre when the fire had destroyed his bonds, but the executioner plunged his knife into him, and flung him back into the flames.

The following happened in June, 1532. A young fellow, good-looking, and with most fascinating manner, but by no means well enough in worldly goods, courted a more or less well-preserved widow, notwithstanding her nine children of her first husband, which subsequently she increased by another nine of her second. Tempted by the amiability, the appearance, and the demeanour of the youngster, the dame consented to be his wife. The happy day was already fixed, the viands ordered, and the preparations completed, but the bridegroom was at a loss how to pay for his wedding clothes, the customary presents and other things. Hence, one fine evening he left the city, and in the early morn reached the village of Putten, where, espying a ladder on a peasant's cart, he puts it against the wall of the church, breaks one of its windows, gets inside, forces the reliquary, possessing himself of the chalices, other holy vessels, all the gold and silver work, not forgetting the wooden box containing the money. After which, taking the way whence he had come, he flung away the box and entered the city laden with the spoil.

A local cowherd, driving his cattle to the field, happened to pick up the box. At the selfsame moment the sight of the ladder and of the broken window sets the whole of the place, rector, beadle, clerk, and peasantry, mad with excitement. The whole village is up in arms; the neighbouring roads are scoured in search of the perpetrator of the sacrilege. At twelve o'clock, the cowherd comes back with the box. He is arrested; the patrons of the church, who reside in the city, have him put to the torture. He confesses to the theft. There was, nevertheless, the absolute impossibility for him to have got rid of the stolen objects, inasmuch as he had been guarding his cattle during the five or six hours that had gone by between the robbery and his arrest; the slightest inquiry would have conclusively proved his innocence. In spite of this, the confession dragged from the poor wretch by unbearable pain, appears most conclusive. Condemned there and then, he is there and then put on the wheel. The real culprit watched the execution with the utmost composure.

The proceeds of this first crime were, however, by no means sufficient to defray the cost of the wedding, and the bridegroom forced another church. He took a reliquary and a holy vessel, reduced them to fragments, and tried to sell them to some goldsmiths at Greifswald. This time he was unable to lead the pursuers off the scent. Having been arrested in the house of my wife's parents, he was racked alive, and his body left to the carrion birds.

A similar tragedy took place between the Easter and Whitsun of 1544. I anticipate events, because the horror of them was pretty well equal, but there was a great difference in the procedure. In the one case, deplorable acts, at variance with all wisdom, and disgraceful to Christians; in the other place, a thoroughly laudable conduct, consistent with right and reason. On his return from Leipzig, whither he had gone to buy books,

Johannes Altingk, the son of the late Werner Altingk, a notable citizen and bookseller of Stralsund, was killed on the road from Anelam to Greifswald. In consequence of active inquiries, two individuals on whom rested grave suspicions, were incarcerated at Wolgast. But the case was proceeded with more methodically than the one I have just narrated. The magistrates went with the instruments of torture to the prisoner, who seemed the least resolved. He made a complete avowal. His companion and he had put up for the night at an inn at Grosskistow; Johannes Altingk had taken his seat at their table and shared their meal. Then, before going to bed, he had paid for all three, showing at the same time a well filled purse. The scoundrels had at once made up their minds between them to kill him at a little distance from the inn on the foot-road, intersected here and there by deep ruts, and where consequently there was only room to pass in single file. "Next morning, then, when the young bookseller was marching along between his fellow-travellers, I struck him at the back of the head;" said the accused. "The blow knocked him off his feet; we soon made an end of him altogether, and flung his body to the bottom of the deep bog. With my part of the spoil I bought myself this hat and this pair of shoes."

After this interrogatory, the judges, accompanied by the executioner and his paraphernalia, went to the second prisoner, who denied everything. It was in vain they pressed him and told him of his accomplice's avowal; he went on denying everything. When they were confronted, the one who had been first examined repeated all the particulars of the crime, beseeching the other to prevent a double martyrdom, inasmuch as the truth would be dragged from them by torture, and the punishment was unavoidable. No doubt the Stralsund authorities, those who had judged the above named perpetrator of the sacrilege, would have put the accused on the rack without the least compunction or ceremony, *de simplice et piano, sine strepitu judicii, quemadmodum Deus procedere solet*. At Wolgast, on the contrary, though the hangman had orders to hold himself in readiness, *ad actum propinquum*, the magistrates preferred to exercise some delay. The prince had the bog examined, but no body was found there. When taken to the spot, the prisoner who had confessed his guilt recognized the place of the murder, without being able, however, to point it out accurately. The landlord and his wife at Gross-Kistow, when examined carefully, denied having lodged any one at the period indicated.

Finally, a messenger of the Brandenburg March brought the news that an assassin condemned to death confessed to having killed in Pomerania a young librarian, for which crime two individuals were under lock and key at Wolgast. When taxed with having almost caused the death of innocent people by false avowals, the self-confessed murderer replied that death seemed to him preferable to the "criminal question," as that kind of torture was called. Their acquittal was pronounced on their taking the oath to bring no further action.

But this only shows the precautions to be taken before applying the instruments of torture to merely suspected men. On the other hand, it has been shown over and over again that some of the guilty hardened to that kind of thing will allow themselves to be torn to pieces sooner than avow.

In that year (1531) Duke George died in the prime of his life. His second wife was the sister to Margrave Joachim; they got rid of her for about 40,000 florins, and she subsequently married a prince of Anhalt, but finally she eloped with a falconer.

My mother having realized all her property at Greifswald, my parents really possessed a considerable fortune in sterling coin, and they called my father "the rich man of the Passen Strasse." It wanted, however, but a few years to shake his credit and to impair the happiness of his family. Without exaggeration, two women, named Lubbeke and Engeln were the principal causes of our reverses. Not content to buy on credit our cloth, which they resold to heaven knows who, they borrowed of my father, fifty, a hundred, and as much as a hundred and fifty crowns on the slightest pretext. The crown in those days was worth eight and twenty shillings of Lubeck. They promised to refund at eight and twenty and a half, and to settle for their purchases at the same rate; but if now and again they happened to make a payment on account of a hundred florins, they took care to buy at the same time goods for double the amount. My mother did not look kindly upon those two customers; she imagined that her money would be better invested at five per cent., and she spared neither warnings, prayers, nor tears to dissuade my father from trusting them. She even took Pastor Knipstrow and others into her confidence to that effect. Finally, the account came to a considerable amount, while the debtors were unable to pay as much as twenty florins. Then it transpired what had become of the cloth. The mother of one townsman, Jacob Leveling, had had 800 florins of it; the wife of another, Hermann Bruser, 1,725 florins. Hermann Bruser was a big cloth merchant who sold retail much cheaper than any of his fellow-tradesmen.

My father having taken proceedings against his two customers as well as against the woman Bruser, the latter and her husband promised to pay the 1,725 florins. Nicholas Rode, who had married Bruser's sister, and the syndic of the city, Johannes Klocke, afterwards burgomaster, induced my father to accept that arrangement, and Bruser secured conditions after having signed an acknowledgment beginning as follows: "I, together with my legitimate wife, declare to be duly and lawfully indebted to etc., etc." The syndic had drawn up this act with his own hand. He had affixed his signature to it, and his seal, and Rode had in the latter two respects done the same. But the period of the first payment coinciding with the tumult against Nicholas Smiterlow, Bruser, one of the ringleaders, thought he could have the whip hand of my father as well as of the burgomaster. On his refusal to pay, the case came before the court once more; and then, while denying his debt, in spite of the formal terms of his declaration, Bruser denounced as usurious agreements obtained by litigation. Klocke and Rode assisted him with their advice and influence; the first-named, in his capacity of a lawyer, conducted the suit, and quoting the *leges et doctorum opiniones*, easily convinced his non-legally educated colleagues of the council. The Westphalian Cyriacus Erckhorst, the son-in-law of Rode, and a velvet merchant, plotted on his side. There were golden florins for the all-powerful burgomaster Lorbeer, and pieces of dress-material for Mrs. Burgomaster; so that, after long arguments on both sides, Bruser was allowed to swear that he was ignorant of the affair, which, moreover, was tainted with usury. My father could not conceive that this personage would have the audacity to deny his signature, and, supported in his supposition by Burgomaster Nicholas Smiterlow, he did not appeal against the judgment, and at the next sitting Bruser appeared at the bar of the inner court, took the oath, and offered to comply with the second part of the order; only, in consequence of the absence of his witness he claimed a delay of a twelvemonth and a day, which was accorded to him; after which my father appealed to the council of Stralsund and afterwards to that of Lubeck.

In due time my father started for Lubeck, and took me with him. At Rostock, we lodged at the sign of *The Hop*, in the Market Place. My father had a considerable sum upon him to pay cash for his purchases of salt, salted cod-fish and soap, and as a measure of precaution, he carried that money in his small clothes, for Mecklenburg was infested by footpads and highwaymen. While undressing, he dropped his purse under the bed, an accident which he did not notice until next day about twelve o'clock, when we had reached Bukow. As the court was just about to open it fell to my lot to take the road back to Rostock *per pedes*. On that day I could get no further than Berkentin, but very early next morning I was at Rostock. Naturally, I rushed to the inn and to the room. Luckily the servants had not made the beds. I soon espied the little bag and was in time to take the coach to Wismar. My father, uneasy on my account, was already reproaching himself for having let me go.

Their worships of Lubeck condemned Bruser to keep his written promise; he then appealed to the Imperial Chamber. The suit dragged along for several years; finally, the supreme decision was to the effect that it had been well judged, but improperly thrown into appeal in the first instance, and that in the second it had been faultily judged and properly sent for appeal. The defendant was condemned to pay the costs to be determined by the judge.

And now I may be permitted to give an instance of the disloyalty of the procurators of the Imperial Chamber. Doctor Simeon Engelhardt, my father's procurator, did not hesitate to write to him that he had won his case, and asked for the bill of costs of the two previous instances, so that he might hand them to the taxing judge and apply for execution. He added that the trouble he had taken with the affair seemed to him to warrant special fees. My parents, elated with the news, promptly transmitted the bill of costs and their fees for the execution. Engelhardt produced the *cedula expensarum*; Bruser's procurator requested copy, not without pretending to raise objection. Engelhardt delivered the required copy, leaving to the judge the case of designating the winning party; in other words, the one who had the right to present the *designatio expensarum*. Well, that right was adjudged to Bruser, who drew up the *cedula* after *ours*. Engelhardt was compelled to hold his tongue and my father had to pay 164 florins.

That point having been settled, they passed to the second *membrum* of the Stralsund judgment; namely, whether the conditions stipulated for by my father were tainted with usury? After such an expensive and protracted lawsuit, the court, considering that Bruser had failed in his attempt to bring proof, condemned him to fulfil his engagements. Against that sentence he appealed to Lubeck. Having been non-suited there, he wished to have recourse to the Imperial Chamber, but we signified opposition to the *exceptio devolutionis*. According to us, he had not complied with the privilege of Lubeck. Bruser's procurator maintained the contrary. The whole of the discussion bore entirely on the sense of the word "*wann*" inserted in the Lubeck *vidimus*. Was it a *conjunctio causalis, cum posteaquam*, or an *adverbium temporis, quando*? After long-drawn debates, the appeal was rejected, and Bruser had all the costs to pay.

Then, to frustrate his adversary, he pleaded poverty on oath, although he gave to his daughter as many pearls and jewels as a burgomaster's girl could possibly pretend to. Foreseeing the upshot of the lawsuit, he had already disposed of one of his houses; after which he bestirred himself to safeguard his dwelling-house, his cellar and his various other property from being seized. Nicholas Rode, he who had signed the obligation, deposed to that effect, a document professedly anterior to my father's claim, an act constituting in his favour a general mortgage on all Bruser's property. As a matter of course, this led to a new lawsuit, which occupied respectively the courts of Stralsund and of Lubeck and the Imperial Chamber. The latter registered Rode's appeal at the moment the Protestant States denied its jurisdiction. A suspension of six years was the result, but after the reconstitution of the chamber and the closure of the debates, I did not succeed, in spite of two years' stay at Spires, in getting a judgment.

Weary of being involved in law for thirty-four years, my father wound up by acquitting the heirs of Rode of all future liabilities in consideration of a sum of one thousand florins. As it happened the original debt was seventeen hundred and five and twenty florins; in addition to this, my father had refunded to Bruser one hundred and sixty-four florins expenses, his own costs exceeded a thousand florins and he had waited forty years for his money. The whole affair was nothing short of a downright calamity to our family; it interrupted my studies and caused the death of my brother Johannes. "*Dimidium plus toto*," says Hesiod, and the maxim is above all wise in connexion with a law-suit at the Imperial Chamber.

Writing, as I do, for the edification of my children, I consider it useful to mention here the subsequent fate of our godless adversaries. The seventy-fifth Psalm says: "For in the hand of the Lord there is a cup, and the wine is red, and he poured out of the same, but the dregs thereof all the wicked of the earth shall wring them out and drink them." Yes, the Almighty has comforted me, he has permitted me to see the scattering of my enemies. The two principal ones, Hermann Bruser and his fraudulent wife, fell into abject misery; they lived for many years on the bounty of parents and friends; finally the husband became valet of Joachim Burwitz who from the position of porter and general servant at the school when I was young had risen to be the secretary of the King of Sweden. The devil, however, twisted Bruser's neck at Stockholm. He was found in his master's wardrobe, his face all distorted. His daughter, dowered *in fraudem mei patris*, did, for all that, not escape very close acquaintance with poverty. She sold her houses and her land; and at her death her husband became an inmate of the asylum of the Holy Ghost, where he is to this day. Bruser's son, it is true, rose to be a secretary in Sweden, but far from prospering, he committed all kind of foolish acts everywhere. His first wife, the daughter of Burgomaster Gentzkow,[16] died of grief at Stralsund, where he had left her with her children at his departure for Sweden. He was found dead one morning in his room; his descendants are vegetating some in the city, some in the country.

The author of the plot, the honest dispenser of advice, Johannes Klocke, managed to keep his wealth, but he was racked with gout and had to be carried in a chair to the Town Hall; he died after having suffered martyrdom for many years. The four sons of Nicholas Rode were reduced to beggary; the house Bruser sold in order to cheat my father actually belongs to my son-in-law. As for Burgomaster Christopher Lorbeer, so skilled in prolonging lawsuits, does he not expiate, he and his, every day, the wrong in having lent himself to corruption. Erckhorst, the man who tempted him, was robbed while engaged in transporting from one town to another two large bundles of velvet, silk, jewellery and pearls, the whole being estimated at several thousands of florins. His second wife was the byword of the city for her levity of conduct; at every moment she was caught in her own dwelling-house and in the most untoward spots committing acts of criminal intercourse with her apprentices. What had been saved from the thieves was devoured by his wife's paramours. Absolutely at a loss to reinstate himself in his former position, Erckhorst made an end of his life by stabbing himself.

My father's other debtor, the woman Leveling, was left a widow with an only son. Her property in houses and in land yielded, it was said, a golden florin and a fowl per day. That fortune, nevertheless, melted away, and Leveling, worried by her creditors, was obliged to quit her house with nothing but what she stood up in. Lest her son, a horrible ne'er-do-well of fifteen, should spend his nights in houses of ill-fame, she kept a mistress for him at home; after that she married him at such an early age as to astonish everybody, but he cared as much about the sanctity of marriage as a dog cares about Lent. During the ceremonies connected with rendering homage to Duke Philip, the duchess lodged at Leveling's and stood godmother to his new-born daughter, which honour had not the slightest effect in changing the scandalous life he led with a concubine. One night, in company with a certain Valentin Buss, he emptied the baskets in the pond of the master of the fishmongers. An arrant thief, he was fast travelling towards the gallows. Buss, who wound up by going to prison, would have been hanged but for Leveling, who in order to redeem himself parted to the council with his last piece of ground, namely, that in which his father's body rested in the church. One day at the termination of the sermon, Leveling, sword in hand, pursued my father, who had just time to reach his domicile and to shut the door in his face. On the other hand, Master Sonnenberg, who sheltered the old woman Leveling while she was negotiating with her creditors, was not content with egging on her son to all sorts of evil deeds, but had the effrontery to say to my father: "I'll tame you so well that you shall come and eat out of my hands."

After having squandered his inheritance, Leveling died in the most abject poverty; his daughter Marie, the duchess' goddaughter, sells fish in the market. Such was the end of the wealthy popinjay. Mother and son followed the traditions of their family without having profited by the lessons of the past; one of the woman Leveling's relatives was, in fact, that Burgomaster Wulf Wulflam, reputed the richest man on that part of the coast,[17] whose wife was so fond of show and splendour that at her second marriage she sent for the prince's musicians from Stettin and walked from her house to the church on an English carpet. For her own wear she only used the finest Riga flax. So much vainglory was punished by the God of Justice, who expels from His kingdom the proud and haughty. The only thing she had finally left of all her magnificence was a silver bowl with which she went begging from door to door. "Charity," she cried, "for the poor rich woman." One day she asked from one of her former servants a shift and some linen for a collar to it. Moved with pity, the latter did not refuse. "Madame," she said, "this linen was made of the flax you used for your own wear. I have carefully picked it up, cleaned and spun it."[18]

The arrangement made by the Levelings with their creditors gave to my father the passage of the Muhlen-Strasse. Inasmuch as the premises were tumbling to pieces, masons, carpenters, stonecutters and plasterers were soon set to work and began by expelling the rats, mice and doubtful human creatures that had taken up their quarters there. The best tenement adjoining the city wall with a beautiful look-out on the moats and the open country was occupied by the concubine of Zabel Lorbeer. She was one of the three Maries, and had presented him with either seven or eight bastards. My father, finding the door locked one morning, ordered the workmen to knock down the wall which fell on the bed where the scamp and the girl were sleeping; the only thing they could do was to get out of the way as quickly as possible. Lorbeer brought up his progeny according to the principles that guided him; and finally had his son beheaded to save him the disgrace of the gallows.

A short digression is necessary in connexion with the three Maries. [19] They were sisters, exceedingly good-looking, but the poet's "*Et quidem servasset, si non formosa fuisset*," essentially applied to them. Many traps are laid for beauty, and they one after another fell into them. They lived on their charms, being particularly careful about their appearance and dress in order to attract admirers. Their attempts to obtain such notice were seconded by an unspeakable old crone, Anna Stranck, who had been a downright Messalina in her time, and of whom it was said that she could reckon on the whole of the city among her parentage, although she had neither husband nor children, but that she had had illicit intercourse with every male, young, old and middle-aged, fathers, sons and brothers. Anna Stranck invented for the use of the three Maries a kind of loose coif, the fashion of which our womenkind have religiously preserved; even those who have discarded it wearing a velvet hood based upon that model. They brought their hair, black or grey about two inches down on the forehead. Then came as many inches of gold lace or embroidery, so that the real cap, intended to keep the head warm did not in the least cover the brain. I am purposely quoting the name of Anna Stranck, for it is well to remind people to whom the headgear was due in the first instance; and may it please our dames to preserve it for ever in memory of the woman, mother, grandmother and great-grandmother of their husbands.

I now resume my personal narrative. During the rebuilding of this new property, I was fetching and carrying all the while. One day my father sent me to our own house for the luncheon for himself and for the carpenters. The workmen were just knocking down a chimney; they were working higher than the chimney on a gangway made of boards which at each extremity overlapped the stays. A great number of large nails were strewn about the scaffolding. I climbed up, with my arms full of provisions, but scarcely did I set my foot on the gangway than the gangway toppled over and I was flung into space, the nails descending in a shower on my head. I just happened to fall by the side of the open chimney; half an ell more or less and I should have been through its aperture on the ground floor. As it was, the accident proved sufficiently serious. I had dislocated my right elbow and horribly bruised my arm. They took me home, whence my mother took me to Master Joachim Gelhaar. He was absent, and inasmuch as the case seemed urgent, they had recourse to the barber in the Old Market, who dressed the bruises without noticing that the bone was dislocated. Next morning Master Gelhaar came. A simple glance was sufficient for him; he grasped my arm, pulled and twisted it and put the bones back into their sockets. But the limb was bruised and swollen and twisted. I shall never forget the pain I suffered. In a little while, though, I was enabled to go about the house as usual with one arm in a sling, and the other available for our childish pastimes.

The old beams and rafters of the premises under repair were stacked at our place. One day, while perched on one of the piles, I struck out with a hammer in my left hand; one of the beams rolled down and my leg was caught between it and the other wood. The pain made me cry out lustily, but it was impossible to disengage my leg. My mother was not strong enough for the task, and making sure that my leg was crushed, she shouted and fetched the navvies and the brewery workmen; they delivered me. When she was certain that no harm had come to me, my mother, still excited, treated me to a good drubbing. On New Year's Day, 1533, my father was elected dean of the Corporation of Drapers.[20]

CHAPTER III

The ecclesiastical affairs of Stralsund had assumed more or less regular conditions; the Gospel was preached in all the churches without opposition either on the part of the princes or of the council. Smiterlow had sanctioned the return of Rolof Moller. Nevertheless, peace was not maintained for long, Lubeck, Rostock, Stralsund and Wismar having revolted against their magistrates. In fact, at the death of King Frederick of Denmark, George Wullenweber,[21] burgomaster of Lubeck, having for his acolyte Marx Meyer, decided to declare war upon Duke Christian of Holstein.

According to Wullenweber, the conquest of Denmark was a certainty; and inasmuch as the magistrates of Lubeck, belonging to the old families, looked with apprehension on the enterprise, they were deposed and sixty burghers added to their successors.

Marx Meyer was a working blacksmith with a handsome face and figure. Being a skilful farrier he had accompanied the cavalry in several campaigns, and his conduct both with regard to his comrades and the enemy had been such as to gain for him the highest grades. He was created a Knight in England and amassed a considerable fortune. His rise in the world filled him, however, with inordinate pride and vanity. Nothing in the way of sumptuous garments and golden ornaments seemed good enough to emphasize his knightly dignity. He had a crowd of retainers and a stable full of horses, for like the majority of folk of low birth, he knew of no bounds in his prosperity. Odd to relate, he was courted by people of good condition; women both young, rich and well-born fell in love with this, and it would appear that he gave them no cause to regret their infatuation. I have read a letter written to him by one of the foremost ladies of quality of Hamburg: "My dear Marx, after having visited all the chapels, you might for once in a way come to the cathedral." May his death be accounted as an instance of everlasting justice.

In June 1534 the councillors of the Wendish cities,[22] apprehending a disaster and being moreover exceedingly grieved at this struggle against the excellent Duke of Holstein, foregathered at Hamburg to consider the state of affairs. Wullenweber, however, presumptuous as was his wont, became more obstinate than ever and rejected with scorn most acceptable terms of peace. Hence, the Stralsund delegate, Burgomaster Nicholas Smiterlow, addressed the following prophetic words to him: "I have been present at many negotiations, but never have I seen matters treated like this, Signor George. You will knock your head against the wall and you shall fall on your beam end." After that apostrophe, Wullenweber, furious with anger, left the council-chamber, made straight for his inn, had his and Meyer's horses saddled and both took the way back to Lubeck, where immediately after his arrival Wullenweber summoned his undignified council and the aforementioned sixty burghers, who between them decree in the twinkling of an eye a levy of troops; dispatching meanwhile to the council of Stralsund a blatant sedition-monger, Johannes Holm, with verbal instructions and a missive couched substantially as follows: "Wullenweber is zealously working to bring principalities and kingdoms under the authority of the cities, but the opposition of Burgomaster Smiterlow has driven him from the diet. In spite of this, the struggle is bound to continue, so it lays with you to act."

Nothing more than that was wanted to stir the whole of the citizens against Smiterlow. The Forty-Eight came to tender their condolence to Burgomaster Lorbeer who was secretly jealous of his colleague. Pretending to be greatly concerned, he exclaimed: "This is too much, impossible to defend him any longer." His hearers took it for granted that Smiterlow was left to their discretion, while, according to Lorbeer himself, the ambiguous words merely signified: "Smiterlow has so many enemies that I can no longer come to his aid."

At Smiterlow's return, the fire so skilfully fed by Lorbeer broke into flame. People hailed each other with the cry, "Nicholas the Pacific is here." The delegate had to deliver an account of his mission to the burghers summoned to that effect at six in the morning, at the Town Hall, with the city-gates closed and the cannon taken out of the arsenal and placed in position in the Old Markets The crowd poured into the streets, and at the Town Hall itself people were crushing the life out of each other. When Nicholas Smiterlow came to his statement that he had opposed Wullenweber's warlike motions, there was a hurricane of cries, curses and insults; it sounded as if they had all gone stark mad at once. It was proposed to fling the speaker out of the window; an axe was flung at the Councillors' bench and in endeavouring to intercept the weapon the worshipful Master Kasskow was severely wounded. One individual placed himself straight in front of the burgomaster. "You scum of the earth," he yelled; "did you not unjustly fine me twenty florins? Now it is my turn." "What's your name?" asked Smiterlow. "That's right," he said on its being given; "it was a piece of injustice, he ought to have had the gallows. I was sheriff at the time and the council instructed me to fine you twenty florins. My register of fines can show you that I did not keep them for myself, but spent them for the good of the city." His interlocutor wished to hear no more and disappeared in the crowd.

It should also be noted that the beggars who generally hung about the burgomaster's dwelling were all the while vociferating under the windows of the Town Hall. "Fling Nicholas the Pacific down to us," they shouted; "we'll cut him up and play ball with the pieces." One of the Forty-Eight having asked, "What do you think of it, my worthy burghers?" the rabble yelled, "Yes, yes," without the faintest idea of the nature of the question. Somebody thereupon observed, "Why are you shouting 'Yes'? Are you willing to hand over the public chest?" Thereupon there was an equally unanimous and stentorian "No." Unquestionably the devil had occasion on that day to laugh at the people in his sleeve.

This martyring of the first burgomaster, an eminent, virtuous man, who had, moreover, attained a certain age, was prolonged till seven o'clock at night. Finally, he received the order not to leave his quarters. Similar injunctions were inflicted on my father in his capacity of nephew by marriage to the burgomaster, and to Joachim Rantzow for having exclaimed, "Gently, gently; at least give people a chance to explain themselves."

The soldiers and sailors were enjoined at the sound of the drum to man the galleys, and a strict watch was kept. At night a strong squad encamped in front of Smiterlow's dwelling; the soldiers, among other pastimes, amused themselves with firing at the front door; the bullets passed out at the other side of the passage through a circular glazed aperture. There were many hours of anguish for the burgomaster, his wife and children, who expected at every moment to have their home invaded by the mob.

On the Monday of St. John they elected two burgomasters, namely, Joachim Prütze, the erewhile town clerk, an honest and sensible man, and Johannes Klocke, the actual town clerk and syndicus. Seven burghers were elected councillors; with the exception of Secretary Johannes Senckestack, who had had no hand in the thing, they were all honest, uninteresting folk, as simple-minded as they were upright and virtuous. Johannes Tamme, for instance, a worthy and straightforward man, replied to the artizans and others who came to complain of the bad state of business: "Make your mind easy; it will change now that seven capable people form part of the council." Antique simplicity indeed. Nicholas Baremann boasted of earning ten marks each time he left his home. One day he went into the cellar to look at a barrel of salt-fish, he was accompanied by a servant who was not altogether right in his head. In those days men wore round their necks a very narrow collar of pleated tulle. While the master was bending over the fish, the servant with one blow of his hatchet clean cut his head off. Instead of taking flight he quietly went back to his work. When interrogated about the motive of his crime, he replied that his master presented his neck so gently as to make the operation merely child's play. In spite of his unquestionable mental state, the murderer was broken alive on the wheel.

My father was practically imprisoned for fifteen months in his own house, whence resulted an enormous loss to his own business, for in view of the coming herring-fair at Falsterbo, in the province of Schonen,[23] his cellar and hall were packed with Luneburg salt; there was also a considerable quantity of dried cod, besides a big assortment of cloth, and amidst all this he was forbidden to cross the threshold of his house and no one was allowed to come and see him. My mother was, moreover, pregnant at the time, and as the date of her confinement drew near my father asked for leave to take up his quarters with a neighbour until it was over. His petition was refused, and at the critical moment he found himself compelled to get into the adjoining house by the roof. He was also prevented from personally inviting the godparents.

George Wullenweber and his undisciplined followers opened the hostilities by sea and by land. In this bitter struggle the Duke of Holstein preserved the advantage, though he fought as one against two, but the Almighty was on his side. Humiliated by these reverses, with their prestige diminished and threatened with an ignominious fall, the fribbling authors of the war expected to save everything by substituting another chief for Wullenweber. After a week of negotiations the emissaries of Lubeck, Rostock, and Stralsund assembled at Wismar offered to Duke Albrecht of Mecklenburg the throne of Denmark. The act, drawn up in due form and signed and sealed by Lubeck, Rostock and Wismar was dispatched to Stralsund, the signature and seal of which was wanting to it. The fine phrases of the Lubeckian message got the better of the opposition of the council; the Forty-Eight broke open the casket containing the great seal, affixed it to the document and sent it back to Wismar.

Every rule had been strictly observed; the Duke of Mecklenburg invited the representatives of the cities for the next day to a banquet, at which the act was to be handed to him. But during the morning itself the delegates of Stralsund, under the pretext of wishing to examine the parchment, asked to look at it, and Christopher Lorbeer, borrowing a pocket-knife of his colleague, Franz Wessel, cut the strings of the Stralsund seal, after which they made off as far as their carriage would let them. They were half-way to Rostock while the other ambassadors were still waiting for them with dinner. Undeterred by this, Albrecht, accompanied by his wife, her ladies, servants, horses and dogs, took the road to Copenhagen, like a legitimate sovereign.

Lorbeer himself, his children, and the rest of his relations have sung in all manner of keys the resolute--others would say, the audacious--conduct he displayed on that occasion; nobody, whether townsman, rustic or alien was to remain ignorant of the feat; and to this day people keep repeating that Burgomaster Lorbeer, scorning all danger (*non enim sine periculo facinus magnum et memorabile*), made himself illustrious by this signal act, by this heroic exploit. If, however, we turn the leaf, what do we read? *Qui periculum amat peribit in eo*; real courage will never be confounded with reckless audacity. That the act was provided with the great seal of Stralsund is a fact known to the representatives of Lubeck, Rostock and Wismar, who handled the document on the strength of which, when ratified by the Forty-Eight, Duke Albrecht went and shut himself up in Copenhagen, where he sustained a siege, and practically obliged Stralsund to make the same sacrifices for him the other cities had made. Consequently, one has the right to ask: "Where was the advantage of detaching the seal?" If Lorbeer had utilized his energy in keeping in port vessels, soldiers and ammunition, then he would have rendered a signal service, and, besides, prevented the waste of much money. Do Lorbeer's admirers imagine that Duke Albrecht would not have avenged the outrage when once his throne was consolidated? The least he would have done was to close the Sound against us, and to hamper our commerce everywhere. Verily they are right, the citizens who keep on praising the mad trick of Lorbeer.

Burgomaster Smiterlow bore his enforced retirement with admirable patience. Instead of meddling with public affairs, he assiduously read the Holy Scriptures, and spent most of his time in prayer. He finally knew by heart the Psalms of David. As a daily visitor to his home, I can say that no bitter word ever fell from his lips. He often repeated, "They are my fellow-citizens; the Lord will move their spirit. It is my duty to suffer for the love of my children."

Our gracious prince, Duke Philip, sent to request the liberation of the burgomaster. The envoys were told that the answer would be sent to them to the hostel. The discussion was a very long one, after which they deputed the very host of the envoys, Hermann Meier, together with Nicholas Rode, the one as illiterate as the other, and both densely ignorant on every subject. Hermann Meier, who was a native of Parow, had amassed much property in cash, in land, and in houses. Being the owner of the two villages of Parow, he had practically for his vassals his uncles and his cousins, whom he ruled at his will. Nicholas Rode was a well-to-do merchant, but who had never associated with people of condition. Hermann Meier had undertaken to address the envoys, but he began to stumble at the first sentence, and finally, stricken dumb altogether, he left his colleague behind, rushed from the room, and went helter-skelter down the stairs. When he reached the yard, he fell altogether ill with excitement. Nevertheless, he plucked up his courage and went back--to apologize, as one would suppose. Not at all. Scorning all exordium, and without even giving the envoys their titles, he went straight to the point. "The council and the Forty-Eight," he said, "have decided in the name of the citizens that we should signify to you as follows: Inasmuch as they did not consult the prince to inflict the confinement, they shall not consult him to annul it." Verily, a speech worthy of the orator and of those who sent him, *similes habent labra lactucas.* I wonder what would happen if somebody took it into his head to-day to address a prince in that manner. Considering that all the magistrates of that period were of most mediocre capacity (I am using a mild term), two suppositions are admissible. It was either the intention of the Forty-Eight to make the young duke ridiculous by choosing such delegates, or the three or four intelligent members of the council declined this foolish mission.

The embassy had, however, one result. My father was summoned to the Town Hall, where he was told that he could recover his freedom in consideration of a fine of a hundred marks. He wished to know what fault he had committed, and was told not to "argufy." "Hundred marks or the collar. You can take your choice." As a matter of course my father chose the former, although the only crime that could be imputed to him was his marriage with the niece of Burgomaster Smiterlow. The same mode of procedure was applied to the case of Joachim Rantzow, an honest and honoured citizen, who subsequently became a member of the council.

Shortly after this Councillors Nicholas Rode and Nicholas Bolte came to enjoin Burgomaster Smiterlow, in conjunction with two of his relatives, to sign a document already engrossed and provided with the wax for three seals. According to them it was the only means to end his captivity and to avoid all further and even more serious dangers. In this piece of writing Burgomaster Smiterlow confessed to having been a traitor to the city, a perjurer, guilty of the most infamous conduct, and to have forfeited all his rights. The two councillors made it their special business to paint the situation in the most sombre colours. Terror-stricken and dissolved in tears, the burgomaster's wife implored her husband to accede to the request of these two fanatics until the Lord Himself could come to his aid. Unmanned by all this, Smiterlow asked my father to seal the act with him. "No," exclaimed the latter, "I shall not sign your dishonour." But his two sons-in-law, overcome by the tears of their mother-in-law, affixed their seals. Thereupon the burgomaster, escorted by the two councillors, his two sons-in-law and my father, repaired to the Town Hall. On their way, he went into the St. Nicholas' Church, knelt down in the stall near the great St. Christopher, and said a short prayer.

The council of the Forty-Eight was holding its meeting in the summer council-room. Requested by Christopher Lorbeer to resume his usual seat, Smiterlow refused. "I cannot do so," he said, "after the document I have just signed." Nevertheless, they insisted until he took his seat. Then he addressed them, reminding them that he had travelled in the city's service a hundred and odd days (I have forgotten the exact number, for I was only sixteen years old). "If it can be proved that I have spent one florin unnecessarily, been guilty of one neglect or caused a single prejudice, I am ready to yield all I possess and my life besides. If, on the other hand, I can show my innocence, then can I count upon the same protection as that enjoyed by the other citizens; that is, frequent the churches, cross the bridges, appear in the market place, and attend to my business in all freedom and security." The reply being affirmative, he rose from his seat, wished the council a peaceful term of administration, and, followed by his nearest relatives, went back to his home.

The situation remained the same until 1537. Strong in the consciousness of his own honesty, and leaving the Forty-Eight to govern at their own sweet will, Smiterlow remained perfectly tranquil in his retirement. He was an assiduous churchgoer, and when the weather was fine, took excursions into the country accompanied by his daughters, his sons-in-law, my parents and their family. His jovial disposition delighted them all.

On the other hand, the Forty-Eight were constantly assailed by fear. The success of the war became more and more doubtful, in spite of the sacrifice of hundreds of lives, in spite of the pillaging of the Town Hall, in spite of the enormous sums wasted--thrown into the water, it would be more correct to say. They converted the bells of the city and of the villages into money; all these took the road to Lubeck, where, to our disgrace be it said, the mark of Stralsund can still be seen on a bronze pile-driver. Twice did the citizens, from the highest to the lowest, pay the tax of the hundredth halfpenny on the strength of their oath.

When they saw their power tottering, the Forty-Eight imitated the unjust steward of St. Luke, and compelled the community to confirm, renew and extend the infamous declaration violently dragged from the council of 1522. The new act had apparently some good in it. It enjoined upon the magistrates judicious rules of conduct which, however, were not at all within their competence. In reality, the ancient council acknowledged to have incurred by its resistance a fine which was remitted to them by their magnanimous successors. It took the engagement to favour the cause of the Forty-Eight. No dissension, misunderstanding, accusation or recrimination, whether relating to the past or the present, would in future be tolerated. Any contravention to that effect entailed upon the councillors the loss of their dignities; upon other citizens, the loss of their civic rights; upon women and children, a fine of fifty florins, payable by the father or husband, and going to the fund for public buildings.

That much was decided on the Friday after Candlemas, 1535. Nevertheless, the Forty-Eight kept trembling in their shoes. The very next year witnessed the promulgation of another decree, threatening with the utmost bodily penalty any and every one, young or old, rich or poor, magistrate or simple burgher who should decline the responsibility of the expedition to Denmark, or should influence others on the subject. This act was transcribed sequentially to that of 1535, with the formula: Given under our administration anno and day as above. Hence it was antedated. It was a clumsy trick, for a unique act does not admit of a codicil. But does the ass ever succeed in hiding its ears?

In 1536, on the day of *Esto Mihi*, Duke Philip married, at the Castle of Torgau, Fräulein Marie, sister of the Duke of Saxony, Johannes Friedrich. The marriage rites were performed by Dr. Martin Luther, who after the ceremony said to the husband: "Gracious prince and lord, Should the event so much desired be somewhat tardy in coming, let not your Highness be discouraged. *Saxum* means stone, and nothing can be drawn from a rock without time or patience. Your Highness shall be included in my prayers: *semen tuum non deficit.*" The duchess, in fact, gave birth to her first child only about four years later.

The punishment of the wicked and the triumph of the just marched abreast, *inclusio unius est exclusio alterius et e contra*. Amidst the torments of hell the damned watch the bliss of the happy ones whom they have persecuted on earth. I am bound to insist upon this antithesis while pursuing my narrative. I expect no thanks, for men are so thin-skinned as to cause them to quiver at the slightest touch; and that is the reason why all those who have written on Stralsund, such as Thomas Kantzow, Valentin Eichstedt,[24] and Johannes Berckmann passed their pens to their successors when they got as far as 1536. I have no desire to flatter or to find fault, but I intend to speak the real truth, however disagreeable it may turn out to be. My sole concern is to preserve the dignity of history. If people will take the trouble to read carefully the authors just named, and especially Berckmann, otherwise the Augustine monk, his impertinent libels will enable them to appreciate the usefulness of the present pages. The approval of honest folk is the only reward I care for; the rest is of no consequence.

It is almost incredible that the Duke of Mecklenburg should have committed the blunder of yielding to the suggestions of Wullenweber, whom all good citizens virtually disavowed. Never was there a more unjust war. In disposing of a country which, on no assumption whatever, could possibly belong to them, the cities caused an incalculable prejudice to the Duke of Holstein, the Lord's anointed, the legitimate, well-beloved, and expected sovereign. He showed great firmness. The leader of a powerful army, and master of its communications by sea and by land, he was fully aware of his superiority to an adversary who, shut up in Copenhagen, only thought of pleasure, hunts and banquets. In spite of his just resentment, magnanimous Christian obtained a victory over himself, and while the surrender of the city was being negotiated, he sent provisions to the Duchess of Mecklenburg, at that time in childbed. This was tantamount to giving her charity. After the retreat of Duke Albrecht, Charles made a triumphal entry into Copenhagen, where he was crowned in 1537, and the presence at the pomp and ceremony of the coronation of the ambassadors of the cities was calculated to give him complete satisfaction. As for the Duke of Mecklenburg, he had learned to his cost the folly of disregarding the words of the Holy Spirit: "My son, fear thou the Lord and the king, and meddle not with them that are given to change: for their calamity shall rise suddenly; and who knoweth the ruin of them both?" (Proverbs xxiv. 21, 22).

At Lubeck the pitiful collapse of the council brought about the reinstatement of the old magistracy. In a spirit of pacification they gave Wullenweber the captaincy of Bergendorf; but Wullenweber, while crossing the territory of the Abbey of Werden, was seized by order of Christopher, bishop of Bremen, who handed him over to his brother, Duke Heindrich of Brunswick. After a cruel captivity at Wolfenbüttel, and in consequence of indictments as numerous as they were grave (especially from Lubeck, represented by his secretary), he was sentenced to death in September, 1537, and his body quartered. At the taking of the fortress of Wardenburg, Duke Christian captured Marx Meyer, his brother Gerard Meyer, and a notorious Danish priest. These three were executed by the sword, quartered, and their bodies shown on the rack to the great satisfaction of the Danish people and the honest Lubeckenaars so long oppressed.

Nicholas Nering, a citizen of those parts, had sold to Johannes Krossen a farm with all its live stock and belongings, but, according to him, he had reserved for himself the foal of a handsome mare, if it should happen to be a colt, and a colt it turned out to be. At the period of its weaning, in 1535, he claimed the young animal. Krossen contested the claim. Thereupon, according to the evidence of his step-son, Peter Klatteville, who was about fifteen, and whose evidence was recorded in the black register of the court, Nering, not to be outdone, mounted his black horse, the lad trotting barefooted by his side, and both went at five a.m. to Krossen's farm. Nering got the colt out of the stables while the youngster kept watch. Nering hid his spoil for three weeks at Schwartz's, at the new mill, and after having made Peter promise to keep the secret on the penalty of the most terrible punishment.

Different is the version recorded in the new register, written on parchment and bound in white sow's skin. "In 1536, on the Monday after *Reminiscere*, Nicholas Nering, accused of pillage, has confessed before the court that riding along the Frankische landstrasse, after passing the gate, he noticed three colts; that moved by a wicked inspiration, he had gone up to them and thrown the leash over one of these, and fastened it to the pommel of his saddle, and in that way brought it to his own stables. After having heard the above confession, it was decided to take Nicholas Nering outside the city and hang him on the gallows."

Nicholas Nering's bad reputation did not dispose the council in his favour; hence all his friends had employed him to restore the colt in order to prevent the matter going into the courts, but he had proved obstinate. While he was in his cell, he repeated that he was indifferent to death, but that he deplored the calamities which his execution would entail. It was an evident proof of his having concocted a scheme of vengeance with his confidants. This became obvious enough after his death, when his kindred left the city and began setting fire to mills, homesteads and villages of the neighbourhood, and recruiting accomplices by sheer weight of money. Two of these malefactors were taken at Bart, and put on the rack. At Stralsund they arrested ten individuals at once, among others, Christian Parow, the dean of the drapers, and Johannes Blumenow, the dean of the shoemakers. Young Peter Klatteville confessed to having set the New Mill on fire at the instigation of his mother, Nering's widow. Three were put on the rack; they declared having received of Parow ten marks for committing the crime, and the ministers who conducted them to the execution had much trouble to make them retract the accusation in the presence of the crowd. The following is the version in the *Annales* of Berckmann, one of the ministers: "This is what I have personally seen. When Parow took his stroll in the market place, the raven of Barber Grellen ran to peck at his legs, so that Parow considered it the best part of valour to quit the place. I am bound to admit, though, that this bird was in the habit of annoying the peasants who happened to wear wide linen breeches. Parow, who was an old man, did not pay sufficient attention to his appearance as to have his breeches properly pulled up like those of his companions; hence, there is nothing to prove that Providence made use of the raven to declare which kind of death Parow deserved."

Berckmann is simply nothing more nor less than Satan's slave when he tries to make Parow odious. It is true that this worthy man signed and sealed the avowal of his forfeit; the act happened to fall into my hands when I was secretary of the city. I destroyed it, in that way saving an honourable family from future affronts, without causing any damage to the public welfare. Besides, this concession was known to every one. It had in the opinion of those who gave themselves time to think the same value as that of Burgomaster Smiterlow branding himself as a traitor and an infamous creature. During the inquiry, everybody could see how incensed Parow was with the Nerings. If he did give them ten marks, it was because the money was extorted from him bit by bit by a certain Smit who perished on the rack. Nering's stepson Klatteville even declares that Parow came one day to his mother and had a long conversation with her. He does not know what Parow said to her, but he seemed heartbroken at the behaviour of the Nerings, for he wept like a child and went away weeping. In the draper's company no one ever objected to sitting next to him at table, except Olaff Lorbeer, a ridiculous personage, and the son of one of the principal faction-mongers. He always overwhelmed the good old man with his coarse allusions.

Johannes Blumenow, condemned to death on Tuesday, was only led to the scaffold on the following Thursday. I saw the execution. The corpse remained on the wheel, wrapped up by means of a cord in the blue dress he wore every day. This was done in order to prevent the crows from going to work too quickly. This Blumenow, a lively, though grey-haired fellow, the dean of the shoemakers, was the wealthiest of the Forty-Eight. He was very ambitious for the burgomastership which, he flattered himself, he could discharge better than any body. At the last burgomaster's banquet, that of Nicholas Sonnenberg, Frau Blumenow said to the matron next to her: "I did not wish to come, but I ought to know what to do when our turn comes to give the banquet." I have seen Blumenow busy cleaning skins and during that time many a notable personage clad in furs bowed down before him with more respect than before any former burgomaster. Berckmann attributes no other wrong to him than that of having induced Nering to renounce his citizenship (that is honest enough); but, he insinuates they had made up their minds to ruin him because he had in his possession the famous act elaborated by the Forty-Eight. What a pity it is that Berckmann sets so little store by the truth. Who compelled him to commit so many foolish fabrications to paper? With a little trouble on his part he could have learnt that about forty years previously a priest had been assassinated in his dwelling. The murderer remained unknown until Blumenow, being put to the torture, confessed to being the author of the crime. He had counted upon a big sum of money, but the victim did not possess more than a few pence. That, my very dear Berckmann, was what brought Blumenow to the scaffold. The sedition mongers had taken their precautions so well in the act of 1535 and in its appendix that, but for the Nering lawsuits, the honest part of the community would have never had the joy of seeing their oppressors pay for their misdeeds.

I have already recounted the pitiful end of Rolof Moller; the whole of his line was overtaken with similar punishment. His eldest son, George, who had been my schoolfellow at Rostock, was only a stripling when he caught a nameless disease through frequenting a certain class of women. He wanted to play the young country squire, did little work and spent much. His stepfather took him away from his studies, and sent him to England to learn the language of the country, and then to Antwerp, to get an insight into business. The young fellow, however, continued his spendthrift ways, and it became necessary to recall him. Rolof Moller's second son, for a mere trifle, stabbed in the open street his cousin with whom he had been drinking claret at an apothecary's. The name of Moller is fated to be extinguished in a short time.

What shall I say about Burgomaster Lorbeer, the instigator of the three riots, and especially of the third against Smiterlow? Everybody is aware of the contempt into which he fell even during his lifetime, and of the horrible malady that carried him slowly to the grave. After his death his wife and daughters still believed themselves to be the masters, as in the days when visiting an estate of the city they were greeted with the formula of reception, "Be welcome, dear ladies, on thy lands," and when the passers-by hailed them with a "God preserve you, young and dear burgomasters." This deference had inflated their presumption to such an extent that they lost all respect for both the council and the law courts. They ended up by exhausting the Divine patience.

The master-miller Nicholas Hildebrand was not the least influential among the Forty-Eight. A busybody, self-interested, he meddled with everything that could bring water to his milldam. Having had certain private reasons for retiring to Wolgast, he intrigued so barefacedly as to compel the duke to imprison him; and inasmuch as nobody dreamt of interceding for him, he spent the whole winter in a cell. At his discharge his legs were frost-bitten and he was eaten up with vermin. Another active and restless firebrand, the erewhile tailor Marschmann, who came to Wolgast to escape his creditors, kept Hildebrand company the whole of the winter. Knigge took to making false coin; but for Doctor Gentzkow, whose step-daughter he had married, the capital sentence passed on him would not have been commuted into banishment. Christian Herwig died in abject misery. They had given him the nickname of Count Christian, because in his prosperous days he strutted about in his best dress, one hand on his hip, and taking up the whole width of the street by himself. His wife became an inmate of the St. John's Asylum. One of his daughters, a downright slattern, had to beg her bread and was found dead one morning; the rest vegetated in the most sordid conditions. Nicholas Loewe, a quarrelsome creature who tried to look like a captain in his white dress set off with red velvet, in the end considered himself lucky at the St. John's Asylum to don the grey small clothes provided for him by charity. Long before his death he became stone blind. His daughter Anna was the talk of the town. I could easily extend this list, for, as far as I recollect, not one of those sedition-mongers escaped the punishment inflicted by the Almighty on rebels unto the third and fourth generations.

Stralsund, there is no doubt, is likely to feel for a long while the pernicious effects of Rolof Moller; but just as history praises Cambyses, that arch-tyrant, *monstrum hominis el vera cloaca diaboli* for having ordered the death of the prevaricating judge and for having had his skin nailed on the judgment seat; so on one point, and on one only, are the sedition-mongers entitled to commendation. They replaced the banquets of the burgomaster and the councillors by presents of goldsmith's work or by a piece of silver. Nowadays the city receives from the burgomaster a piece of silver-gilt; a councillor merely gives a piece of silverwork. The guilds have also done away with the banquets of reception and election. Instead of foolishly wasting their money in gormandizing, the new dean or the new companion offers a present of silver which does duty at the fêtes and gatherings, so that nowadays the wooden and pewter goblets have made room for silver tankards. On Twelfth Night the council and the corporations make a display of their treasure, to show to the public that it is not only intact, but increased.

After the tragedy of the Passion comes the glory of Easter Day. Nicholas Smiterlow had suffered civil death; and among certain individuals on the magistrates' bench the password had gone round to prevent his resurrection. When, however, the disastrous issue of the war but too plainly confirmed the prophecies of the old burgomaster, the ironical nickname of "pacific" became the chief claim to his glory. Councillors and burghers in plenary meeting assembled, dispatched two of the former to him with the request for him to repair to the Town Hall. Burgomaster Lorbeer tried to stop the mission by rubbing his arm and saying that the letter of avowal signed by Smiterlow was a most indispensable document on that occasion, inasmuch as it was a question of annulling it. His attempt to redress the balance of his own game by a delay of twenty-four hours was a failure. His objection was simply put aside, and the secretary went at once to Blumenow's for the said letter, together with the pact imposed by the Forty-Eight. When Smiterlow entered the council-room all the burghers cried, "Here is our beloved father, Nicholas the Pacific." He was conducted to his former seat, above Lorbeer's; they begged him to give them the help of his experience, and they promised that henceforth he should be exempt from all missions and embassies. Standing on the treasury chest, so as to afford a sight to everybody, the secretary tore the famous agreement into two, and detached Smiterlow's seal from it. But the burghers were not at all satisfied, and shouted to him to stick his penknife into and to lacerate the letter of avowal in a similar fashion. And thus ended the domination of the Forty-Eight.

Faithful--perhaps too faithful--to his habit, the ex-Augustine monk Berckmann limns Smiterlow in the falsest colours. He fancies he is using irony when he exclaims, "Burgomaster Nicholas Smiterlow was a fine specimen of a man, conscious of his own worth, handsome, eloquent, prudent and wise, and enjoying much consideration from princes and nobles." It so happens that all this is simply so much bare truth, and added to all these merits, Smiterlow had the fear of God and a wide knowledge of the Scriptures. The *Annales* of Master Gerhard Droege quote him as the oldest patron and protector of the Evangelical ministries; hence, everything that Berckmann writes in connexion with or about him is inexact. Here is an instance. Berckmann states that Smiterlow was confined to his bed twelve weeks, while in reality he was taken ill one Sunday and died the next Tuesday, in 1539. His son George, my junior by a twelvemonth, was burgomaster for twenty-two years. He had inherited all his father's virtues; he went through similar ordeals, and was vouchsafed the same comforts from on high, and I see no reason to modify my letter to Duke Ernest Ludwig. That prince, egged on by the caballers of his court, exclaimed at the news of Smiterlow's demise, "I had two enemies at Stralsund. Smiterlow is dead, and the devil will soon take Sastrow." I wrote to His Highness as follows:

"Gracious prince and lord,--The defunct burgomaster was neither bad naturally nor of base condition. His loyalty towards your Highness and Stralsund never failed, as could be proved by his numerous services. If he could have changed a farthing into a florin to the advantage of the city he would unquestionably have done so. Neither he nor his ever cheated the treasury. Hard-working, just and incorruptible, his speech expressing the feelings of his heart he, was a slave to duty, and severe or lenient as circumstances and persons dictated. Not at all obstinate, he was particularly amenable to reason, for the public weal was his sole guide. He administered the law with the strictest impartiality. A foe to dissipation and excess, he led a useful and retired life; though frugal and saving, he never remained behind where honour demanded the spending of money. The greatest harmony prevailed between him, his wife, and his servants. Though he had not pursued the ordinary course of studies, he was endowed with supreme wisdom. He had a most wonderful memory, and an equally wonderful gift of elocution. As a loyal subject, I can but address to God one prayer. The King of the Persians, Darius, prayed for as many zopyres as a pomegranate contains pips; may your Highness be enabled to count as many Smiterlows in the city and in the fields, not to mention the court; and while including the latter I wish to cast no reflection on any one. What then are we to think of those who dare to slander the defunct and to blacken his character in your Highness' eyes, besides causing grief to his wife, his children and his friends?"

Everybody on the other hand would freely admit that Rolof Moller was overbearing, presumptuous, crafty, greedy, ungrateful, relentless, and turbulent. Smiterlow and Moller were so utterly different in character as to be unable to breathe the same air. At the council, in church, nay in the city itself, the presence of one was sufficient to drive away the other. Great, therefore, was the surprise when George Smiterlow married Moller's niece. How would people, for whom the space of a large city seemed insufficient, agree under the same roof, at the same board, in the same bed? What strange *communicatio idiomatum* was going to result from that marriage? Hence, I should openly disadvise the election of such a Smiterlow for the council, and least of all should I make him a burgomaster, for they have many more of their mother's than of the father's characteristics; *in hac lucta duarum diversarum naturarum* the Mollers appear to have had the advantage.

Nevertheless, this new generation is still sufficiently young to be susceptible of improvement. From the bottom of my heart I wish it may be so, for the sake both of its reputation and its welfare.

I have written the foregoing pages somewhat oppressed by the thought of the ill-will I am drawing on my devoted head in praising Smiterlow at the expense of Rolof Moller. The descendants of the latter will never forgive me. But I derive consolation and strength from the appreciation of educated men. They know that the historian's duty is to go straight for his aim, and to proclaim the truth, whether for good or evil, whether it pleases or displeases, and let come what may. I recommend to my children submission to the authorities, no matter whether Pilatus or Caiaphas governs. For the good of their soul and the welfare of their body they ought never to make pacts with sedition-mongers.

CHAPTER IV

My parents recalled me in 1538, having discovered that at Greifswald I more often accompanied my grandfather in his strolls than sat over my books. I attended school during the stay of a twelvemonth at the paternal home.

One instance will show into what kind of hands the chief power had fallen. In 1539, Duke Philip, travelling to Rügen with his wife, made his first entry into Stralsund, and Burgomaster Christopher Lorbeer, who fancied himself to be the incarnation of eloquence, made the following speech to him: "Philip, by the grace of God, Duke of Stettin, Pomerania, of the Cassubes and the Wends, Prince of Rügen, and Count of Gutzkow, the council is indeed very pleased to see you. Be welcome." In subsequent days I have often been chaffed about this speech; usher Michael Kussow, among others, never opened the door to me without crying out, the moment he caught sight of me, "And indeed Philip, by the grace of God ..."

My brother Johannes had been admitted *magister*--the first of thirteen--at Wittemberg, and on leaving he brought with him a letter from Dr. Luther to my father, who, in consequence of the Bruser-Leveling lawsuit, had stayed away for many years from the Communion table. The letter was couched as follows: "To the honourable guildmaster, Nicholas Sastrow, my good friend: Grace and peace be with you. Your dear son, *magister* Johannes, after having expressed to me his sorrow at your having kept away for many years from the Holy Communion table--which absence is calculated to create a bad example--has requested me to rescue you from that dangerous path. Not one hour of our lives in reality belongs to ourselves. His filial solicitude, therefore, induced me to send you these present lines. Let me exhort you as a Christian, as a brother, according to the precept of Christ, to change your resolution, and well to remember the much greater sufferings of the Son of God, who forgave His executioners. Bear in mind that at your last hour you will be bound to forgive, as a brigand who is tied to the gallows forgives. Wait for the decision of the court before whom your suit is pending, but do not forget that nothing prevents you from participating in the Holy Supper. If it were otherwise I myself and our princes would have to remain away from the Holy Board until our differences with the papists be settled. Leave the matter in the hands of the law, and say to yourself for the comfort of your conscience: 'It is the judge's place to decide where lies the right; meanwhile, I forgive those who have wronged me and I will partake of the Holy Communion.' You consider yourself as having been wronged. You have had recourse to the courts; it is they who shall decide. Nothing can be more simple. Take in a friendly spirit this exhortation which was prompted to me at the instance of your son. May God watch over you, Amen. Wednesday after *Miser. Dni.* 1540. Martinus Luther."

I trust my descendants will transmit religiously from generation to generation the autograph of the saintly man to whom the whole world owes gratitude and affection. Together with this letter, and as a proof of the wise outlay of the paternal allowance, my brother brought home with him a number of his *poemata* printed in a volume. My parents' means not admitting of his being maintained in a foreign land, he spent nearly four years at home, studying all the while. Besides the *Progymnasmata quaedam*, issued from the Lubeck press in 1538, he published in 1542 at Rostock an *Elegia de officio principis* dedicated to Duke Magnus of Mecklenberg; and in the same year at Lubeck, a *Querela de Ecclesia* and the *Epicidion Martyris Christi Doctoris Ruberti Barns*, which caused a good deal of trouble both to him and his printer.[25]

At the advice of my brother, my parents sent me to study at Rostock with Arnoldus Burenius and Henricus Lingensis. My brother, who became intimately acquainted with the latter, wrote to him that I had already gone through the ceremony of initiation; but the students found out that since then I had gone back to school at Stralsund, and each day my entrance at the *lectorium* caused a fearful tumult.[26] The *depositor* having pulled me by my cloak, I hurled a large inkstand which I happened to have in my hand at him. The ink soaked his long grey mantle with black fastenings, a fashionable garment of the time. Verily, I got my reward, when, for the sake of peace, I submitted a second time to the ordeal. It literally rained blows. The *depositor* pressed my upper lip with his wooden razor and the wound was a long while healing, for no sooner did it close up than my food, and, above all, salted things inflamed it once more.

The two *magistri* directed in common the purses (scholarships or otherwise) of the Arnsburg, which was the most numerous, as it consisted of thirty students. We took our meals at Jacob Broecker's, and we paid sixteen florins per annum for our breakfast and two other meals, *plus*, in the summer afternoons, some curdled milk or other refreshments.

At the end of two years my parents complained of the expense involved in my stay at Rostock; they were, moreover, displeased at my leaning towards theology. In fact, I felt neither old enough nor sufficiently advanced in learning to choose between the different faculties, but being unwilling to relinquish my studies I exposed my difficult position to my tutors, who at once decided to forego their fees, and also induced our host Broecker to feed me for eight florins per annum.

Truly, I had to lay the table, attend at meals, to clear it, and in addition to this to look after young Broecker, who was about my size and who was afterwards confined at Ribbenitz, to dress and undress him, to clean his shoes and to arrange his books. On the other hand, there were certain services to be rendered to *magister* H. Lingenfis. I had to brush his shoeleather, make his bed, keep his room heated, accompany him to church and to other places, and to carry his lantern in winter. It seemed very hard to me at first not to be served any longer, and not to sit down to meals with my college chums, but there was no help for it.

Besides, we had fallen into good hands. Arnoldus Burenius read us twice Cicero's *Offices*, which he interpreted in a thoroughly artistic manner, and afterwards the orations *pro Milone, pro rege Deiotaro, pro Marco Marcello, pro Roscio Amerino, pro domo sua,* and the *de Aruspicum responsis,* the *Epistolae familiares,* the long and beautiful chapter *ad Quintum fratrem,* the *Rhetorica ad Herennium,* etc. His colleague expounded Terence, the *Dialectica Molleri,* even the *Sphaera Joannis de Sacrobusto,* the *Theoriae planetarum,* the *Computum ecclesiasticum Spangenbergii,* the *libellus de Anima Philippi,* and finally he presided over useful *exercitia styli et disputationum.*

My bedroom fellows were Franz von Stetten and Johannes Vegesack, the nephew of the Bishop of Dorpat, who kept him on a grand footing, and allowed him the staff of servants of a grand seigneur rather than that of a youngster. Vegesack practised all kind of sword-play, but I have heard that after the death of the bishop, he became a schoolmaster in Livonia. My private tutor, Danquart, coached him in the *praecepta grammaticae,* gave him themes to treat in German, and corrected his exercises.

The money we received from our parents had to be handed to our tutor Lingenfis; he gave it back to us as we needed it. We were bound to make notes of even our most trifling expenses. My tutors showed much interest in me, either out of consideration for my brother or because of my own unwearied application. I, on the other hand; served them zealously and faithfully, and was always at their bidding. The cross looks of my fellow-students, however, suggested the advisability of a change of residence; my brother counselled Greifswald.

In 1540 Duke Philip came to Greifswald for the ceremony of receiving homage. The exiles came with him; some held the tail, others the harness of his horse. My father was specially invited by the prince to hold the stirrup. The duke took up his quarters at Hannemann's, his wife with the Stoïentins. Frau Stoïentin, her daughter, her grandson, and all the relatives, when doing obeisance to the princess, claimed the upholding of the decree of expulsion against my father. The duchess specially recommended two of her principal officers to transmit the request to her august spouse; but the latter's reply effectually prevented her from returning to the charge, and the gates of Greifswald were reopened to my father.

I left Rostock in 1541. My stay at home was, nevertheless, very short. I soon transferred myself and my books to Greifswald, where I rented a room with Joachim Loewenhagen, the pastor that was to be of St. Nicholas' at Stralsund. Master Anthony Walter who shortly afterwards became rector of the Paedagogium of Stettin, instructed me in the *Dialectica Caesarii*. Master Kismann explained and interpreted Ovid's *Fasti*.

On Christmas Day, 1541, a vessel hailing from Colberg, and laden with barrels for Falsterbo, anchored at Stralsund. The coopers were in a great state of excitement, declared an embargo, and would not even allow the cargo to be sold at Stralsund.[27] In vain did the council guarantee proceedings against the purchaser of that merchandise; they went on agitating, refused to buy the barrels themselves, and replied with blows to those who spoke common sense. One burgher died from the consequences of their ill-treatment. They finally destroyed the barrels. Five people were arrested. Johannes Vogt, their dean, fled to Garpenhagen, but he was brought back to Stralsund and placed under lock and key. There was but a narrow escape from the executioner's sword. The coopers were summoned to the Town Hall, where the prisoners made their appearance with the iron collar round their necks and their hands and feet fettered. The corporation was fined four marks per head. Its privileges were withdrawn; it had, moreover, to rebuild at its own expense part of the city walls.

I have already mentioned that my brother *Magister Joannes*, had various *poemata* published at Lubeck and Rostock. From the latter city he returned by stage coach to Stralsund in company of Heinrich Sonnenberg and a woman. By their side rode Johannes Lagebusch and a good-looking young man, Hermann Lepper, who had been to the mint at Gadebusch to exchange 100 old florins for new coin. That money was in the carriage. A gang of thieves, or rather highwaymen, got wind of the affair. In consequence of the mild laws of repression, these gentry swarmed throughout Mecklenburg, and the names of the noblest families figured among them, which fact gave substance to the poet who wrote:

> Nobilis et nebulo parvo discrimine distant,
> Sic nebulo magnus nobilis esse potest.

Of course these lines do not apply to many honourable personages belonging to the nobility. But to return to my story.

When the travellers had got beyond the village of Willershagen they left the coach, and, provided with their firearms proceeded on foot, for the country was by no means safe. Instead of prudently escorting the vehicle the two horsemen went on in front. The brigands came up with them and entered into conversation. Suddenly one of them snatched the loaded pistol Lagebusch was carrying at his saddle-bow--the fashion of carrying two had not come in--fired it at Lepper, who was galloping back to the carriage, killing him there and then, while Lagebusch set spurs to his horse in time to warn Sonnenberg, who hid himself in the brushwood. My brother, armed with a pole, and standing with his back against the carriage to prevent an attack from behind, offered a stout and not unsuccessful resistance. He managed to wound in the thigh an assailant who, carried away by his horse, bit the dust further up the road. But another miscreant, charging furiously, sliced away a piece of my brother's skull as big as a crown (the fragment of bone that adhered to the skin was the size of a ducat), and at the same time dealt him a deep gash at the throat. As a matter of course, my brother lost consciousness; nay, was left for dead while the bandits sacked the carriage, caught the horse of their wounded comrade, but seeing that he could not be transported, abandoned him and decamped with their spoil. They, however, did not take the carriage team. In a little while Sonnenberg emerged from his hiding-place, and, with the aid of the driver, hauled my brother into the carriage. The woman bandaged his head and kept it on her knees. Lepper's body was placed between the legs of the wounded young man, and in that condition they reached Ribbenitz, where the surgeon closed the gash in the neck by means of pins.

The Rostock council promptly sent its officials to the spot. The brigand was conveyed to the city, but almost immediately after his being lodged in prison, he died without naming his accomplices. There was, moreover, no great difficulty in finding them out, but their friends succeeded in hushing up the whole affair; the authorities acted very mildly. The dead robber was nevertheless judged and beheaded. His head remained for many years exposed on a pike.

Lagebusch brought the news to Stralsund, and the Council immediately offered my father a closed carriage with four horses. We started that same night, provided with mattresses, and reached Ribbenitz next morning after daybreak. My brother was very weak. While the horses were stabled and after the court had drawn up a detailed report, we gave Lepper an honourable and Christian burial. We began our homeward journey at dusk, going slowly all through the night, and got to Stralsund at midday. Master

Joachim Gelhaar attended to my brother, but in spite of his acknowledged skill, he did not succeed in curing the wound of the neck; the improvement of one day was counteracted the next. In the end they discovered that the surgeon of Ribbenitz had closed the wound askew; the edges did not join, and one had been flattened by means of a large copper pin, the head of which had disappeared. Master Joachim repaired the mischief, not without causing great pain to his patient, who, however, promptly regained his health.

After reading the *Epicedion Ruberti Barns*, the King of England sent ambassadors to threaten Lubeck, the book having been issued from Johannes Balhorn's presses. Although the author had no connexion with the city, the council nevertheless apologized for him on the ground of his youth. He had simply aimed at giving a *specimen doctrinae*, but to pacify the king, Balhorn was banished, and had to leave the city at sunrise. He was allowed to return a few months later.

The costly Bruser lawsuit had deprived my parents of the means of sending us to study in foreign countries, so they bought two horses and dispatched me and my brother to Spires to watch the progress of the affair, and to do as best we could for ourselves. We started from Stralsund on June 14, 1542. Our parents accompanied us as far as Greifswald, where we stopped one day to bid good-bye to our grandmother and the rest of the family. I was in high spirits. Johannes was dull and depressed. "Dear son," said our mother, "why this sadness? Look at Bartholomäi, how gay he is." "My brother," replied Johannes, "has no care weighing on his mind; he has no thought for the future."

We made for Stettin, then for Berlin and Wittemberg; in fact, "we rode straight on," as people say. At Wittemberg, Johannes ran against Dr. Martin Luther, standing before the bookshop near the cemetery. Dr. Luther shook hands with me. Philip Melanchthon and other learned personages gave us letters of introduction to the procurators and advocates of Spires.

Half-way between Erfurt and Gotha there is a big inn where we halted for half a day to rest our horses and to mend our clothes. We settled our bill before going to bed. Next morning on reaching Gotha my brother found he had lost his purse; he had left it under his pillow. It was a great misfortune, for we were not overburdened with means, and the look of the inn left but little hope of getting our own back again. Immediately after my horse had had its feed, I retraced my steps, galloping all the way. When I reached the hotel I tied up my horse and in the twinkling of an eye ran up to the room with the servant at my heels. We both flung ourselves on the purse. I had the luck of laying hands on it first, but I fancied he was entitled to a tip. If either the girl or the young man had come near the bed after our going we should have never seen our money again.

In spite of the gathering darkness, I was in the saddle again, for it would have been unwise to spend the night alone under such a roof. Half a mile (German) farther there was a nice village, and as night had set in altogether I made up my mind to stop there. The inn was full of peasants. It happened to be Sunday, and these worthy folk, who had noticed my riding by like possessed two hours before, said to each other: "Well, we were mistaken after all. It's His Highness' messenger." Thereupon the host told the servant to look to my horse; nothing would induce him to let me do it myself. He, moreover, insisted on my sitting down to the table immediately; they brought me boiled and roast meats and excellent wine. The peasants in their turn show me all kinds of attentions, and when I mention the settlement of my bill before going to bed, the host declares that he could not hear of such a thing, and moreover swears by all his household gods that he'll not let me go in the morning without a good basin of soup, and that if I were to stay for a week he would not accept a farthing, because he could never do enough for his gracious prince. They put me into a very white and very soft bed, where I slept long and soundly.

While I was enjoying every comfort, my poor brother was bemoaning his imprudence of having sent me to look for the purse. I did not know the country, the hotel had a queer appearance. I had not returned, although it had been settled that the town gates should be opened to let me pass. My brother's anxiety may therefore be readily imagined. He dispatched an express messenger with a description of myself, and that of the horse; the messenger passed the inn at the very moment I was starting. He recognized me and informed me of my brother's anxiety.

At Spires we put up at the *Arbour*, and when our horses were sufficiently rested my brother sold them to the landlord of the *Crown*. We could not afford, though, to stay at the inn, so we rented a small room with one bed, and with this we had to be content for more than five weeks. At meal times we went to eat three or four rolls under the city walls, after which we drank half a measure of wine at the tavern. The days when Bartholomäi Sastrow led the dance, and feasted at the big wine cellars like *König Arthur* and the *Rathskeller* were over.

Philip Melanchthon had recommended us to his half-brother, Doctor Johannes Hochel, procurator, and to Doctor Jacob Schenck, advocate at the Imperial Chamber. Thanks to the latter, Johannes found bed and board, *mensa splendida et delicata* at the provost's of the chapter, a great personage occupying the handsomest mansion of Spires, the habitual quarters of the Emperor. This provost entertained daily a number of guests, but he himself lived upon fowl broth and apothecary's stuff prescribed by his doctor. He was fond of listening to the discussions of his guests, some of whom sided with Luther and others with the pope. If, at the end of the debate, he now and again added a few words, it was simply to admit that he had never read "St. Paul," but that, on the other hand, he had read in Terence: "*Bonorum extortor, legum contortor.*" He was practically in the same boat with the Bishop of Wurzburg, who is reported to have said: "I thank heaven that I have never read 'St. Paul,' for I should have become a heretic just like Luther."

On August 10, Dr. Hochel obtained a place for me at Dr. Frederick Reiffstock's, one of the oldest procurators of the Imperial Chamber, a most learned lawyer and excellent practitioner, who was altogether unlike the majority of the procurators at Spires. He had spent several years of his youth at Rome as auditor of the "Rote" (ecclesiastical jurisdiction). He was very conscientious and energetic. At the issue of the sittings, he immediately wrote to the party whose case had been called; then, the moment the minutes and other documents had been copied by his principal clerk, he sealed the whole, and deposited it in a large box on the table of his office. When this or that messenger came to announce his next departure the procurator examined the box to see whether there was anything to dispatch in that direction, and he marked on the outside wrapper the vail to be given according to the condition of the roads or their distance from the main ones. His practice was made up of princes, nobles, and eminent personages. One day he replied to Duke Albrecht of Mecklenburg who had sent him a case, that, unless new facts could be adduced, he advised the withdrawal of the suit. The fees were nevertheless very considerable. The duke handed the case to Dr. Leopold Dick, who allowed himself to be directed to the *juramentum calumniae* and lost the whole affair.

My master had four sons, all of whom took their doctor's degree. The three elder had returned, one from France, the two others from Leipzig; hence I had three horses to take care of, and three rooms to keep heated. Doctor Reiffstock was determined I should not be idle. One day he placed before me a bundle of documents as thick as my hand but very well written. He told me to copy them, and then to collate them carefully with his second clerk. I was under the impression that it was a most important affair; when it was finished the procurator told me that he simply wished to give me something to do.

On December 14, 1542, an imposing deputation of the Protestant States repudiated as suspect the Imperial Chamber, and declared its decisions and enactments null and void until its complete reformation. The procurators immediately reduced their staff, and Dr. Reiffstock dismissed me, which grieved me very much. As I foresaw, my parents would think me guilty of some grave misconduct, but a letter from Johannes soon undeceived them.

Though a writer's place could easily be had away from Spires, I would not leave my brother or the city before the termination of the lawsuit. We also hoped that the chamber would be reconstituted at the next diet. For all these reasons combined I entered into the service of my father's procurator, Simeon Engelhardt. I might as well have taken service in hell. Dr. Engelhard was an honest man, but he and his family belonged to the Schwenkfeld sect. [28] He had three daughters and a son between eight and nine whom I had to teach his declensions and conjugations. The matron of the establishment was a virago of the worst description, mean and bitter-spoken, who grudged her husband his food. Often and often did I see her snatch the glass from his lips. People may think she did it for the best, lest he should get drunk. Not in the least; she did that kind of thing at the family table; besides, his worst enemy could not have called him a wine-bibber. The pewter goblet of each child (there were two grown-up daughters) held about the contents of a pigeon's seed-box. The cup was filled once with wine, twice with Mayence beer (an abominable concoction), after which you were at liberty to swill as much water as you pleased. As for the two servants and the two scribes, the pittance was meagre indeed. A piece of meat not as big as an egg, floating in beef tea pellucid to a degree. This was followed by cabbages, turnips, lentils, herbs, oatmeal porridge, dried potatoes, etc., even on fish days. At the end of the meal a goblet (?) of wine. Whoever was thirsty after that--a by no means uncommon state of things--could go and pull the well-rope. Truly, it would be difficult to say how much water I swallowed in that house.

Dr. Simeon Engelhardt had nearly as many lawsuits on hand as Dr. Reiffstock, about four hundred. Each document was copied four times. The first remained with the principal bundle of papers, the second was sent to the client, the third and fourth went to the registry of the court which kept one, wrote the word "Productum" on the other, and dispatched it immediately by the beadle to the procurator of the opposing party. There were two sittings per week, sometimes a third for fiscal cases.

The copying of the protocol and of the acts imposed very hard work upon us. Being only two clerks, there was no time, on court days, for swallowing a piece of bread. On the other hand, the mistress of the house took no notice of anything like that. What her daughters or the servant girls could have done, namely, laying the table, bringing the cold or hot water for washing up, clearing the table and getting rid of the dish-water; all this came to Bartholomäi's share, whether he happened to be head over heels in other work or not, and the master of the house did not dare to utter a syllable.

Amidst the biggest stress of business, when we did without our meals, the lady cried across the yard: "Bartholomäi, will you mind troubling yourself to come and throw the dish-water away?" And as if the satire was not obvious enough, she added: "Look at the lazy scamp. He has not attended to the water at all." I was forbidden to go out without asking, even to call upon my brother. Nor was this all. In the morning I saved the servant girls marketing; a basket slung on my arm like Gretchen, I bought the provisions for the household; cabbages, turnips, bread, and what not, and when I came back there was faultfinding without end for not having haggled enough. On washing day, which came round too often to please me, I pumped the water. When the pump was out of order it was I who went down the well to repair the mischief. And I was not a child, but a young man of twenty-three. I was paying for the good times of Stralsund. At each visit my brother was bewailing my fate and preaching patience. "In days to come, when you shall have a wife, children, and servants of your own, you will be able to tell them of your less happy days."

When Mistress Engelhardt was in her "tantrums," she went about for a week without addressing a friendly word to her husband. At such periods her son Solomon would come into the office to tell me that his father was a dissipated brute who had not slept with his mother for a week, etc., etc. The youngest of the girls fell ill and died; her mother put the corpse into a sack in guise of a coffin. An old crone carried it to the cemetery on her back. One can only hope that she dug a grave and placed her burden into it, for no one accompanied the dead child; no one superintended the burial.

Thanks to his capital practice, made up of the nobles and the cities paying him yearly retaining fees, thanks also to the avarice of this virago, Dr. Engelhardt easily put aside two thousand florins per annum. He lent money to the client-cities at interest. For two years running I made payments of two thousand florins each on a simple receipt.

In 1543, on his return from Italy, the emperor hurried on his preparations for a war against the Duke of Juliers. Ulm and Augsburg cast some magnificent pieces of field artillery, with their carriages and wheels; and as it was considered easier to transport the carriages separately, a numberless troop of Swabian carters was engaged. His Imperial Majesty stayed at Spires, the artillery not being ready. Autumn overtook him, and as the roads of the Netherlands were very bad at that season, his Majesty, to his great vexation, had to defer the attack. One day, being on horseback, he hustled a waggoner whose team proceeded too slowly to his taste, and spoke, moreover, very harshly to him. The Swabian, who had no idea of the identity of his interlocutor, merely made a grimace and shrugged his shoulders. A smart rap with a riding crop from the emperor was the result.

So far from submitting, however, the stubborn clown promptly belabours his assailant's head with his whip, uttering imprecations all the while: "May the thunder strike and blast you, you scum of a Spaniard," and so forth. Of course the emperor's suite laid hold of him, and he had to pay dearly for his mistake. Not so dearly, though, as he might have done if the colonels entrusted with inquiries and the drawing up of the indictment had not purposely dragged the thing along to let the emperor's anger spend itself. Charles had forgotten all about the affair. He probably thought that his orders had been carried out and that the Swabian culprit was comfortably swinging from this or that gibbet, when the said colonels and captains humbly submitted the reasons for his being pardoned. There was first of all the ignorance of the waggoner, secondly the often excessive roughness of the Spaniards towards these poor Swabians. Furthermore, there was the august leniency of all great potentates and the gratitude of which the army would feel bound to give proof, if it were exercised upon such an occasion as the present. The prince relented to the extent of deciding that the culprit should have his nose cut off in memory of the assault. The colonels and the captains expressed their respectful gratitude, and the condemned man learnt the commutation of his sentence with great joy. They cut off his nose flush with his face. He bore the operation with a good grace, and for the remainder of his life sang the praises of the emperor. For many years he could be seen urging his cattle along the roads between the Rhine and the Danube. I happened to come several times into contact with him at the inns. I asked him before other travellers about the nature of the accident that had cost him his nose, whether he had left it in the French country. "Nay, nay," he replied, and with great glee recounted his adventure, showering blessings on his Imperial Majesty.

While the emperor was warring in Africa, Martin van Rosse[29] profited by the diversion to work his own will in the Netherlands. He had, for instance, imposed a ransom on Antwerp on the penalty of burning it to the ground. His Majesty, having learnt that he was conducting the expedition as a landsknecht, felt curious to get a glimpse of this personage. Martin van Rosse was warned too late; the emperor was already there. He pulled up his horse before the rebel. The latter, dropping on his knee, begged that the past might be forgotten, and swore to shed his last drop of blood for the emperor, who touched him lightly with his stick on the shoulder, and forgave him everything. "We forgive you, Martin," he said, "but do not begin again."

On February 20, 1544, the Diet was opened at Spires. I have heard it said that the Elector Palatine Lewis always endeavoured to dissuade his Majesty from choosing that town, because his *mathematicus* had predicted that he should die at Spires. In consequence of this, perhaps, he presented himself in person to the emperor at the very beginning of the session, and at the end of a few days took his leave to return to Heidelberg, where he died on March 16.

In default of a church, the Elector of Saxony had religious service performed in a tavern where he had put up a seat for the ministers. Lutes, fifes, cornets, trumpets and violins, instead of an organ, constituted a most agreeable concert. The elector's horse was a most robust animal, and there was a stepping stone attached to his saddle.

On the eve of Maundy Thursday at sunset twenty-four flagellants of both sexes marched by in their shirts, their faces covered with pieces of stuff into which were cut holes for their eyes and mouth, their backs sufficiently bare for the birch provided with steel-pointed hooks to touch the flesh. It was a hideous spectacle, the hooks tearing pieces of flesh away, and causing the blood to trickle down to the ground. The penitents advanced very slowly, one by one, in two single files, divided as it were by Spanish gentlemen of high degree, each carrying a thick wax candle. The whole street was lighted with them. When they reached the church of the barefooted Carmelites the procession fell on its knees and dragged itself from the porch to the crucifix in the choir in that way. Near the entrance the surgeons dressed the wounds; rumour had it that two corpses were carried away.

The emperor washed the feet of twelve poor men; the King of the Romans did the same. Care had however been taken to ascertain that those people were in good health; nay, their feet had been washed beforehand. The two sovereigns with napkins round their waists merely dried the feet, after which they waited upon the poor at table. "Friends," they cordially said to them, "eat and drink."

Like all gatherings of eminent personages, this diet entailed a rise in the prices of food, but especially of fish. A Rhine salmon cost sixteen crowns; for half of one the purveyor of the Duke of Mecklenburg paid eight crowns.

A Spanish gentleman who had taken up his quarters with an amiable widow who was looking to his comfort, became imbued with the idea that she would not refuse him her favours; so one night he crept into her bed; but the widow having got hold of a knife plunged it into his body and killed him there and then. Of course, she did not know how to get rid of the body; but though certain of her own ruin, she did not stir from her home. Her anguish at the prospect of the consequences had reached its height when the emperor, informed of the real state of the case, sent to reassure her. The Spaniards came to take the body of their countryman, and to perform the last duties to it.

On March 20, 1544, the emperor granted the privilege of a coat of arms to my brother Johannes, and conferred the title of poet laureate[30] on him, in recognition of a poem dedicated to him. Johannes Stigelius also offered the emperor a *scriptum poeticum*. His Majesty replied to him through the pen of his vice-chancellor, Seigneur Jean de Naves: "*Carmen placet Imperatori; Poeta petat, quid velit habebit; Si voluerit esse nobilis, erit; si poeta laureatus, erit id quoque; sed pecuniam non petat, pecuniam, non habebit.*" It might serve as a warning to Stralsund not to lavish its money on the first comer who thinks fit to dedicate some poor rhymes to it.

On May 19, 1544, I was made a notary by Imperial diploma. Prelate Otto Truchess, of Waldburg, bestowed upon my brother a gold chain for a *carmen gratulatorium* on the occasion of his recent installation in the see of Augsburg.

Doctor Christopher Hose, ex-procurator and advocate of Stralsund, who had been struck off on account of his evangelical faith, had built himself a handsome residence at Worms. He came to Spires during the Diet. A veteran practitioner, a straightforward and agreeable man, he was a favourite with his colleagues, and especially with the young ones. He was, however, highly esteemed by everybody, and nobody minded him exposing the astute moves of his adversaries. A learned doctor had invited him and several colleagues, Master Engelhardt among the number. When I got there with my lantern to escort my master home, the evening cup was being poured out, and whether I liked it or not, the host and Dr. Hose, who were acquainted with my family's circumstances, made me sit down at the lower end of the table and offered me cakes, pastry, etc. Thereupon Master Engelhardt got up brusquely and wanted to go. "Seeing that my servant is sitting down, I had better go. At any rate I shall not sit down again unless he remains standing to attend to me," he said. Dr. Hose, however, went on with his little speech to me. "Look you here, Pomeranian," he remarked, "the words 'procurator at the Imperial Court' are simply synonymous with those of hardened rogue, and that is the gist of the matter." (The latter was a favourite interjection of his.) "At your age," he went on, "I was also with a procurator who run up costs very heavily with his clients without doing much for them. Now, just listen to this story. A Franconian gentleman entrusted a most important case to my master, gave him a considerable retaining fee, and promised him another big sum at the end of the year. When the case had been put upon the rolls, the procurator put the documents relating to it into a bag, showing the names of the parties to the suit in large letters; after which he suspended the bag in the usual way with many others in the registry room with which you are familiar. At the end of the year he claimed his fees, announcing at the same time the termination of the suit and his hurrying on of the judgment. The client added to the sum agreed upon a gratification and a present for us, the engrossing and copying clerks. Nevertheless, he fancied the affair was dragging along, and one fine day he came to Spires and rung at our door, and on its being opened my master a once recognized the visitor. You are aware that procurators generally have their own rooms facing the door, in order to see who came in and went out. Thereupon my master runs to the registry chamber, takes down the bag in question, and places it on the table. After which he has the Franconian shown in, receiving him very cordially, imbuing him at the same time with the idea that he never loses sight of his documents. He also tells him that he was constantly demanding the execution of the judgment, but that he will insist still more strongly, and will send an express to his noble client. The latter departed exceedingly satisfied, after having offered a rich gift to the procurator's lady. Well, as a fact, the lawsuit was not even in its first stage.

"Take my word for it," he went on, "the procurators of the Imperial Chamber are past-masters of trickery, and that's the gist of the matter. If you have made up your mind to practise at Spires, Pomeranian, you must provide yourself with three bags: one for the money, one for the documents, and the third for patience. In the course of the suit you will see the purse get flatter, the documents grow bigger, and patience desert altogether; but you will comfort yourself with the thought that the emperor writes to you: 'We, Charles V, by the Grace of God Roman Emperor, Perpetual Aggrandizer of the Germanic Empire, King of Spain, the Two Sicilies, Jerusalem, Hungary, Dalmatia, etc., assure our dear and faithful Bartholomäi Sastrow, of our grace and goodwill.' Think of the pleasure and the honour of receiving that missive, while you are sitting in the inglenook amidst your family. Assuredly it is money well spent." That was the manner of Dr. Hose's discourse.

The diet dissolved. King Ferdinand with his two sons, Maximilian and Ferdinand, reconducted the landgrave. At their return there was a terrible storm, accompanied by hailstones as big as hazel nuts. In Spires itself several hundred florins worth of windows were broken. The cavalry, hussars and royal trabans fled panic-stricken; it was nothing less than a general rout, and the gathering darkness increased the confusion. The runaways only reached Spires after the gates were closed, and lay down in the outer moats in order to save their lives. King Ferdinand appeared on the scene, absolutely alone. He called and knocked, shouted his name, and finally succeeded in finding some one who recognized him, when of course the gates were thrown open, and they sped towards him with many torches. The first question of the king was about his sons; nobody had seen them come up. Thereupon more confusion, shouting, questioning, and contemplated saddling of horses; but just in the nick of time the princes rode up, escorted by a small number of men. The trabans pleaded mortal danger in excuse for their neglect of duty, and their wounds in fact confirmed the plea, for the king, having made them strip, could see how the hailstones had literally riddled their bodies. All declared that their mounts no longer answered the bit.

The reconstitution of the Imperial Chamber was adjourned. I should have regretted returning to the paternal roof before our lawsuit was in a fair way of being settled; on the other hand, life at Master Engelhardt's was intolerable in consequence of his accursed wife, who was a fiend incarnate. Her dreadful character inspired me from that day forward with an aversion for petticoat government, and I am likely to preserve it until I draw my last breath. My father's interest dictated resignation, for my stay at Spires in hurrying up affairs also saved expenses of procedure and of correspondence, the latter of which threatened to be heavy now and again, when a messenger had to be dispatched to Stralsund. I was sufficiently versed in the scribal art and in High-German to find employment elsewhere. I was offered a post at the chancellerie of the Margrave Ernest of Baden and Hochberg, Landgrave of Sansenberg, Overlord of Roetteln and Badenweiler, etc., whose residence was at Pforzheim. It was only six miles (German) distant from Spires, and I accepted.

I and my fellow-scribe had been constantly engaged in engrossing deeds. As a rule these were petitions addressed either to the emperor or to some prince in behalf of the Jews of Swabia or of the Palatinate, who paid largely. Our master left us free in that respect. He knew that we were not inclined to work for nothing. Eager to earn money we even encroached upon our hours of sleep in order to get all the possible benefit of the diet. We had, furthermore, the tips of clients in return for our promise not to neglect their affairs. The receipts were dropped into a solid iron box, secured to the window of the office. Dr. Engelhardt kept the key of it. We estimated the treasure at a hundred crowns, and looked forward with joy to its division. When I was about to leave, the procurator came into the office, opened the box in my presence, and emptied it. We gloated over the admirable collection of florins, crowns, and other specimens of beautiful German and Welch coinage. Master Engelhardt gave me a crown, another to my fellow-clerk, and pocketed the rest. Stupefied and dumbstricken we saw him walk away with the proceeds of our vigils and our labour. No! Dr. Hose did not libel Master Engelhardt.

CHAPTER V

My brother accompanied me as far as Rheinhausen. From thence I got to Bruchsall, the residence of the Bishop of Spires, then to Heidelsheim, Brettheim, and at last to *patria Philippi*, Pforzheim. I entered upon my duties at the Chancellerie on June 24, 1544. My brother Johannes went with his master to the baths of Zell, where he met with an honourable, young, and good-looking girl from Esslingen. The young girl's guardian and her kinsfolk (licentiates, the syndic of Esslingen, and other notables) allowed the couple to plight their troth, subject to the consent of our parents. It was agreed that my brother should proceed to Italy to get his doctor's degree, that he should get married on his return, and take his wife with him to Pomerania. Johannes asked me to go to Esslingen to see the young girl and her family; her birth, character and dowry left nothing to desire. We wrote home each on his side; my parents opposed a categorical refusal. After that I never saw my brother really in good spirits. The young girl married a wealthy goldsmith of Strasburg. When my mother informed us that she and her husband gave their consent, it was, alas, too late. Poor Johannes, undermined by regret, was visibly wasting away.

Pforzheim is not a large place, and it has only one church. The town lies in a hollow amidst smiling plains, watered by a clear, health-giving stream, swarming with delicate fish. It is a charming place in the summer. The neighbouring lofty mountains are covered with dense, almost impenetrable forests full of game. Though lying in a valley, the castle commands the town. There are among the population a great many learned, modest, pleasant and well brought-up men. All the necessities of life, both in good and bad health, are at hand: apothecaries, barbers, innkeepers, artisans, etc.; in addition to these there are the canticles and sermons of the Evangelical religion. The life at court was conducted on economical principles, but on a very decent footing, however, and without the slightest attempt at parsimony unworthy of a prince. Yet the difference between their usages and those of Pomerania was great. The meals consisted of meat, fish, vegetables, dried figs, oatmeal porridge, cabbages and a fair ration of bread, and in a pewter goblet some ordinary wine, unfortunately in insufficient quantity, especially in summer. The counsellors were, however, served a second time. There was always plenty of work; there was a secretary of seventy, and a chancellor not much his junior, and the most morose of all doctors of law.

In 1545 Margrave Ernest concluded a pact of succession with his nephews; the negotiations were only waiting for an exchange of deeds. I was entrusted with the engrossing of one copy. The text was so long that it would scarcely hold on one skin of parchment; it was, therefore, necessary to write very close and small. I was rather frightened, for the chancellor was difficult to please; one might scrape and scratch till the erasure was invisible; he would light a candle in plain daylight, hold the deed before the flame, find out the flaw, and tear up the document while giving a strong reprimand.

I had been working at that copy for forty-eight hours, when all of a sudden an omission of at least a line struck me all at once. I had never been in such an awkward position in my life. I might count on several days' imprisonment; the only thing that could save me was a stratagem. The castle was on the heights, the chancellerie at the foot of them in the town itself. When the bugle sounded for dinner I stopped behind till everybody was gone; then in the twinkling of an eye I got hold of a cat, dipped its tail into the ink, and let it loose on the skin of parchment; the deed was all smeared over, the marks of the animals feet as distinct as possible. I shut it up and went to my meal. When it was over I let my colleagues go first; as they opened the door the cat flew at them, and on the table they caught sight of its latest masterpiece. At that moment I entered, and they showed me the disaster, explaining at the same time how the cat "went" for them. Naturally I played at being in despair, equally naturally they all tried to comfort me, and thus I came with flying colours out of what threatened to be an ugly scrape.

Whenever a condemned man was led to execution, Margrave Ernest made him come to him in order to reconcile himself with him. After having asked pardon of him for his compulsory sternness, he recommended him to show himself firm and bold, the blood of Jesus Christ having been shed not in order to save the righteous, but the unjust. Then he shook hands with him, and the wretched man was led away.

The Margrave had his apartments right over the principal entrance of the castle, so as to see everybody that came in or went out. One day he caught sight of the head cook taking away such a magnificent carp that its tail showed from under his cloak. "Just listen," exclaimed His Highness; "the next time you rob me, either take a carp less big or a longer cloak." While they were putting wine in his Highness's cellar, two cooks who were going into the town passed by; one had a couple of capons stuffed away in his belt. The Margrave called them to lend a hand, and wishing to be quick they flung off their cloaks. The scamp was not thinking about the birds, which began to peck at his arms while he was pulling the rope; thereupon they called all the serving wenches out to enjoy the spectacle. There is no need to add that they were the laughingstock of them all.

As there was to be a diet at Worms, I was anxious to have an interview with my brother. In order to save time I hired a trotter, which carried me in a day to Spires, and back the next morning to Pforzheim. The return journey, though, nearly cost me my life. I was leaving the hotel of Brettheim when I was hailed by a horseman coming out of another inn. "Whither are you going?" he asked. "To Pforzheim." "That's capital; that's my road; we'll ride together." A mile farther on a side path of which I knew enabled us to cut across the country, but at its other end they had put down four poles. Instead of turning back I urged my horse, which at first puts a forepaw betwixt the poles; it does not free itself in time, gets its hind leg in the wrong place, and finally falls on its left side. My companion shouts to me to catch hold of the animal's head to prevent its moving; then he jumps down himself, unbridles and unharnesses my mount, and after having told me to leave go its head, starts it with a smart stroke of his riding whip, while I am on the ground seated in my saddle, and with one spur caught in the belly-band. Had I been alone and without Divine help, I should have been dragged along and dashed to pieces. When all danger was over, the horseman told me that our roads parted on that spot. In vain did I remind him of his intention to go to Pforzheim; he wished me good-night, recommending me to the care of God and all His angels. I was anxious to offer him a finger's breadth of wine at the next inn; he declined my offer, on the pretext that its acceptance would cause too great a delay. I shall never cease to believe that my saviour was a holy angel.

Johannes approved of my intention to leave Pforzheim for Worms, where the diet would most probably proceed with the reconstitution of the Imperial Chamber. Then would be the right moment to return to Spires. The Margrave when I left, sent me half a golden florin, besides a court dress.

All at once there grew under my right nostril a pustule as big as a grain of barley; I punctured it frequently, and there came more blood from it than one could have imagined, but the kind of tumour did not disappear, not even when the surgeon whom I consulted cut it. It kept growing again, so, in order to destroy its root, as he said, he rubbed it with what I suppose was *aqua fortis*, for it caused me a horrible pain. I suffered most when going to Spires, owing to the cold and the wind; my nose swelled enormously.

On April 17 my brother accompanied me to Hütten, a mile and a half distant from Spires. There we parted, weeping bitterly; we had a presentiment that we should never see each other again, or even write. Next morning Johannes started for Italy.

His Imperial Majesty being detained in the Netherlands with gout, the king of the Romans opened the diet of Worms on March 24, 1545. Only a small number of princes came, so the emperor, when he arrived, prorogued the diet until the next year.

The spiteful, impious and fiendish wife of Procurator Engelhardt had made my life at Spires a misery, but at Worms I suffered hunger and thirst and all the wretchedness of downright distress. I wish this to be remembered not only by my children, but by all those who happen to read me. I carried the whole of my belongings upon me, namely: the court dress given to me at Pforzheim, two shirts, a sword with a silver tip to its sheath, and the six florins the Margrave had sent me, the whole constituting but a scant provision. The absence of the Emperor interfered with my livelihood; there was little work to do for copyists, and under those unfavourable conditions I stayed for twelve weeks. A canon, brother to Johannes' employer, gave me shelter during the first fortnight, after which he left for Mayence. The envoy of the dukes of Pomerania, Maurice Domitz, captain of Ukermünde, who knew my family very well, put, it is true, his purse at my disposal, knowing as he did that he would be reimbursed at Stralsund; the syndic of Lubeck was also at Worms with Franz von Sitten, my Rostock chum; neither the one nor the other would have refused to do me a service; borrowing meant, however, imposing new sacrifices upon my parents, so I preferred to suffer privation.

My nose caused me severe pain for a long while; when it gave me some respite, my mornings and afternoons were spent in walks, either with my countrymen from Mecklenburg, Pomerania or Lubeck, or with the friends I had made in Worms. Nobody had any idea of my being as poor as I was. At the dinner hour, when everybody repaired to the inn, I bought a pfenning's worth of bread, and the public fountain supplied the drink gratis; it was very rare that I took a little soup with a piece of meat as big as an egg in it, at the eating house. The owner of the establishment allowed me, in consideration of a kreutzer, to spend the night on a wooden seat; a bed would have cost half a batz (a batz was equal to about a penny of those days), and the wooden seat seemed preferable, inasmuch as I had sufficient "live stock" of my own, without picking up that of others. I sold the silver tip of my sword sheath, an iron tip as it seemed to me, to meet all my requirements. I subsequently disposed of one of my two shirts for what it would fetch; the six florins had melted away, and I wanted the wherewithal to buy dry bread. When my remaining shirt was dirty I went to wash it in the Rhine, and waited in the sun while it was drying; all this was so much money saved, no cost of laundry, soap, ironing or pleating.

My small clothes fell on my heels; I myself could no longer repair them. The "snip" at Worms would have asked not less than a batz; at Spires, on the other hand, it would have been done for half the price. So I made up my mind to go to Spires. I only reached the outer fortifications after the closing of the gates. Dying with hunger, thirst and fatigue, I lay down in the moat where I almost perished with cold. Next morning, at the tailor's, after having undressed, I sat huddled up all the while he was mending my clothes. I went back to Worms at a "double quick," having done twelve miles to save half a batz.

The constant want of nourishment had made me weak, and with my blood in a bad state, incapable of holding a pen if I had found any copying to do. My distress was at its worst when one of my kindest acquaintances the secretary of the Bishop of Strasburg, informed me that being in need of a writer, he was going to recommend me to his master, but the prelate said no because Pomeranians professed the Evangelical religion. Finally, through the good offices of the secretary of the Order of St. John, the chancellor succeeded in getting me a place at the receiver's of the said order. Great indeed, was the deliverance, and joy reigned in my heart instead of despondency. It was only later on that my eyes were opened to the dangers of my new condition.

On July 9, 1545, then, Christopher von Loewenstein, receiver of the Order of St. John for Lower and Upper Germany (he had been present at the taking of Rhodes by the Turks), engaged my services as a scribe. He promised me a complete dress and boots, such as his other servants received, but he did not stipulate the amount of my salary; he gave me to understand, though, that I should have no reason to grumble.

The function of receiver consisted in collecting the revenues of the various commanderies on account of the knights of Rhodes actually at Malta. At the demise of a commander, the receiver takes possession of the property of the defunct, and despatches it with the ordinary interest by means of bills of exchange to the Grand Master of the Order, who at that time was a Frankish gentleman, Don Jean de Homedes. The Grand Master confers for life the vacant benefice upon this or that knight who has distinguished himself before the enemy. The right of installing the new commander belongs to the receiver, who derives enormous profits from his office.

My master had, moreover, seven commanderies of his own; he was, therefore, perfectly justified in having eight horses in his stable like a great noble. He gave me the money to take the coach to Oppenheim, whence I was to proceed by water to Mayence, where he himself was to make a stay of several days. Mayence, Frankfurt and Niederweisel were the three commanderies which most often required his personal attention.

Niederweisel is an imperial town of the Wetterau, between Butzbach and Fribourg. Herr von Loewenstein spent the greater part of the year in a magnificent dwelling, replete with every imaginable comfort; spacious dwellings kept in excellent condition had been erected around a vast court; granges, stables, riding school, brewery and bakery, kitchens, atop of which were the refectory and the servants' quarters; at one end of the court the master himself occupied a handsome room and dressing-room, affording an uninterrupted view of the whole. A deep moat crossed by a drawbridge ran round the structure. And I, after having wanted the strictly necessary at Worms, found myself suddenly wading in plenty. The effect of the abrupt change of fortune may easily be imagined.

Though short in height, my master had won his benefices by his bravery at the siege of Rhodes. In his riper age he remained the soldier he had been in his youth. Daily feasting, succulent cheer, washed down by copious libations--a numerous company always around him--his revenues enabled him to lead that kind of expensive existence. The commandery being on the high road, landsknecht and horseman, sure of liberal entertainment, regularly made a halt there; the neighbours themselves were not more sparing with their visits; in short, gaming, feasting and drinking took up all the time.

The commander had practically a concubine under his own roof. He chose her with an eye to beauty, dressed and adorned her according to his means; when he wished a little more freedom, he married her to one of his equerries, gave her a home at Butzbach, and provided her against want. Butzbach being within a stone's throw of Niederweisel, he reserved to himself the option of seeing her when he liked. In my time, he lived with Marie Koenigstein, the daughter of the defunct town clerk of Mayence; she was, moreover, his god-daughter, and by her father's will his ward. Beauty, education, excellent manners, kindliness: all these and many other qualities were hers. Why had she not met with a more staid and sober guardian? She was about eighteen, when one fine day the commander came to Mayence in a closed carriage, sent for the young girl, told her to get in for a few moments and drove her as fast as the horses would carry them to Neiderweisel. So effectually did he hide her that for seven or eight weeks her brothers and relations did not know what had become of her. Finally, by dint of gifts, the commander succeeded in mollifying the brother, whom he sent to the

Grand Master of the Order. As for Marie, she had everything she could wish for in the matter of silken gowns, gold-embroidered cuffs and sable furs.

I was lucky enough to find favour with the commander. Every peasant-tenant of the seven commanderies held his homestead on a lease; and I had a crown for each renewal. I wore a dress like that of the equerries. Madame Marie looked to my shirts, handkerchiefs and night-caps and kept them in good condition. A nice well furnished room, close to the drawbridge did duty both as a bedchamber and study. I had my meals at the commander's board with his guests, Marie, the chaplain and the three equerries. Well fitting clothes, a sword with a silver sheath-tip, and a golden ring on my little finger contributed greatly to transform me into a young gallant; my pitiful figure of Worms was completely transformed; I improved physically and found favour in the eyes of the fair.

As for my duties, they were not very heavy; the only commanderies that gave us trouble now and again were those of the Landgrave of Hesse; they grudgingly settled their dues in consequence of the antipathy of the landgrave, for my master, who did not worry himself much about religious matters, was neither a papist nor a Lutheran, only Knight of the Order. The intrigues of the court compelled Herr von Loewenstein, therefore, to summon the Hessian commanderies before the tribunals; and the results, as far as I was concerned, were frequent journeys to Cassel and to the chancellerie of Marburg.

The commander had a rich collection of bits, bridles, saddles and saddle-cloths; he kept three equerries, though only one bore that title; the stable held seven or eight young stallions from Friesland that had been bought at the Frankfort fair. When the commander went out on horseback, a frequent occurrence, I accompanied him with the equerries; he made us change our mounts each time and entrusted us with horses costing between sixty and seventy, while he himself only rode an indifferent cob not worth half-a-score of florins. His horses were all of the same colour; when he grew tired of that colour he sold the cattle at half-price or gave them away, just to get rid of them. On one occasion he fancied a good ambling animal; he had happened to meet with a dappled grey, strong, clean-limbed and a capital pacer. It was valued at a hundred crowns; he, however, soon afterwards offered it to the Elector of Mayence who was very anxious for it and reserved it for his personal use.

The commander kept a fool of about eighteen, but who had been downright mad from the day of his birth. On one occasion the fellow entered his master's room and told him that he had been embracing the cowherd's daughter in the shed. He spoke out plainly without the least disguise. "After dinner, we mean to begin again in the same spot," he added. "Beware of St. Valentine's evil," said the commander. "Yes, sir, at the stroke of twelve, at the grange; your Grace will be able to bear witness to it." The commander hurried up and arrived *opere operato*. He sent to Friburg for the operator and signified his sentence to the fool who kicked against it. The commander, however, promised him a pair of crimson boots. "True, will your Grace give me your hand on the promise?" said the idiot. The commander gave him his hand; thereupon the fool exclaimed: "Come, Master Johannes, make haste." The operator stretched him on a bench, where the other servants kept him motionless, for at the first cut of the razor he began to resist. Master Johannes proceeded quickly and surely.[31] ... The patient remained for nine days on his back on a narrow couch, bound hand and foot so that he could not move an inch. The commander had given instructions to treat him with every care.

Master Johannes very soon deemed the fool sufficiently recovered to get rid of him, but at the commander's wish he kept him for some time longer in his room to the great annoyance of Master Johannes' young and good-looking wife; the latter had a strong objection to the fool's telling all sorts of tales about herself and her husband, on whose doings he spied night and day. He became a great nuisance, for in spite of his operation he grew fat and saucy, and at the death of the Commander, Landgrave Philippe sent for him to come to Cassel.

The chaplain was a fine specimen of the young debauchee. Instead of preaching the pure doctrine of Luther he performed mass twice a week in the chapel of the commandery. To get to the chapel he had to go through the servants' refectory just at breakfast time. He simply sat down, got hold of a spoon and dipped it into the soup. "Master Johannes," said we, "you know it is forbidden to eat before the mass?" "Nonsense," he replied; "the Saviour gets through bolts and locks; the soup won't stop him."

Herr von Loewenstein owned an old ape, a strong customer, who could get into formidable passions. The animal, which was kept on a chain, would only allow its master, the baker and myself, to come near it. Most dangerous was it when showing its teeth, as if laughing. When I sat down within its reach, I dared not get up without its leave; perched on my shoulder, it amused itself by scratching my head, and I had to wait till it got tired; then I shook hands with it and I was allowed to go. One day a landsknecht, a handsome, well built fellow, tempted by the prospect of a good meal, came into the commandery. He carried a javelin, and the ape, who unfortunately was free of his chain, jumped at him, and after having wrenched the weapon from him, bit him in several places that it was most pitiful to see; after which it crossed the moat, climbed to its master's window, opened it, and made its way into the room. With one glance the commander perceived that the animal was in a rage; he endeavoured to soothe it with kindly words. It so happened that a silver dagger was lying near the window sill; our ape ties it round its waist; thereupon the commander gently draws the weapon from its sheath, plunges it into the animal, and notwithstanding its bites, holds it pinned down until the breath is out of it. There is no denying that an ape is a terrible creature when it gets on in years and grows big.

After the harvest our master wished to go partridge-hawking, for his hawks were well trained. As his dapple-grey was being brought round--the one that ambled so capitally--the unexpected visit of several strange horsemen interrupted the party; the commander gave me his hawk, telling me to go without him. Just as I am getting my right leg over the saddle the bird beat its wings, the horse frightened, gets out of hand of the groom, and I am caught in the stirrup; more concerned for the hawk than for my safety, I drop backward, the horse continues to plunge, drags me along, kicking me all the while, the commander and his frightened guests looking powerlessly on. Luckily my shoe and my left hose give way and stick to the stirrup, while I am left on the ground, with nothing more serious, though, than a couple of swollen limbs. Nevertheless, on that day I had a very narrow escape from death.

The Elector of Saxony and the Landgrave of Hesse constantly raising levies against the Duke of Brunswick, the commandery swarmed with colonels and captains.[32] They offered me the post of secretary; the arrangement was, in fact, concluded, but I did not wish to go except with the consent of the commander. He granted me my leave, though giving me to understand that I should not expect to return to his service after the war. And inasmuch as the war was to be a short one, the warning gave me food for reflection. The winter was coming on; I certainly had no wish for a repetition of my privations at Worms. I remained, for the following lines recurred to my memory:

> Si qua sede sedes, et erat tibi commoda sedes
> Illâ sede sede, nec ab illâ sede recede.

Several companies of landsknechten were reviewed; and nothing could have been more diverting than to watch the inspector examine the weapons and the shape of the men, their dress and their gait. He made them march past him rather twice than once. How each man tried to hide his shortcomings, and how those who were "passed" as fit blew themselves, and swaggered and talked loud and boastfully like the hirelings they were. The war came to an end on October 21, with the capture of Duke Henry of Brunswick and his son, Charles Victor; his second son, Philippe, hastened to Rome to ask for help of the pope.

At the autumn fair Herr von Loewenstein took up his quarters at Frankfurt with the whole of his household for six weeks. My old chum, Franz von Stiten, coming across me once more, I told him everything about my position, and when I had given him the address of the House of the Knights of St. John, he arranged to come and pay me a visit one morning before the commander was stirring. And, in fact, he came, and had a long conversation with Marie, to whom he gave particulars about my parents, birth, and family circumstances. The information still further disposed the damsel in my favour; in short, I am bound to confess that I lost all claim to the meritorious reputation of Joseph the chaste. Since then I have acknowledged my sin to the Almighty, and I have sufficiently expiated it during my journey to Rome to count upon my pardon; besides, amidst the privations, dangers and trials which I am about to relate, however just the punishment may have been, the Divine mercy has never failed me, sending me protection and deliverance as it did in its admirable ways.

While my master drank and gamed with his guests (he was rarely alone, and in Frankfurt less than elsewhere) I read, in the quietude of my own room, the *Institutes*, which I nearly always carried about with me. In vain did Herr von Loewenstein tell me again and again not to expect to become a doctor of law while I was with him. I did not fear any opposition from that quarter.

In February 1546 my master having been summoned to Spires, the habitual residence of the superior of the Order for Germany, only left Marie and myself behind at Mayence. A letter from my parents, telling me of the death of my brother in Rome, made me decide upon my journey to Rome. There was not the slightest trace left of the sufferings I had undergone at Worms; my health was excellent, I had a well-stocked wardrobe, and my purse was fairly lined. On the other hand, the loose morals of the Knights of St. John were calculated to take me to hell rather than to heaven; the money earned in such a service could not bring luck; it was better to spend it on the high roads, and to cut myself adrift from such a reprehensible mode of life. Undoubtedly the time had come. Besides, it was absolutely necessary to ascertain the circumstances of my brother's death; I knew the sum of money he had with him, and the idea of his having spent it in so short a time was inadmissible. I told my reasons, though not all, to Marie; we parted on the most amicable footing. In the letter she gave me for the commander, she informed him of the sum she had given me at my departure, leaving it to him to increase it. Herr von Loewenstein wished me happiness and luck, and advised me, if I valued my life, to abstain in Italy, but above all in Rome, from all theological controversy; finally, he added a double ducat to Marie's gift. From Spires I went a little out of my way to see my friends at Pforzheim; after having said goodbye to them I began my long journey, alone and on foot, under the holy safeguard of the Almighty.

CHAPTER VI

I started from Mayence on April 8, 1546, and after crossing an unknown country by bad roads, I reached Kempten, an ancient imperial city at the foot of the Alps, and the see of an important abbey. The unpleasant parts of the journey hitherto had been solitude and fatigue, when at a quarter of an hour from Kempten there appeared two wolves of very good size. They were making for a plantation of oaks on the other side of the road, but when they got to the highway, at a stone's throw from where I was, they stopped "to take stock of me." Evidently they were going to make a mouthful of my poor, insignificant person. What was I to do? To beat a retreat was practically to invite their pursuit. To advance was to lessen at every step the distance dividing us. Trusting to God's good will, I kept marching on, and the wolves disappeared in the underwood. I hurried on, to escape the double risk of meeting the carnivora again or to find the city gates shut against me, for night was coming on apace. At the hostelry nobody seemed surprised at the meeting, for the neighbouring mountains swarmed with large packs of the animals. What they wondered at was the manner in which I got out of the danger. I offered thanks to the Lord.

I lay two nights at Kempten, because I was told not to venture alone in those mountains, where wild beasts and murderers prevailed. Meanwhile three Hollanders, proceeding to Rome and to Naples, arrived at the inn; it was the very opportunity I wanted; other travellers going to Venice joined our little caravan. Every evening, or at least one out of every two, we plunged our feet into running water; it proved a sovereign remedy against fatigue, recommended by the Hollanders.

The council was sitting at Trent. Before that town we made a halt in the middle of the day, in one of the burghs called markets, because they are too large for a village and too small for a town, notwithstanding their having a few stone houses. After having cooled our feet in the running stream we prepared for ourselves a meal of hot milk, eggs, and other eatables we had managed to find. The host and hostess who had been invited to the feast were most obliging; they foresaw a fat bill. Having had a good rest and plenty of food and drink, and having paid our reckoning, we bade them goodbye, and we already were at a considerable distance when a horseman came galloping after us, signalling us to stop by raising his hat. He brought me the satchel of brown damask that contained the whole of my fortune. I had left it behind lying on the table. The man absolutely refused to accept any reward. I wonder if I could find any instance of such disinterestedness in our country?

At Easter I heard most delicious singing in the Trent churches. I have heard the musicians of Duke Ulrich of Würtenberg (and they were a subject of pride with him), of the Elector of Saxony, of the King of the Romans, not to mention those of the Emperor, but what a difference. Old men, with beards almost reaching to their waists, sang the upper notes with a purity and skill fit to compare with those of the most accomplished youngster. Trent boasts of the most elegant castle of Germany and Italy. I also saw there the tomb of the child Simeon, the innocent victim of the Jews.[33]

A great personage had posted from Venice to the council; the rider, who was to take the carriage back, allowed me for a trifle to mount the second horse. It was agreed that I should wait for my companions at *The White Lion* in Venice.

At a short distance from Trent one gets into Lombardy. After a lone and difficult journey across the Alps, during which there is nothing to be seen but the sky and the mountains rearing their heads against the clouds, it was like entering into another world. The air was balmy, the country revelling in green; and if I had wanted a thousand florins' worth of cherries, I could have got them far more easily than in Pomerania in the middle of June. Lombardy is a beautiful land, of fertile and well cultivated plains. The trees are planted at thirty feet from each other, with an interval of sixty feet between each row; the vine extends its branches from one tree to another, and the grapes ripen between pears and apples. The corn grows between the trees; at the end of the fields there are reservoirs the water of which is distributed every morning by means of locks into the irrigation canals. The country resembles a vast prairie. The sun sheds his rays the whole day; no wonder that the earth is so fruitful. There are two crops of grain every year. From Trent to Venice there are also many important towns and castles.

I reached Venice towards the end of April. The public promenade helped me to kill the time while waiting for the arrival of my companions; and as my dress attracted the notice of the children in the street, who pursued me with the cry: "*Tu sei Tedesco, percio Luterano!*" I had it altered to the Welch fashion.

An aged priest, travelling with a servant to attend to his horse, had left the Low Countries with the mad intention of visiting the Holy Sepulchre; my companions practically catechized him on the subject of religion, and the poor man showed himself so little versed that I came to his aid by pretending to be a Roman Catholic. In acknowledgment of the service I had rendered him, he paid my reckoning at the inn, and wished to take me with him at his expense to Jerusalem. I cannot say if he saw his own household gods again, but he did not shake my resolution to proceed to Rome.

Venice and its environs, especially Murano, where the most precious glass is manufactured, would be sufficient to claim one's interest and attention for a whole twelvemonth; but our resources required husbanding, and we proceeded to Chioggia to embark in a big ship sailing for Ancona. Contrary winds kept us in port a considerable time; to pass the time we played skittles outside the walls. We carried our daggers at our backs in Walloon fashion, which caused us to be summoned before the authorities. How did we dare to appear in public armed with daggers--a crime which was punished with hanging in Italy? In consideration of our presumed ignorance of the law, mercy would be shown to us this once, but we ought to take it as a warning. The magistrates inquired whence we came, and whence we hailed, etc., and their astonishment was intense when they learnt that my country was two hundred leagues away on the shores of the Baltic, and was called Pomerania. Then the interrogatory went on: "Do you profess the Catholic religion?" "Yes," I answered. "Do you admit the doctrine of our holy father, the pope?" "What is your opinion with regard to the Mother of God, the saints and the celebration of mass?" "In our country the Church teaches that at the moment St. John baptized Christ, God the Father spoke these words: 'This is My beloved Son, in whom I am well pleased; listen to him.' The doctrine of the Son of God and of the apostles is, therefore, the pure Catholic doctrine; and whosoever preaches it deserves belief. With regard to the blessed Virgin Mary, the saints and the mass, we entirely submit to the word of God." Finally, on our statement that we were going to Rome, the magistrates, inclining their heads with a smile, recommended us to God's keeping and to His holy angels.

At the first favourable wind we took ship, provided with the quantity of provisions the pilot had told us. After having passed Ravenna and other beautiful cities of the Adriatic, we cast anchor at Ancona, a town driving a considerable trade, and provided with an excellent port in the shape of a half moon, affording shelter from the most violent tempests. Here our company was still further increased by a certain Petrus from the Low Countries, a handsome young fellow, tall and well set up, who for a long time had been soldiering in Welch countries. He made us go round by Our Lady of Loretto, a locality famed for the indulgences granted to its pilgrims. It would be difficult to conceive anything more wild than the country--a veritable brigands' haunt. The town has but one long street, at the end of which there is a small chapel, the tenement reputed to have been occupied by the Virgin Mary at Nazareth and transported thence by the angels. In a niche there is an image of the Virgin, alleged to be the work of St. Luke. For a certain consideration a priest will rub the rosaries against the image, and under those conditions the pilgrim obtains so many indulgences that he would not part with them for an empire. The quills of the porcupine constitute one of the principal articles for sale at Loretto. I saw a great many of those animals alive; they are about the size of a hedgehog. I ornamented my hat with a large leaden medal of the Virgin surmounted by three quills fastened with a silken thread, and each with a small flag at the end. I also saw at Loretto a live chamois, the only one I ever beheld, though chamois are not rare in that country, and above all in the Alps. The flesh of the chamois is preferred to that of the deer. I have tasted it; I have even worn several pair of small clothes of chamois leather; it is excellent, and you can wash it like linen, and the skin remains as soft as ever.

Petrus was known everywhere, and principally in the mountains. Without ever having studied to that effect, he could pride himself upon being a good musician and being able to sing at sight. In every town he took us straight to a monastery, where the young monks hailed him by his name, feasted him, bringing him wine and refreshment; then they sang a piece of music, drank a cup of wine, and we took our leave. This Petrus was a precious travelling companion; added to his knowledge of the country, he had a most agreeable disposition, *et comes facundus in via pro vehiculo est.* He told us where he was born and how many years he had lived in Italy, far away from his parents, whom, however, he was most anxious to see again. I, in my turn, told him the business that called me to Rome; he offered to accompany me on the return journey. The voyage from Milan and across France was delightful, he said; he was familiar with the roads as far as the Low Countries. I was delighted with the proposal, which, as will be seen, was wellnigh fatal to me. In Rome, after having settled us in a hostelry, Petrus gave me his address, and we agreed to meet often.

On May 26, 1546, I presented myself at the house of Doctor Gaspard Hoyer, who, at the first glance, knew my identity by my likeness to Magister Johannes. He changed my straw hat, ornamented with the holy relic which I had bought at Loretto, for a black biretta of Italian fashion, a headgear very much worn in those days at Rome. He had with him Gerard Schwartz, the younger brother of Master Arndt Schwartz, and in talking together we discovered that we had left Trent on the same day without having fallen in with each other, Schwartz having travelled by way of Ferrara. He was a very scholarly young man, and a near kinsman of Dr. Hoyer. I never saw him again; and one day, when I asked Master Arndt Schwartz, he told me that Gerard had come back to Stralsund mentally affected, and that subsequently he disappeared. I have got an idea that he had contracted an illness in Rome which he dared not avow to his relatives.

Master Gaspard Hoyer had only learnt of the death of my brother thirteen days before my arrival, in a letter from my father. The news had grieved and surprised him, but there remained the fact that my parents in Pomerania had been informed more promptly of the misfortune than an inhabitant of Rome. I conceived many tragic suspicions, on the subject of which I could only trust to God. Dr. Hoyer proved his goodwill by accompanying me to the Cardinal Count de St. Flore,[34] whose servant my late brother had been; he presented me, exposed my wretched situation, and renewed the request he had preferred at the receipt of my father's letter. The cardinal was exquisitely sympathetic; he had promptly communicated with his steward at Acquapendente, and he expected the reply, together with my brother's belongings, at every moment. Nevertheless, Master Hoyer had to wait until July 1 without receiving another summons to call. He considered my presence necessary, and on our way he told me that he and the cardinal had offered my brother a canonry at Lubeck, and that in consequence of his refusal my brother had become strongly suspected of Lutheranism.

We were taken at once to the cardinal, who handed me five-and-twenty golden crowns, three double ducats, two golden florins, two rose nobles, one florin of Hungary, three angelots (French money), a golden chain of twenty and a half crowns, three golden rings (the first being a seal, the second a keepsake, and the third set with a turquoise), worth seven and a half crowns, another half-crown in gold, and three Juliuses. I was told at the same time that my brother had spent thirty crowns in clothes, that during his illness he had bequeathed twenty crowns to the poor, and that his tombstone had cost another thirty. According to Roman custom, the servants had divided his wardrobe among themselves. The cardinal said also to me: "*Legit aliquoties libros mihi admodum suspectos, et quanquam admonui eum, ut non legeret, tamen deprehendi saepius legentem.*"

After this he asked me several questions of interest about Pomerania. Was it as hot there as in Rome? The cardinal, in fact, was sitting in his shirt sleeves, in a large room whose window panes were made of linen instead of glass; the floor was constantly sprinkled with water, which by a nice contrivance ran away. My reply caused the cardinal to exclaim: "*O utinam et Romae ejusmodi temperatum aërem haberemus.*" After Master Hoyer had thanked him in both our names, we took our leave. "Did you hear what the cardinal said?" asked the doctor, when we were in the streets once more. "No doubt I did," was the answer. "Yes," he remarked, "Master Johannes' stay at Acquapendente was a very short one; and yet, no German was ever less fond of Italian fruit, fresh figs, melons, etc., than he." People ought to know that those fruits are delicious, but harmful to those who are not used to them. Many a German on his first arrival yields to the temptation, and pays for the imprudent act with his life. Besides, Dr. Hoyer had not had the slightest anxiety with regard to my brother, whom only very recently he had met in the street. I left the money and the trinkets with Dr. Hoyer until my departure.

Master Gaspard Hoyer was an honest, loyal and obliging little man; may the Lord watch over him. In order to make my money hold out, he took a good deal of trouble to find me a place with the superintendent of the hospitium of Santa-Brigitta, an aged Swedish priest, who took boarders from among the advocates, procurators and suitors of the Tribunal of the Rote. To cook, to wash up, to make the beds, to lay the table, and to clear it, to bring the wine from the cellar, and to serve it, these were my functions, for which I received half a crown per month. Apparently they were satisfied with my culinary talent; it is true, I had only to prepare the soup, called "minestra"; the other dishes came from the tavern. In Rome, where there are so many people who cannot publicly live with a woman, and where it swarms with suitors and pleaders who would find it difficult to keep up a house, there are excellent taverns, providing fish, flesh, game, poultry roast, boiled pasties, and delicate wines; in short, everything necessary to a princely banquet.

One day, while at meat, my master announced the happy tidings of the death of Dr. Luther; the heresiarch had met with the end he deserved; a legion of devils had swooped down upon him, and a horrible din had put all those around him to flight. Luther himself had bellowed like a bull, and at the last moment he had uttered a terrible yell; his spirit went on haunting the house. The boarders vied with each other in falling foul of "that abominable Luther," that limb of Satan, doomed, like all the other demons, to everlasting fire. The only one who did not join in this charitable colloquy was a procurator of the Rote; he only opened his lips to murmur now and again: "*O Jesu, fili Dei, miserere mei,*" to the tune of that famous Italian song, to which there seems no end, "*Fala lilalela.*"

My master, who performed mass at the chapel of the hospitium, hit upon the idea to take me as his acolyte; my ignorance of the various movements and my lukewarmness to learn, made him exclaim: "*Profecto tu es Lutheranus!*" "*Sum Christianus,*" I replied, "my schooling in my native country, and my daily work at Spires by the receiver of the Order of St. John, left me no leisure to think of mass." I am bound to confess that as we went on, the suspicions of my new master did not fail to inspire me with fears for my safety. My master officiated at all the masses on saints' days, both in town and in the neighbourhood; there were as many as three on the same day; and as the journey from one church to the other was long, and we left at daybreak to return very late at night, our satchel contained a large flagon of wine and substantial food. Each altar was completely prepared for mass; our master halted before the altar nearest to the entrance, put on his chasuble and said a mass. The first one I heard; then we departed for another church, and there, while my master officiated, I sat down behind the altar, my satchel on my knee, and ate a comfortable morsel, and washed it down with a moderately full cup. At meal time the priest noted the deficiency, and asked me for an explanation; I frankly confessed my inability to prolong the fast, which after all I was not bound to observe, inasmuch as I did not say mass. The explanation was more or less graciously received.

This visit to the various stations enabled me to see and to learn a great many in a short time, for my master, who knew the city thoroughly, was very pleased to show me its curiosities, and often went a long way round for my sake. Rome has close upon one hundred and fifty churches, seven of which count as principal ones. There are many abbeys, convents and asylums. I did not see all these buildings, and the majority of those I saw did not strike me as remarkable. At the door of each church a tablet tells the dates of the pilgrimages and the number of indulgences to be gained; the general list of the pilgrimages and of the indulgences is also sold separately. The annual number of stations or pilgrimages exceeds a hundred; hence, one can redeem all one's sins at least a dozen times; that is, eleven times more than is necessary, and one is furthermore gratified with a hundred thousand years of indulgences. O, good Jesus, why didst not thou remain in heaven, if our salvation is after all to depend upon holy popes and their magnificent indulgences, notwithstanding which they have to go and join the devils in hell.

A special mention is due to the Asylum of the Holy Spirit, the pride of Rome, and which is considered by the wise as the most meritorious work of Christendom. Rome contains a mass of single folk of both sexes; the pope's *entourage* consists of fifteen or sixteen cardinals, whose establishments are kept on a footing as good as that of the courts of our princes of Germany. Then there are about a hundred bishops having servants, and several thousand prelates, canons and priests with their servitors. I refrain from numbering the young monks, who keep their vow of chastity as a dog observes Lent. Nor should we forget the assessors, advocates, procurators, notaries and pleaders of a hundred different countries who crowd the law courts. All these are forbidden to have a wife. Nevertheless, thousands of them shelter under their roofs persons of the fair sex, supposed cooks, washerwomen and chambermaids. And now calculate the number of disorderly women.

They, however, enjoy a wonderful liberty, and it is safer to wound or even to kill a man in Rome than to treat roughly an importunate harlot. At Vespers, great lords, pope, cardinals, bishops and prelates send for these "damsels of joy." They come to their homes in male disguise; the others know exactly where to find them.

The courtesans sell their wares at a high price, for they stroll about attired in velvet, damasks, silks, and resplendent in gold. They cannot sell their favours cheaply, inasmuch as they pay a heavy tax, which, together with the proceeds of masses, constitutes the revenues of the priests with which Rome swarms. If one wishes to ascertain the revenues of an ecclesiastic, he asks: "How many harlots?" and the figures show whether he, the ecclesiastic, is more or less favoured. No wonder, then, that, privileged in that manner, magnificently dressed and kept in splendour, prostitutes come to Rome from all parts. It is worthy of notice that the young girls of Rome emulate the others with zest. (Dr. Hoyer's cook, a native of Nuremburg, must have been once a beautiful creature. Her master always called her madonna Margarita.) At thirty or thirty-five, when they find their admirers desert them, these persons become cooks, laundresses, serving wenches, without, however, disdaining a good windfall. The result was this: they smothered, they flung into the cloaca, they drowned in the Tiber more new-born than there were massacred at Bethlehem. Herod after all was an impious and barbaric tyrant, and resorted to this butchery in order to defend his crown. Yet by whom were the poor innocents in Rome deprived of baptism and life? By their mothers, by those to whom they owed their birth, by the saints of this world, the vicars of Christ.

To cure the evil by means established by God Himself was not to be thought of, marriage having been declared incompatible with the sacerdotal office. Pope Sixtus IV, however, having set his heart upon stopping those horrible murders, restored from roof to cellar the Asylum of the Holy Spirit, tumbling to ruin, and enlarged it by several handsome structures; he established an important brotherhood there, at the head of which he inscribed his own name, an example followed by many cardinals. Each member of the fraternity has the privilege of choosing for himself a confessor; and power was given to said confessor to give plenary absolution once when the penitent was in a state of good health; when dying, an unlimited number of times, even for the cases usually reserved for the Apostolic See.

The wards of the hospital are handsome and roomy, the beds and appurtenances leave nothing to desire. The sick of every country are treated with unremitting care; when they are cured they pay, if they are able and willing; but the very poor are sent away dressed in new clothes from head to foot, and provided with some money. The staff is composed of sick-nurses of both sexes, physicians and surgeons; the establishment has, moreover, an excellent dispensary abundantly stocked with everything, and recourse to which was often had from outside. The institution--apart from the hospital--brings up foundlings and orphans; the governors have the boys taught this or that trade, according to their aptitude or taste, nor are the girls allowed to remain idle. While still very young they begin to knit, to spin, to sew and to weave; in fact, under the direct supervision of the mistresses attached to the establishment, they are taught all the occupations of their sex. If one of the inmates wishes to get married, he or she must inform the administrators either directly or through an intermediary. Inquiries are made about the suitors, about their means of maintaining a family, etc. The girls get a modest marriage-portion, an outfit, household goods and utensils, and at Whitsuntide six or seven unions are celebrated at the institution on the same day.

Truly, it is a great institution, which seems to defy all criticism. In spite of enormous expenses, the existence of the establishment is assured by its resources. Of course Sixtus IV. has contributed largely from his private purse, but those contributions were as nothing to the practically incredible sums collected by the courtesans throughout Christendom in aid of the hospital, Germany included, and even Pomerania, if I may trust to the recollections of my young days. One day, while taking a stroll with Dr. Hoyer, I ventured to ask him if he had no wish to come back to his native country, where he had friends, relatives, property and livings. He said he had not such a wish, in consequence of the difference of religion, adding: "May my countrymen amend their ways and become converted, like all those who have turned away from the true and primitive Catholic doctrine." "But," replied I, "it's we who have the true and primitive Catholic doctrine in its purity." Dr. Hoyer retorted: "It is written, 'Ye shall know them by their fruits.' Well, let them show me anywhere in Germany an institution to be compared to the hospital and the Asylum of the Holy Spirit." "I know this saying of Christ," I remarked, "and I turn it against the papists. Good fruits, indeed; a life of abomination, the murder of innocent creatures, a premium on debauch by picking up the new-born. The pope, the cardinals, bishops, prelates, canons, their servants, monks, assessors and other hangers-on of the priesthood, would not all these be better off in taking to themselves wives? for as much as the Almighty condemns fornication, as much does he recommend to the priest, as well as to the layman, the holy state of marriage, the antidote to the Roman horrors of a certain kind. Do not we read in the Epistles of Paul:

'Marriage is honourable among all things'? And if so, there would be no more murdering of innocents, mothers and fathers would themselves look after their offspring, the Asylum of the Holy Spirit would become useless, an immense saving would be effected, and everybody would have a clear conscience with regard to that kind of thing." Dr. Hoyer did not answer me, but what a wry face he pulled!

Rome contains a great number of handsome mansions, for the popes, in order to perpetuate their memory, erect three-storied and four-fronted palaces; whole streets of houses are demolished if in any way they obstruct the view. The material employed is a magnificently hard stone; there is a popular saying to that effect: "In Rome, great blocks of marble, great personages, great scoundrels." Nor are the cardinals and bishops satisfied with modest buildings, least of all with humble huts; as a consequence, the stone masons always have their hands full. Buffaloes, a species of very strong oxen, convey the stones, which are hoisted up in the easiest possible manner, by means of curious engines.

On Corpus Christi day there is a grand procession, in which the pope takes part. The streets through which he passes are bestrewn with green, the houses are ornamented with rich hangings, there is the firing of cannon, and clever pieces of fireworks are let off from the various palaces; naturally there is an immense crowd, and people could walk on each other's heads; the smallest window has a number of spectators. At the Castle of St. Angelo there was an admirable piece of fireworks in the shape of a sun; the whole structure seemed to be ablaze. At St. Peter's there was a discharge of heavy artillery, and the cannons of St. Angelo and of the cardinals replied to the salute. There was so much smoke and so much noise that one could neither hear nor see anything. At last both subsided, and then the pope appeared on the balcony, where they presented a book bound in gold to him, from which he read, but I could not catch a word he said. All at once the whole of the enormous throng, thousands of people, fall on their knees, I alone remain standing; those around me stare at me with stupefaction, thinking, no doubt, that I have taken leave of my senses. When the reading was over (it was a short one) the pope blessed the people, who cried: "*Vivat papa Paulus, vivat.*"

Close to the Church of Maria de Pace stands the huge statue of Pasquin, which every morning denounces, without ceremony and with impunity, as it were, the mistakes and crimes of the great ones of the land, the cardinals and the Pope Paul III were often taken to task; numberless were the allusions with reference to his acquisition of the cardinal's hat. A German, who had come to Rome for absolution, confessed, among other things, to having spoken ill of the pope. The confessor was greatly perplexed. It was difficult to account this as a sin to the penitent, when at any minute the latter might hear the pope insulted openly; on the other hand, to refrain from condemnation on the ground that the case was a common one at Rome was virtually discrediting the papacy in the estimation of the Germans. Clever man that he was, the confessor asked: "*Ubi maledixisti Pontifici, in patriâ vel hic Romae?*" "*In patriâ.*" was the answer. "*O!*" exclaimed the priest, "*commisisti grande peccatum; Romae licet Pontifici maledicere, in patriâ vero non.*"

At that time the pope was recruiting, to the sound of the drum, troops to aid the emperor against the Lutherans. About 10,000 foot soldiers and 500 light horse, both exceedingly well-equipped, enlisted. They mustered at Bologna; the pope's grandson Octavius, Governor of St. Angelo,[35] received the command of the contingent. The Spanish Inquisition grew more and more energetic in order to arouse the religious ardour of the horse and foot soldiers. A Spaniard, convicted of Lutheranism, was paraded seated on a horse, covered to its hoofs with placards representing the devil; the gallows were erected close to the pyre in front of Sancta Maria super Minervam. The poor wretch was hanged and his body burnt; after which a chattering monk demonstrated at length the temporal and spiritual dangers of the Lutheran heresy.

The cardinals gave a grand banquet in honour of Duke Philip of Brunswick. A well-born Spaniard slipped in among the servants of the prelate where the entertainment took place. That nation is greatly addicted to pilfering. Most people know the answer of Emperor Charles V to the Spaniards, who wished to induce him to suppress the habitual drunkenness of the Germans: "It would practically remove the opportunity of Spaniards to do a bit of robbery now and again," said Charles. Fancying that such an opportunity had come, the Spaniard got hold of some bread and a flagon of wine, hid himself under the table, the cloths of which reached to the floor. In the event of his being caught, he was ready with the plea of a practical joke, knowing that the host was himself very fond of them. Two of his servants were posted near the great mansion. The banquet was not over before midnight, and the stewards of his Eminence, worn out with fatigue, considered that the silver would not take wing when the doors were shut. They therefore left it where it was, merely shutting the doors behind them. Emerging from his hiding-place, the Spaniard introduces his confederates, and they all carry away as much as they can. The spoil is sold to the Jews, with the exception of the least cumbersome pieces, which the scoundrel intends to keep for making a show of his own; and then the three depart in the direction of Naples as fast as their horses will carry them.

His Eminence's retainers having gone to bed late, were not up betimes, and their astonishment on entering the banquetting hall may easily be imagined. Their flesh crept. How were they going to avoid being sent to prison? Were they to preserve silence about the affair, or inform the cardinal? They decided upon the latter course. They were locked up, and couriers were dispatched in hot haste to warn the innkeepers; the express order of the pope was to bring back to Rome any person in whose possession the stolen objects were found.

It so befell that, tired and hungry, the Spaniard stopped at a hostelry; they laid the table for him, but at the sight of the earthenware he waxed indignant. "What's the meaning of this?" he bellowed. "Am I a nothing at all?" Thereupon he orders his servant to bring out his own silver. The landlord, who had ample time, in the kitchen, to look at it, recognized it from its description, sent for reinforcements, and his three customers were taken back to Rome. When interrogated, the Spaniard denounced the Jews as receivers; his money was taken from him, the silver was found at the Jews' houses, and they were immediately put under lock and key.

A great number of Jews dwell in Rome, practically confined to one long street, closed at both ends. Any one who should be imprudent enough to come out of that street during Passion week, commemorating, as it does, the martyrdom of Christ, would infallibly be murdered. When Easter is gone Jews are as secure as they were before; they go everywhere, and transact their business without being hampered or molested. The two receivers were the principal and the richest members of their tribe; thousands of crowns were offered for their ransom, but it was all in vain. The five criminals perished on the gallows, erected by the St. Angelo bridge, the Spaniard in the centre, a copper crown on his head, to single him out as king of the thieves.

In fact, no week went by without a hanging. I was an eye-witness of the following. The hangman was about to push a condemned man from the ladder, when a friendly voice in the crowd cried: *"Messere Nicolao, confide in uno Dio!"* to which the thief replied: *"Messere, si."* At the same moment he was hurled into space.

I have often seen the strappado given; among others, to priests guilty of having said more than one mass per day, a practice considered hurtful to the interest of their fellow-priests. A pulley is fixed to the coping of the roof; in the middle of the rope there is a stick which stops the rope running along the groove farther than that. The culprit, his hands tied behind his back, is attached to the one end of the rope, which is in the street. After that he is hoisted up and left to fall suddenly to within a yard of the ground. In that way the wrists pass over the head, and the shoulders are dislocated. After three hoistings he is unbound, taken into the house, where his limbs are set, an operation which the *lictores* perform with the greatest ease in virtue of their great practice. There are, however, patients who remain maimed all their lives; on the other hand, I have known a priest, who, in consideration of a Julius, consented to suffer those three turns.

I was beginning to think about my homeward journey, and felt greatly perplexed about it. The dog-days were drawing near, and Northern folk are unable to bear them in Italy. On the other hand, along the whole of my route war was raging, and the Welch soldiers are a hundred times greater devils than the Germans; though in Germany itself it would have been a difficult task to get through the lines of those formidable imperial cohorts, the savage bands of Bohemians, and, in fine, the Protestant army. Was I to prolong my stay in Rome? Wisdom said no. I remembered but too well Cardinal St. Flore remark about my brother, *"Frustra eum admonui, ut non legeres libros suspectos."* Moreover, my opinion on the Asylum of the Holy Spirit had scandalized Dr. Hoyer, and the provider of the St. Brigitta institute had exclaimed with an oath: *"Profecto tu es Lutheranus."* The Spanish Inquisition was acting with the utmost rigour; and inasmuch as the wine was excellent I was very nigh forgetting for a little while the prudent counsel of my former master, the commander of St. John. Consequently, after ripe reflection, full of trust in the Almighty, and also counting on the faithful company of Petrus, I told Dr. Hoyer of my impending departure. He considered it incumbent on him to point out the dangers of the journey, but perceiving that my mind was fully made up, he handed me my brother's property and gave me a letter for my father. I parted with the Swede *bonâ cum veniâ*, seeing that he gave me a crown for the six weeks I had served him.

I had told my friend Petrus that until my going I should confide to Dr. Hoyer the valuables the cardinal had restored to me. From that particular moment he talked about leaving Rome, especially as the enlisting had begun, and the mercenaries were almost immediately after their registration dispatched to Bologna. We finally fixed our departure for July 5. God, once more, took me under His wing. I had become acquainted with a companion of my own age, named Nicholas, the son of a tailor at Lubeck. He told me that after many years stay at Rome he wished to see his own country again, but that he had not the necessary money for the journey. If I did not mind paying his expenses on the road, he would reimburse them at Lubeck, and consider himself my debtor ever afterwards. I was really glad at his request, for I considered him a man of honour and most loyal. He was, moreover, thoroughly master of Italian, which I knew very badly. I therefore thanked Providence who sent me a *comitem mente fideque parem*.

On the eve of our departure I went to inform Petrus of the excellent news. He turned pale, grew low-spirited, and did not utter a syllable. I ascribed his coolness to something that had annoyed him, and told him that we should come for him very early in the morning. After a moment's hesitation he said "yes," and walked away. Next morning Nicholas and I, prepared and equipped for our journey, knocked at his door. Petrus lodged with poor people; he was a simple landsknecht, and, according to his landlady, he carried all his belongings on his back. The woman then told us that Petrus, after leaving us, had promptly enlisted and betaken himself off, from fear of his creditors and in spite of his promise to pay them all with the money he was shortly expecting. Let my children give praise to the Almighty who saved my life at the moment I was blindly going to trust it to the mercy of a vagrant mercenary. No doubt that, shortly after leaving the city, he would have killed me in some solitary spot, of which there is no lack in the neighbourhood of Rome. Not a soul would have troubled about what had become of me. The least he would have done to me was to rob me of everything I possessed before letting me go free, and, as I am ignorant of the language of the country, I cannot help shuddering at the thought of the fate that was in store for me.

And here I record, for the benefit of my children, the prediction of that sainted Doctor Martin Luther. "War," he had said, "will make Germany expiate her sins. It shall be staved off while I live, but the moment I am gone it will break out." Now, he went to sleep in the Lord on February 18 of this year (1546) at Eisleben, his natal town; and the historians have stated that the preparations for war commenced in February at the moment he fell ill. I myself had superabundant proofs in April of both the emperor and the pope arming on all sides; and it was at the beginning of June that the Cardinal of Trent reached Rome, dispatched by his Imperial Majesty to hurry the departure of the 10,000 Italian foot-soldiers and the 500 light horsemen.

CHAPTER VII

On the morning of July 6, 1546, in my twenty-sixth year, I left Rome with my faithful companion Nicholas. My gold was sewn up in my neck collar, the chain in my small clothes. In the way of luggage I had a small satchel containing a shirt and the poems composed by my brother at Spires and in Rome; slung across my shoulders I wore a kind of strap to which I tied my cloak in the day. I had my sword by my side and a rosary dangling from the belt, like a soldier joining his regiment. We had agreed (it being a question of life and death) that I should pretend to be dumb; hence Nicholas did not stir from my side for a moment wherever I went. The landsknechten, who spoke to me on the road without receiving an answer, were informed by him of my pretended infirmity. "What a pity," they said; "and such a handsome fellow, too. Never mind," they added, "he'll none the less split those brigands of Lutherans lengthwise." "You may be sure of that," replied my comrade, and thanks to this stratagem we got across the lines of the Welch soldiery.

On the morning after our leaving Rome, Duke Octavius went by, posting. He was accompanied by five people. When we got to Ronciglione, about two miles from Viterbo, we made up our minds to sup there, and go to bed afterwards, in order to arrive early in the city fresh and hearty, though not before daylight, inasmuch as we wanted to lay in a stock of things. Scarcely had we sat down to table when a turbulent crowd of soldiers invaded the inn; the host told us to remain quiet, for he was shaking in his shoes for himself. The bandits commenced by flinging him out of his own door; the larder was pillaged, and after having drunk to their heart's content, they staved in the barrels and swamped the cellars with the wine. It was an abominable bit of business and unquestionably the Welch, and Latin mercenaries are greater ruffians than the German landsknechten; at any rate, if we are to judge from what they did in a friendly country, and virtually under the very eyes of the pope. They invited us to accompany them to Viterbo, in spite of Nicholas pointing out to them that night was coming on apace, and that the gates would be shut. "We'll get in for all that," they said. We were bound to follow them. We got there about midnight, and they were challenged by the guard. "Who goes there?" he asked. "Soldiers of Duke Octavius," was the answer, and thereupon the gate was opened.

I recommend the following to the meditation of my children; let them compare my adventure with that of Simon Grynaeus, related at length in the writings of Philip Melanchthon, Selneccerus, Camerarius, Manlius and other learned personages. In 1529 Grynaeus, then professor of mathematics at Heidelberg, came to see Melanchthon at the diet of Spires; he heard Faber, one of his old acquaintances, emit from the pulpit many errors in connexion with transubstantiation. Having gone up to him when they came out of church, they started a discussion, and Faber, on the pretext of wishing to resume it, invited him to come to his inn the next morning. Melanchthon and his friends dissuaded Grynaeus from going. The next day, at the dinner hour, a weakly-looking old man stopped Manlius at the entrance to the hall asking him where Grynaeus was to be found, the process-servers, according to him, being on the look out to arrest him. Thereupon the various learned men who had foregathered there immediately conducted Grynaeus out of the town, and waited on the banks until he had crossed the Rhine; they had come upon the law-officers three or four houses away from the inn; luckily the latter neither knew them nor Grynaeus. As for the old man, there was no further trace of him; they made sure it was an angel. I myself am inclined to think it was some pious Nicodemus who, having got wind of the wicked designs of Faber, made it his business to frustrate them without compromising himself. Now for my own adventure.

We entered Viterbo in the middle of the night. Prudence dictated the avoidance of the mercenaries' lodgings, for a meeting with Petrus would have been fatal to us; as it happened, the soldiers swarmed everywhere. Wandering from house to house, and devoured with anxiety, we invoked the Lord, our last hope. And behold a man of forty and of excellent appearance accosted us. We had never seen him, and not a syllable had fallen from our lips. We were dressed in the Welch fashion; everybody, even in plain daylight, would have taken us for soldiers. Well, without the slightest preamble, he addressed us in our own language. "You are Germans," he said, "and in a Welch country; don't forget it. If the podesta lays hold of you, it means the strappado, and perhaps worse. You are making for Germany." (How did he know, except by reading our thoughts?) "Let me put you into the right road." Dumb with astonishment, we followed him in silence as far as the gates of the town; he exchanged a few words with the custodian, who, in his own gibberish, said to us: "For the love of you, friends, I'll disobey my orders, which expressly forbid me to open the gates before dawn. You'll find nothing in the faubourg, I warn you; the soldiers have pillaged and burnt everything, but you'll not die for being obliged to do one night without food and drink." Saying which he showed us out and promptly shut the gates upon us.

Who had been our guide? I am still asking myself the question. As for us, reassured by the consciousness of the Divine presence; and in our hearts we gave praise for this miraculous deliverance. The faubourg, destroyed by fire, was simply a mass of ruins. We slept in the open air on the straw of a barn where the wheat is threshed out by oxen and horses. It was daylight when we opened our eyes, and the first thing we saw was a gallows. Towards midday we got as far as Montefiascone, a pretty town famed for its Muscat wine. Thanks be to God, we continued our journey without being again alarmed, and we did not catch sight of any mercenaries until we came to Bologna.

We halted at Montefiascone until the evening and enjoyed the roast fowls and savoury dishes, but the oppressive heat interfered with our appetite, though the bottle was more frequently appealed to. A story is told a of traveller who was in the habit of getting his servant to taste the wine at every hostelry they stopped.[36] "*Est*," said the latter if the wine was bad, "*Est, Est*" if it was passable, "*Est, Est, Est*" if it was good. And his master either continued his route or dismounted according to the signal. At Montefiascone, however, the servant did not fail to cry: "*Est, Est, Est*," and his master drank so long as to contract an inflammation, of which he died. When the relatives inquired about the cause of his death, the servant replied: "*Est, est, est facit quod dominus meus hic jacet*," and in his grief he kept repeating: "*O Est, est, est, dominus meus mortuus est.*"

On July 9 we reached Acquapendente, where my brother died, I visited the church without being able to discover his burial place. To ask questions would have been tantamount to betraying ourselves, considering that the Germans were the butt of public hatred.

Sienna, an important town with a celebrated university, is called *Siena Virgo*, though it lost its virginity long ago. From a neighbouring mountain one notices two small burghs; the one is called Cent, the other Nonagent. The pope being at Sienna, a monk undertook to show him *Centum nonaginta civitates*. When he got his Holiness to the top he showed him the two places in question.

Lovely Florence is the pearl of Italy. At the entrance to each town they said to us, "Liga la spada" (Tie the hilt to the sheath). At Florence we had to give up our weapons. If we had only crossed the city a man would have accompanied us to restore them at the other gate, but on our declaring that we were going to stay until the evening our swords were taken from us, and the hilts provided with a wooden label, part of which they gave us to keep. Besides, some one came into the city with us, and, among other useful information, showed us a beautiful hostelry where they treated us remarkably well for our money. A magnificent palace, a church entirely constructed of variegated marble, adjusted with marvellous skill and art, a dozen lions and lionesses, two tigers and an eagle, that is all I remember. There were ever so many other curiosities to see, but our heads were full of Germany. When the heat of the day abated we pursued our journey; our arms were restored to us on our presenting part of the label.

After having crossed Mount Scarperia, which fully deserves its name, seeing that it constitutes the most fatal passage of Italy to shoeleather and feet, we got to Bologna in the morning of July 13. Bologna is a big city belonging to the pope (*Bononia grassa, Padua la passa*), and endowed with a famous university. The town was teeming with mercenaries, so we were not particularly anxious to stop in it.

At some distance from Bologna begins a canal dug by the hand of man. There the Lord caused us to meet with an inhabitant of Mantua who had just enlisted. We proposed to hire a boat as far as Ferrara together. "Whither are you going?" he asked. As we had the appearance of soldiers, and as he might conceive some surprise at seeing us turn our backs on headquarters, we hit upon the idea of telling him that our master was at the Council of Trent. "Oh," he remarked, "you are going farther, then?" We said neither "yes" nor "no." He knew a little Latin, like myself, and so I no longer kept up my part of a dumb man before him. He professed but small regard for the pope and papism. "How dare you," I exclaimed, "talk in that way in Italy, and on the very territory of the Church? And why, if these are your opinions, do you take service against the Evangelicals?" "What does it matter?" he replied; "I am not risking the loss of a cardinal's hat. I am a fighting man, and fight for those who pay me." When we got near to the Pô, he said: "Ferrara lies no doubt in your most direct road to Germany, but what could you see there of interest? It is only a big town of the old style. You had better come to Mantua, the country of Virgil, a handsome, pleasant, and strong city, with a superb castle. The rest you are likely to get in the boat will compensate for your coming out of your way. I'll go on shore just before Ferrara, and will get a boatman; the place is famed for its fat geese, which, at this season of the year, one eats smoking hot from the spit. I'll bring one back with me, together with bread and wine, and I shall only be gone a little while."

Ferrara, with its famous university, its actual importance, and ancient origin, unquestionably aroused our curiosity. Nevertheless, the advice of our soldier-friend was not to be despised, because by going up the Pô, we advanced in spite of the heat. Our guide soon came back, bringing with him everything he had promised. The boatman whom he brought was simply in his shirt sleeves, and drank at one draught a whole measure of heavy wine we offered him; then, flinging the towing rope over his shoulder, he towed us to Mantua, Ostiglia being our halting place for the night. Having got to Mantua in the morning of July 15, we were enabled to wander through the town before dinner time. Our expectations were in no way disappointed. After having shown us the castle and the principal buildings, our amiable soldier-friend insisted upon entertaining us at the inn. "Are you provided with small change that is current everywhere?" he asked us. "The fact is," he went on, "that the landlords pursue a regular system of cheating. They refuse to take your small money, so that you are obliged to change a crown, and then at the next inn they decline to accept the coin given to you except under its value. Give me a crown, and I'll get you money for it which is current as far as Trent." He brought back good pieces of silver, not to the amount of one crown, but of two crowns, asking us to accept the value of the second as a present, "because," he said, "I consider you very honest and straightforward companions." When we were outside the walls, he gave us full particulars of the route we were to take, recommended us to the safeguard of all the angels, and gave us his blessing. "It is worth more in the sight of the Almighty and against the devil than the blessing of Pope Paul at Rome by his own sacred hands." This was indeed a happy meeting, and we had reason to be grateful to the Lord.

Not far from Mantua, at a spot where the road branches off into four different directions, we came upon two travellers coming from Verona. If we had said one pater more or less with our good friend we should have missed them, which would have been a pity, for they turned out to be my former fellow-travellers from Kempten to Rome, who, having pushed as far as Naples, had returned by way of Venice; they were making for home by Milan and France. They wished me to go their way, and I was very willing; but as Nicholas was altogether of a different mind, it would have been wrong to vex the comrade God had so marvellously provided for me.

When I told them all about Petrus, my interlocutors had no doubt about the danger I had incurred by my imprudent confidence. Italians are not of much account. Germans, after a long stay in that country, end up by not being worth anything at all; and the proverb to that effect is a true one: "*Tedesco Italianato è un diavolo incarnato.*" I learnt later on, both from writing and from oral news, about the troubles between France and the Low Countries, and about the obstacles we should have encountered if we had selected the route of Milan. It gave me a new subject for being grateful to the Lord.

We passed near enough to Verona to catch a glimpse of the buildings, to judge by which it must be a big town. At Trent, where both languages are spoken, and even more German than Italian, my pretended infirmity ceased, and it was Nicholas' turn to be mute, for the Lubeckian dialect is not understood until one gets to Brunswick.

In Italy the scorpions slip in everywhere; into the rooms, under the beds, in the sheets. Hence they place before the windows scorpion oil, that is oil in which one of these reptiles has been drowned. When put on the sting the oil stops the effect of the poison. Personally, I never caught a glimpse of a scorpion during the whole of my stay in Italy.

On July 18 we reached Botzen, a town of importance, famed for its rich mines. On the 19th we were at Brixen, a pleasant burgh, prettily situated. Its chapter enjoys great consideration. Dr. Gaspard Hoyer was its canon, and died there.

The Augsburg troops under the orders of Sebastian Schaertlin[37] had carried the castle of Ehrenberg. King Ferdinand tried to enter the place with the aid of the miners of Botzen, but the pay ran short, and, greatly vexed, the savage horde, which, though by no means devout, after all preferred Luther to the pope, made its way home. Between Brixen and Sterzing we had the misfortune of falling in with them. At the sight of our Italian dress, and our soldier-like equipment, they shook their spears. "Kill the papists; down with the Welch scum," they cried. Nicholas, who was accustomed to enact the spokesman, uttered a few words in his own dialect; thereupon the imprecations grew louder. "They belong to the Low Countries; they are no better than the Italians." "Brothers," I shouted, "you make a mistake. We are faithful Germans, Lutherans and Evangelicals like yourselves. Hence, no violence."

Thereupon we fell a-talking to each other. They complained bitterly of the king, and of his pretensions to carry on a war without a red cent. "Kicks instead of pay," they said. "We are much obliged. We are going back to our mines, where, at any rate, we can earn something." We parted quite cordially, and I once more recommended my faithful Nicholas to hold his tongue for the future, and to let me do the talking.

Innspruck, the capital of the Tyrol, is a moderately big town with long streets, consisting largely of stables for some thousands of horses, for the kings, the Austrian archdukes and their suites frequently halt there. The objurgations of the miners of Botzen induced us to change our dress according to the German fashion.

Our most direct route lay by Ulm, Cannstadt, Spires, Frankfurt, then by Hesse and Brunswick. There are, as it happens, two routes from Innspruck, the one for Bavaria, the other for Swabia. Having met at the city gates some people who professed to be going to Germany, we followed them without further inquiry. What then was our surprise at getting, not into Swabia, but into Bavaria, to Hall and to Ratisbon. Well, as we learnt later on, at that very moment the numerous troops the emperor was expecting from France and Spain were preparing to enter Swabia; the papal troops, whom the Imperial messages left little or no truce, arrived at Landshut, while all the Protestant forces, with the Elector of Saxony and the Landgrave of Hesse at their head, occupied the country. But for the Lord constituting Himself our guide we should have run innumerable perils.

We intended to go from Hall to Ratisbon on a raft, but on the overladen craft there was a horse stamping about in a most disquieting manner, causing the water to well up between the disjointed timber. We preferred to land and to tire our legs to swallowing more water than was necessary to our thirst. Half a league down the stream, the pole-men having got rid of the horse, drew near the shore once more to renew their offers of service. We remained faithful, however, to solid earth.

When we got to the beautiful monastery of Ebersberg, our curiosity tempted us to get an idea of the results of a mendicant's life. As such we humbly and contritely addressed the chancellor, when we entered the abbot's presence. "We have come all the way from Rome; our resources are exhausted," we said. After having promised us to do what he can, the chancellor begins to inquire about the Italian army. "We left it at Bologna," we replied; "it was being reviewed. You'll see it very shortly." This had the effect of turning the saintly dwelling upside down. The monks crowded round the abbot and took to running hither and thither as if bereft of their senses, because for a monastery situated as this was, in the open country, Roman mercenaries or Schmalkalden soldiers were practically one and the same thing.

And inasmuch as our humble persons were forgotten in all this confusion, I said to Nicholas: "Let us go to the inn and show these 'frocked' individuals that we can do without their soup. A snap for that business, unless we have been too inexperienced at it." We ordered the best dishes and washed them down with generous wine. The echoes of our gay repast must have reached the monastery, and when we had paid our reckoning, we pursued our journey.

We stopped four days in the big and beautiful city of Ratisbon. King Ferdinand, his wife, his daughters and the court ladies in gorgeous dresses, lodged in the principal square, the houses of which where elegantly decorated. We saw the carriage sent by the Duke of Mantua to his betrothed. It was entirely white, and perfectly built; the iron was replaced everywhere by silver, even for the smallest nail. The team consisted of four magnificent white mares, without the tiniest spot; the harness was of silver, and their crups were ornamented with three rings of the precious metal. Dressed in white silk, with boots and whip of the same colour, and silver spurs, the coachman slowly drove thrice round the square.

It was very evident that both the emperor and the king were using all their energy. Night and day, at home and beyond the frontier, strict guard was kept. The army of Bohemia was encamped beyond the Danube, while the Germans occupied the head of the bridge on the side of the city. We were warned of the danger of venturing among the Bohemians; between these madmen and the German soldiers there was nearly every day a fresh dispute resulting in wounds which often proved fatal. On the other hand, the Protestant troops were on the move, and it was most difficult to cross their lines. We could, however, not remain in Ratisbon. So we plucked up our courage and started, decided not to lose our heads in case of arrest, but to ask to be taken before the superior officer, for, after all, we had no need to fear an interrogatory. What was the danger of saying whence we came and whither we were going? Our lot was, moreover, in the hands of Him who in Italy had confided us to the protection of his angels.[38] We trudged straight on to Nuremberg. The weather was fine, the roads good, and the inns well provisioned.

Nuremberg is the *oculus Germaniae*. "Germany," according to the Italians, "has but one eye, Nuremberg." Nuremberg harbours the tradesmen, Augsburg the big merchants. We stayed three days in this interesting city, the study of whose civil and ecclesiastical institutions is by no means a waste of time. We there completed our German attire by doublets with short waists. It seemed to me unnecessary to hide the gold and jewels any longer in my clothes, for in spite of the eighty miles from our own native land, we already fancied ourselves in it.

The lord of Plawe had taken up his quarters at our hostelry. He was a Bohemian of important station, an experienced soldier, and a cool-headed, prudent, and clever personage, enjoying much favour with the electors and the princes. He was known by all the dignitaries of France, Germany, and Italy. His history may prove interesting to my children. The lord of Plawe had no children, and to prevent the lapse of his fiefs to the suzerain lord, he prevailed upon his wife to pretend being pregnant, and arranged with a shepherd of the neighbourhood, a strong, robust fellow, whose wife was genuinely in that condition. The newborn being of the male sex, it was carried clandestinely to the castle, where they had great rejoicings, a magnificent christening with high-born godparents. Seven years later, however, the lady of Plawe really gave birth to a son; the two children were brought up like brothers. When he came of age the elder visited the courts, and received a cordial welcome everywhere. The father died, and the elder, feeling himself cramped at home, abandoned the property to the younger in consideration of a yearly allowance. The mother is taken ill in her turn, and before her death reveals to her own child the whole of the secret. The elder, whose allowance is stopped, institutes a claim, and is answered that he is the mere son of a shepherd. The affair is referred to King Ferdinand, the suzerain lord, the lords of Prawe bearing the title of Burgrave of Mesnia, and first chancellor of the kingdom of Bohemia. To prove his parentage he produced the many letters in which his father recommended him in special terms to the emperor, and to the princes as his lawful heir. Several important personages, the majority belonging to the Evangelicals took an interest in his case, and provided largely for his maintenance. The principal Welch and German universities all declared that he proved his affiliation. King Ferdinand, though, leant to the other side, no doubt *ratione papisticae religionis*.

Under these difficult circumstances, this gentleman considered it better not to take service in the war between the emperor and the League of Schmalkalden, inasmuch as he would neither be unfaithful to his master nor to his conscience. The catastrophe which he dreaded nevertheless overtook him. About six months after the termination of the war, when, probably, he felt exceedingly pleased with himself on account of his clever abstention, he was laid by the heels by order of King Ferdinand, shipped on a raft, and taken to Hungary; and from that time he was no more heard of.

On August 11 we only reached Nordhausen in the Harz mountains, just as they were closing the city gates, but sufficiently early, though, to notice ten corpses tied to as many posts. The guard, which had been reinforced, was inclined to leave us outside. They pointed to the men that had been executed. "If they are there, it is because they deserved it," we answered; "ours is a different case." When we got inside we could not find a shelter anywhere. I inquired for the dwelling of the burgomaster and found him at home.

After the few customary inquiries about our names, our place of birth and our destination, the burgomaster questioned us about the beginning of the hostilities. We told him what we knew, and then exposed our embarrassing situation to him. "Never during this painful journey, not even in Italy, had we met with such inhuman conduct," we said. "We are not asking for charity. We are willing to pay for what we get; nobody shall have cause to complain of us. We ask you, therefore, to direct us to a respectable place of shelter."

Our very sordid appearance did not prevent the burgomaster from considering us altogether inoffensive, and, like a man of sense, he explained apologetically, "Our citizens," he remarked, "are still under the influence of a strong alarm, for we know for certain that a band subsidized by the confederate of hell who reigns at Rome is scouring the Saxon country, poisoning wells and pastures and setting fire to everything else. The proof of it is in the ten executed men whom you must have noticed at your arrival. Their crime admits of no doubt." "Agreed," I replied, "but if our conscience were in the least reproaching us, do you think we should have the courage to present ourselves before the first magistrate of the town?"

The burgomaster told one of his servants to take us with his compliments to a certain private individual, who happened to be a butcher with a stock of beautiful, luscious meat. On the hearth the beef was simmering in a large pot, no doubt to be retailed hot next morning. We asked him for some of that; then inquired about the liquor he could offer us. "I have got some excellent Nordhausen beer," he said. We, however, were used to wine. "Cannot you give us some wine? That's what we want with our meat." "If you care to pay for it. It's so much per measure." "Here's the money." "Do you want any fish?" "Yes; let us have a comfortable evening after this rough day. Come and sit yourself down with us and keep us company." He stared at us very hard, not knowing what to think. In spite of his knowing look, he behaved very well to us.

When our hunger and thirst were appeased, the butcher asked us whether we would go to bed or remain where we were. "Bring us some clean straw, and that will be enough for us. We shall not have the trouble of dressing in the morning," we answered. Besides the straw he gave us pillows, downright excellent beds, and snowy sheets; hence, in wishing him good-night, we assured him that we were born to understand each other. Next morning, the one who was the first to rise found the door bolted; we were obliged to wait for our host. We settled the reckoning with him, and the servant who had prepared our couch got a tip.

We stopped a day and a half at Luneburg, which we reached on August 15, and in view of our approaching meeting with our nearest and dearest, we paid attention to our dress. We crossed the burgh of Moelln, where Eulenspiegel lies buried, but at Lubeck a messenger who caught us up informed me that my uncle Andreas Schwartz was living at Moelln with his wife and children, and begged of me to retrace my steps. I spent a whole day with him, and when we had chatted to our heart's content he provided me with a horse and attendant as far as Lubeck.

At the city gate I wanted to turn short; perhaps I was still feeling the effect of the stirrup cup. My horse gave way, and for a moment the rider and the animal lay motionless. They were under the impression that I had broken the left thigh bone; but I got up safe and well.

At Lubeck my faithful travelling companion loyally repaid his debt. I took the coach, and at last, after a journey of eight weeks' (eighteen days of which had been spent in resting at various places, the distance from Rome to Stralsund being 250 German miles, and consequently five times as many Welch ones), I heard the "welcome" from my father, mother, brother and five sisters, all of whom were in excellent health. Together with Dr. Hoyer's letter, I handed over the objects restored by Cardinal St. Flore according to the inventory. My parents gave me two of the rings. As I was as sore as the most foundered horse, my mother had a bath prepared for me twice a week, and she herself rubbed my thigh with curd soap, so that my limbs soon recovered their usual suppleness.

PART II

CHAPTER I

When I had recovered from the fatigue of my travels, I came to the conclusion that a life of monotony and frequent visits to the tavern were not at all to my taste. The day would come when I had a wife and children to maintain; I therefore wanted a means of livelihood. I voted for the scribal occupation, and had recourse to the influence of Superintendent-general Knipstrow to obtain a position at the chancellery of Wolgast. Our friend's efforts having been successful, I was summoned to Wollin, where the prince was going to hold a diet. The journey by coach enabled me to make ample acquaintance both with the councillors and with my colleagues. I entered upon my duties on November 14, 1546.

The staff of the chancellery was composed of Jacob Citzewitz, chancellor; Erasmus Hausen, accountant-general; Joachim Rust, proto-notary; Johannes Gottschalk, Lawrence Dinnies, Christopher Labbun and Heinrich Altenkuke, secretaries. I need only mention for form's sake Valentine von Eichstedt, a student from Greifswald, whom the chancellor wished to initiate in the dispatch of current affairs.

Valentine hung about the office, now and again copying a fragment of a letter. He was wretchedly dressed; his poor blue jacket scarcely reached to his waist, while, on the other hand, his hose fell over his boots. Rust and Gottschalk refused to have him at the clerks' table; he had his meals lower down with the servants. In spite of this, Valentine, at the retirement of Erasmus Hausen, was appointed to the audit office through the influence of the chancellor. In order to get him into the habit of pleading he was entrusted with the cases that were settled by mutual agreement; after which he was sent to Wittenberg to finish his studies, and in a very short period he became accountant-general. A few years later Citzewitz gave up his position of chancellor to him. The protégé paid his benefactor in the usual way of the world, and on that chapter I myself could say a great deal.

The experience I had gained at the Imperial Chamber and in the chancelleries compelled Rust and Gottschalk to acknowledge that I could handle my pen, and inasmuch as the chancellor preferred my work to theirs, they seized every opportunity to do me harm. I had only to ask them for a few materials for this or that work to be sure to get it badly done and teeming with inaccuracies.

The dissolution of the League of Schmalkalden[39] and the threatening attitude of the emperor imparted a feverish activity to the correspondence which was being exchanged between our princes, the Elector of Brandenburg and the Elector of Saxony. The latter spent the winter very sadly at Altenburg. Chancellor Jacob Citzewitz was the soul of these negotiations; his experience of imperial and provincial diets, his learning heightened by eloquence, the personal consideration he enjoyed, his imposing figure, his lofty mind, and his assiduous labours all these, in fact, singled him out to represent the princes both in the councils and on more solemn occasions. Being fully aware of the weightiness of his task, he wholly devoted himself to it; all the enactments of the princes were drawn up by his pen and defied criticism. When Citzewitz at the termination of a debate asked: "Who undertakes the inditing?" all the councillors cried in chorus: "That's Solomon's business," for that was the nickname they had bestowed upon him.

Day and night, on horseback or on wheels, I scoured the highways in company of the chancellor. Starting from Berlin in the evening, we reached Stettin the next afternoon in sufficient time to present the report. Then there were the nights spent at work with the chancellor, who dictated to me the decisions to be submitted to the council on the morrow. I made a fair draft of them before the sitting, so that immediately after their having been read they could be sealed and dispatched. If my children should wish to compute the amount of labour I gave to the court and to Stralsund they will derive a salutary lesson from the reward these labours have brought me in my old days: *in fine laborum*, ingratitude.

Owing to those constant journeys I did not spend four weeks in six months at Wolgast, and still less at the chancellery. I lodged with Master Ernest, the cook of his Serene Highness Duke Philip, and of his august father and grandfather. Ernest was an honest and God-fearing man.

The year 1547 was an anxious one for the courts of Stettin and Wolgast, and the news that the Duke of Wurtemberg had tendered his submission accelerated the departure of a mission to the emperor. It was instructed to deny all participation of the princes in the League of Schmalkalden. The envoys of Duke Barnim were Dr. Falcke, in the capacity of chancellor, and Captain Jacob Putkammer; those of Duke Philip, Captain Moritz Damitz and Heinrich Normann. I was designated to accompany those four personages, and on March 10 we started by way of Silesia.

At Zittau we were obliged to leave Damitz in the doctor's hands; after which we crossed the Forest of Bohemia and reached Lertmeritz; next to Prague, the principal and best fortified town of the kingdom. We spent several days there in order to get an idea of the condition of affairs. The dislike of the Bohemians to march against the Elector of Saxony was evident, but King Ferdinand brought heavy pressure to bear upon them, he called up many of his troops both from Silesia and from Hungary. These Hungarian horsemen, called Husards, happen to be pitiless brigands. The King had placed them under the command of Sebastian von der Weitmülen, who, at the beginning of the war, had been appointed regent of the kingdom. The headquarters were at Eger, where this soldiery cut the children's hands and feet off to put them into their hats instead of plumes.

The councillors sent me to reconnoitre in the direction of Eger, at Schlackenwerth, and at Schlackenwald. My guide followed on foot. He was an intelligent lad, speaking both German and Bohemian. I ascertained that the Bohemians had cut down the trees in the wood, and as such made the route impassable for the horse and artillery, it was even impossible for the landsknechten to cross it with their standards flying.

After that, the councillors sent me to the castle of Gaspard Pflug, to whom the States of the country had entrusted the command of the troops. [40] He was very reserved. "What are we to do?" he said, looking perplexed. "The Elector of Saxony is our ally, our co-religionist; we cannot leave him to his fate. On the other hand, Ferdinand is our king. Are we to jeopardize our liberties?" Gaspard Pflug, having taken refuge at Magdeburg after the capture of the elector, built himself opposite the cathedral an elegant dwelling, where he ended his days, the king having confiscated his property.

While the elector encamped before Leipzig, the emperor overran the Algau and Swabia, imposing heavy fines and big garrisons to the towns forced to capitulate. The Spaniards committed every excess, and above all, in Wurtemberg.[41]

On April 23 and 25 the sun assumed so sombre an aspect that everybody rushed to the threshold of his house; both experts and scientific men foretold strange events.

One day I was strolling alone outside Lertmeritz around the walls (for the time hung heavily on my hands), when an individual, his eyes blazing with anger, assailed me without warning, vilifying me and trying to fling me into the moat. He was evidently under the impression of having come upon a spy. I endeavoured to convince him to the contrary; the difficulty was to understand each other. Finally, with hands clasped together as if they were bound, I gave him to understand with a sign of the head that I was ready to enter the town with him. Thanks to heaven, he consented to this, although he did not cease his imprecations. Before I had fairly entered our hostelry two members of the council came to ask our deputies to forbid their people to leave the city and the promenading on the walls. "We know very well that we have nothing to fear from you," they said, "but our citizens are quick to take umbrage, and just now one of your folk narrowly escaped coming to grief."

On April 16 the news came to Lertmeritz that two days previously the Elector of Saxony had been made a prisoner. Immediately leaving Bohemia we started in the direction of Torgau, but to get to the camp at Wittemberg the perils were endless, for the Spanish troops, whose lines we had to cross, shrank from no misdeeds.[42] Hence it was resolved that I should go to Wittenberg to get a safe-conduct--a decision against which I protested. "How am I to pass without the smallest bit of parchment?" "Never mind," exclaimed Damitz; "the Lord is the best safeguard." "In that case," I retorted, "are you not yourselves under the Divine protection?" My argument was, however, in vain; my life weighed less in the balance than that of my superiors.

In my capacity of a member of the missions to Bohemia and to the camp of the elector, I wore a yellow gorget which was the insignia of the Protestants. I was obliged to hide it in my breast and to replace it with the one bought for me, the red gorget of the Imperialists. And thus I started. If they had caught me with the double insignia upon me, my account would soon have been settled. I should have been slung up on the nearest tree.

I crossed Mühlberg, where the elector, wounded in the cheek, had been made a prisoner on the very spot where his passion for the chase caused so much damage to his unfortunate subjects. Wherever the eye turned there were signs of the recent battle; broken lances, shattered muskets, and torn-up harnesses littered the ground, and all along the road soldiers dying of their wounds and from want of sustenance. Around Wittenberg itself all the villages were deserted; the inhabitants had taken flight without leaving anything behind them. Here, the corpse of a peasant, a group of dogs fighting for the entrails; there, a landsknecht with just a breath of life left to him, but the body putrefying, his arms stretched out at their widest, and his legs far enough apart to put a bar between them.

At the end of my journey and within sight of the Spanish troops I passed a Spaniard, who said to me: "My good and handsome horseman, your service with the emperor is but of recent date." I rode a few steps further; then, undoing my gorget, I rubbed it against my boot to make it appear less new. At last, I reached the camp, where I lost several days in fruitless endeavours.

Every now and again there was firing from Wittenberg. Some Pomeranian horse-troopers with whom I had made acquaintance warned me not to keep to the high road if I should venture in that direction, but to go at random in order to avoid becoming a butt. A couple of steps in front of me a ball whizzed so closely past an individual's head that the shock or the fright felled him to the ground, where he was picked up for dead. From that moment I suspended my strolls.

Dr. Seld, the vice-chancellor, whom I succeeded in seeing,[43] did not disguise the deep irritation of the emperor. I answered that neither Duke Philip nor his brother, Barnim, notwithstanding the former's marriage with the sister of the Elector of Saxony, had given the slightest assistance to the Protestants, either in money, men or deeds, and that it would not be difficult for his Majesty to convince himself of this. Nevertheless my negotiations made no progress.

It was said in the camp that after the defeat of the elector, when Christopher Carlowitzi[44] the principal counsellor of Maurice, came to salute the emperor, whose docile instrument he was, the latter exclaimed: "Well, Carlowitz, what is going to happen?" "Everything is in your Majesty's hands," Carlowitz replied. "Yes, yes, something will happen," was the retort. And when the elector bent the knee before the emperor, saying, "Most clement emperor and lord," King Ferdinand interrupted with, "Ah, so he is your emperor now? But what about Ingoldstadt?[45] Wait a while. We shall soon settle your account." And when the death sentence was delivered, Ferdinand insisted upon its prompt execution. The Marquis de Saluces, on the other hand, repeated to the emperor, even before the arrival of the Elector of Brandenburg, that the best sheep in his flock was the Elector of Saxony, and that his execution would rouse the whole of Germany.

As I found it impossible to get a safe-conduct, I returned to Torgau, and immediately after hearing my report, our embassy ordered its carriages and took the direct road to Stettin.

Inasmuch as the Elector of Brandenburg loudly promised his good offices with the emperor, the princes dispatched me with a letter of thanks to him to the camp at Wittenberg. They also prompted the language I was to hold to the vice-chancellor and to the other Imperial counsellors.[46] To accelerate matters they prepared six relays of horses for me, with precise indications on paper as to their whereabouts, though I started from Wolgast on a pitiful cart-horse, equipped anyhow, for neither saddle, bridle nor stirrups were in condition. They thought that it did not matter, as I had to change animals at a short distance. So far so good. But neither at the first, second, third, fourth nor fifth stage was there a sign of a horse. The last stage was Brandenburg--the Old. Abraham Gatzkow, a gentleman of Lower Pomerania, had indeed provided a downright good and properly equipped saddle-horse for me, only on the day of my arrival he had mounted it for a ride to the camp, so that the same jade carried me to the end of my journey.

On June 1 I alighted at the tent of the Elector of Brandenburg, and when presenting my dispatch, I begged of Chancellor Weinleben to spare me a long stay. Next morning when I called again, he exclaimed: "Oh, the affair takes more time than you think," which remark did not prevent my insisting upon an answer on June 3, inasmuch as the elector went several times a day to the emperor, and that therefore he had no lack of opportunity to broach the subject. Moreover, there was need for urgency; they had just thrown a bridge across the Elbe and the emperor had transferred his quarters to the other side of the river, a sure sign of his approaching departure. To all which arguments on my part, Chancellor Weinleben angrily replied: "The interests of princes are discussed with minds at rest. Just look at the presumption of a simple messenger. Wait till you are told to go and then go. Here, this is the elector's reply. Take it, go, and leave me in peace."

I stopped at the first dense clump of trees in the wood, opened the letter, and immediately turned my horse's head. "What do you want now?" yelled the chancellor, when he caught sight of me. "Am I not to have any peace from you?" "My gracious masters," I replied, "have authorized me to open the letter of his Electoral Highness and to act in consequence. The letter I have just read proves once more the brotherly feelings of the elector, but as he is striking his tent, I think it necessary respectfully to remind him of his generous assurances. I shall wait for him at his leaving the emperor's presence, for I am bound to bring back to Wolgast something more than vague words." At this little speech the chancellor altered his tone. He ceased to address me familiarly as "thou," and, in fact, made somewhat exaggerated apologies, swearing by all his gods that in reality he had not the faintest idea of the affair, but that henceforth he was my staunch ally and that his master should not leave the emperor without ardently pleading the cause of our princes.

When the elector went to the imperial tent I followed him at a distance, and the moment he got into the saddle again I galloped on his track, for I foresaw his departure for Berlin. I was just at the head of the bridge of boats, which was entirely unprovided with parapets or barriers, when I espied coming from the opposite side a heavy cart. Time was precious. I pursue my quarry, and my right stirrup catches in the wheel and my valiant mount, in spite of its prancing and rearing, cannot extricate itself, or even hold its own against four strong draught horses. There is no room to turn, and there seems not even a possibility of saving myself by sacrificing the animal; both it and I seem inevitably doomed to perish by drowning. As for any human help, I do not as much as expect it. Even if they could have assisted me, the Spaniards at the end of the bridge would have been particularly careful not to do so. Just fancy their delight at seeing a German making a plunge with his horse into the Elbe; the sight would have been too delightful willingly to forego it.

When our distress is at its height, when neither our father nor our mother is able to save us, Providence stretches forth his protecting hand.

It happened then, by this merciful grace; the rotten strap suddenly gave way, leaving the stirrup entangled in the wheel and freeing my leg. It was a startling confirmation of the Divine word that the righteous shall see good come out of evil; for had the equipment been brand-new, of the most solid leather and even embroidered with gold and pearls, that harness would have sent me into the stream as food for the fishes.

At last I managed to join the elector. He sent me word that the opportunity for interceding with the emperor in behalf of the princes of Pomerania had not presented itself, but that the counsellors he left behind with the emperor would look to the affair and keep the dukes informed of everything. Why had I not gone to the bottom of the Elbe?

In the camp itself the tale went round that the King of the Romans, Duke Maurice, and after them, the emperor had made a very careful inspection of the church of the Castle of Willemberg, having been led to believe (the emperor and the king especially) that lamps and wax tapers were constantly burning day and night on Luther's tomb, and that prayers were said there just as in the Romish churches before the relics of the saints.

At Treuenbrietzen I made my report to Chancellor Citzewitz. As he was awaiting the arrival of the Pomeranian counsellors who were to accompany the emperor to Halle, he sent me to retain quarters and to give notice to the Brunswicker captain, Werner Hahn, to have twenty horsemen ready at Bitterfeld on June 12. On the morning of the 12th, in fact, the mission alighted at the general hostelry outside Bitterfeld. The captain of the husard-escort had, however, given the preference to an inn in the town. Seeing no sign of the Brunswickers, the counsellors put up their carriage, so that the captain at his return was under the impression that the mission was gone, and meeting with the horsemen, ordered them to face about, he being convinced that the deputies had taken another route.

Evening was drawing near; my business was finished, the quarters had been retained, the supper ordered, and the beds ready. I had taken advantage of the opportunity to renew my wardrobe, and, with my new clothes on, I took a stroll outside the gates through which the mission had to pass. Espying from the top of a mound a troop of advancing horsemen, I went back in hot haste afraid of a reprimand. At the same moment two Spanish bandits, half-naked, for their rags scarcely covered them, ran after me across the fields, the one on foot, the other on a kind of wretched farmer's cob--apparently stolen--and with a pistol at the saddle bow. Casting a careful look round to assure themselves that there were no witnesses to their contemplated deed, one had already raised his pistol when the Brunswicker horsemen arrived on the spot. "*Sunt isti ex tuâ parte?*" he asked. "*Senior, si,*" I quickly answered. "Ah, landsknecht, landsknecht," he said, replacing his weapon, and followed by his companion, making off as fast as he could.

The adventures of that evening were, however, not at an end. I found the gates of the town shut, and a trumpeter galloping along the walls and blowing with all his might. I had not the faintest idea of what it all meant, when the captain of husards appeared upon the spot, recognizes, and hails me. "What are you doing here, and what has happened?" he asked. "Why are the gates shut, and why is the alarm being sounded?" While confessing my total ignorance, I began to ask about the ambassadors; thereupon great surprise of the captain at their being waited for. The matter seemed all the more strange to him in that he on the road fell in with some Spanish horsemen, who told him that they had been sent to meet a mission. What if our counsellors should have been attacked by these people, decoyed into the wood, and plundered? Of course, I felt very anxious to inform the Brunswicker captain, so that he might send a reconnoitring party in the direction of Bitterfeld. Finally, the noise ceased in the town, and the gates were reopened. I immediately reported matters to W. Hahn, who in the early morning sent out his horsemen. An hour afterwards there appeared upon the scene Abraham Gatzkow, the same gentleman from Lower Pomerania who had been instructed to keep a fresh horse for me for the last stage from Brandenburg-the-Old to the camp at Wittenberg. The envoys had sent him on in front, impatient to know why the escort had failed to appear at the appointed spot, a mishap which prejudiced them against me.

Odd to relate, neither Sleidan nor Beuter mentions the alarm to which I referred just now; hence, some further particulars will not be deemed superfluous. Nothing is more frequent in the army and less easy to prevent than the stealing of horses. If an animal takes your fancy, some scoundrel is ready to get it for you for a matter of six or eight crowns. If you keep it six or eight weeks elsewhere, so as to change its habits, and change its tail, its mane and other peculiarities, you may safely bring it back to the camp. A certain German gentleman proceeded in that way with the stallion of a Spaniard; he sent it away to his estates. When the affair had been forgotten the animal reappeared. It so happened that the German horsemen (eight squadrons at the lowest computation) encamped in the middle of a delightful plain, watered by the Saale, while the whole of the infantry of their nation was quartered in the town; a providential circumstance, for if the foot had come to the aid of the horse, there would have been nothing short of a massacre. The emperor, therefore, was well inspired in ordering at once the closing of all the gates.

The Spaniards occupied the height around the castle. At dusk, when taking the horses to be watered, a Spanish lad recognizes the stallion, cries out that it belongs to his master and wants to lead it away. The young German groom resists, and is supported by three or four of his countrymen. The Spaniard rallies a dozen, and the German immediately finds himself at the head of a score. The two parties increase every minute, and the first shots are fired. Posted on the heights, the Spaniards have the advantage of the position, their balls going through the walls of the tents, kill several gentlemen who are seated at table; the Germans give as good as they get. A Spanish lord issues from the town with words of peace from the emperor; he has magnificent golden chains round his neck and is riding a superb animal. At the sight of him there is a general cry: "Fire on the dog of a Spaniard." He advances, nevertheless, on the bridge, but a projectile brings down his mount, which rolls into the Saale, and is drowned there with his master, the wearer of the beautiful collar. Nine days before this, at Wittenberg, a rotten strap had, with the help of God, saved my life. The gentleman covered with gold and dressed in velvet, on the other hand, miserably perished.

The emperor, while all this was going on, sent the son of King Ferdinand, the Archduke Maximilian (afterwards emperor). He felt convinced that it would suffice to restore order, but the moment the archduke opened his lips the Germans repeated the cry: "Down with the Spaniard." The archduke was wounded in the right arm, which he wore during several weeks in a black sling. The emperor himself had to come forth. "Dear Germans," he said, "I know you to be without reproach. I therefore ask you to be calm. You shall be indemnified fully and in every respect, and on my Imperial word, to-morrow you shall see the Spaniards strung up on the highest gibbets." This promise had the effect of quieting the riot, and the gates were opened. The inquiry having shown that the loss of the Germans amounted to eighteen grooms or stablemen besides seven horses, and that of the opposing party to not less than seventy men, the emperor, though professing to be ready to make good the value of the horse and even to punish the Spaniards according to his promise, expressed the hope that the Germans would consider themselves sufficiently avenged, inasmuch as their adversaries had suffered four times more than they had.

During the evening of June 19, the Electors of Saxony and Brandenburg made their entry into Halle with the Landgrave Philip of Hesse in their midst. At six in the afternoon of the next day the landgrave "made honourable amends" in the great hall of the Imperial quarters in the presence of the electors, princes, foreign potentates, ambassadors, counts, colonels, captains, and in one word, of everybody who could find room inside or catch a glimpse of the scene through the windows. But while his chancellor, on his knees, close against him, humbly craved pardon, Philip, ever inclined to raillery, smiled with an air of bravado, and to such a degree as to make the emperor exclaim, while threatening him with his outstretched index: "Go on; I'll teach you to laugh." Alas, he kept his word.

Our counsellors decided to leave me behind incognito at the Imperial camp with a gentleman of Lower Pomerania named George von Wedel, who having murdered his cousin and having been exiled by Duke Barnim, had entered the emperor's service with nine-and-twenty horse troopers. His goodwill towards our mission and my instances finally got him his pardon. That was how the horse on which I had left Wolgast was to carry me as far as Augsburg.

Having started from Halle on June 20, the emperor stopped three days at Naumberg. On the 24th, very early in the morning, he was at the general headquarters at some distance beyond the wall. He wore a violet cap and a black cloak trimmed with velvet several inches wide. Suddenly there was a shower, and immediately the emperor sent for a hat and a grey felt cloak to the town; but meanwhile he turned the cloak he wore and kept his headdress under it. Poor man, who spent untold gold on the war, and who stood bareheaded in the rain rather than spoil his clothes.

The Spanish escort of the landgrave preceded his Imperial Majesty by a day's march, and committed unheard-of excesses. Next morning the corpses were strewn where the emperor passed. Women and girls suffered the most terrible outrages; as for the men, after having suspended them by their genital parts, the barbarians tortured them to make them reveal the places where they had hidden their money, after which, with one stroke of their swords, flush with the abdomen, they detached the victim.

The emperor slept at Coburg, in Franconia. The German horsemen took up their quarters in the adjacent villages. Every house was deserted, the dwellings of the nobility as well as the peasant's farms; nowhere was there a soul to be seen, for, having been sorely tried the previous day by the passage of the Spaniards, the population dreaded renewed scenes of horror. In one house we found a *membrum virile*; elsewhere, stretched on a bed a bloodstained body, exactly in the condition in which those abominable miscreants had put them one after the other. The servants of Von Wedel dug a grave by my orders for the corpse and the *membrum virile*.

Our first encampment after that was a village amidst fertile plains. I unsaddled my horse in order to let it graze in peace until the morning. In the same spot there was a handsome gentleman's dwelling, in its open courtyard a wagon with four strong horses; on the wagon two barrels of exquisite wine. Capons, poultry and pheasants were running about in all directions. I leave people to imagine the massacre, and how, on our return to our tent, we quickly plucked, boiled and roasted the game. We were the absolute masters. There was nothing to fear; the granary was full to overflowing, and we replenished our sacks to the very edge. In short, horses, vehicle and wine, and everything else was carried away. The barrels were emptied on our way; the team was sold at Nuremberg for what it would bring, for we ourselves had had it very cheaply.

The sight of our plenty attracted the notice of Duke Frederick von Liegnitz,[47] so we invited him to share it. Two joyous damsels in gorgeous silk attire were of the party and performed their duty well. The servants also shared in the feast which was prolonged till dawn. The nights, however, were very short.

It was full daylight when, wishing to saddle my horse, I discovered it had been stolen. Immediately, according to 'the usages and customs of war, I chose the best nag at hand, currycombed, bridled and mounted it in the space of a few minutes.

On July 1, towards midday, the emperor made his entry into Bamberg with a numerous suite. The Elector of Saxony occupied a house on the outside of the town on the right, just at the turn of the road, so that he could watch the city and the country. The captive was at the window just as his Imperial Majesty passed, mounted on a small Spanish horse. He made a profound bow; thereupon the emperor burst out laughing sarcastically, and stared at him as long as he could.

The Spaniards took with them from Bamberg four hundred women, girls and female servants, and did not let them go until they reached Nuremberg. The fathers, husbands and brothers followed in their wake; the father looking for his daughter, the husband for his better half, the brother for his sister; at Nuremberg each found his own again. Oh, those Spaniards! What a nation, to dare do such things after the cessation of hostilities, in a friendly country and under the very eyes of the sovereign. The latter, however, displayed a relentless severity. Each evening they put up a gibbet as well as his tent, and the former did not remain long untenanted, but it was all in vain.

I suddenly came across my horse in a meadow near the Nuremberg gates. I put my saddle on its back, and left the animal I had taken at Coburg.

His Majesty journeyed by small stages in consequence of the excessive heat. The diet, in fact, was summoned only for September 1. This slowness gave me the leisure to ride with George von Wedel on the flank of the army, from its head to its tail. It was an interesting spectacle, this mass of men under arms and in battle order; here Germans, farther on Spaniards. In the evening we returned to our own. Far from keeping to the highway, the soldiers marched straight in front of them, making a roadway four times wider than the ordinary one, upsetting all obstacles, knocking down enclosures and filling in moats and ditches. One day the restive horse of George von Wedel insisted on getting into the ranks of the Spanish, who could not or would not get out of the way, and as the rider cried angrily: "Very well, let the French kill thee, then," a half-drunken soldier, mistaking the words, retorted: "*Senor mio, no soy Frances, mas soy un Espanol.*" The Spaniards, in fact, think themselves much superior to the French.

As we were getting near Nuremberg there was no longer any need for me to hide myself. I took up my quarters at the hotel selected by Duke Frederick von Liegnitz, at that period trying to interest the emperor in his paternal affairs. That prince was never sober, and at the refusal of his counsellors, he caroused with the suite of Margrave Johannes.

One day the duke and six servitors of the margrave cut the right sleeves out of their doublets and their shirts. With bare arms, their hose undone so as to show their shirts, their heads uncovered, and list slippers on their feet, the seven persons marched in single file behind the town musicians, playing with all their might, and went after dinner to the Duke Henry of Brunswick's. Prince Frederick held in one hand a set of dice, and in the other a quantity of gold pieces; naturally the crowd ran with them, the foreigners foremost, Italians and Spaniards delighted to see "these sots of Germans" go by. The wine produced such a strong effect that Liegnitz, on entering the apartment of the duke, stumbled across the table, both hands foremost. There was only one dice left, and not a trace of the gold. He was unable to utter a syllable, and dropped on the floor. Four Brunswick gentlemen carried him to a bed on the story above. The emperor, it is said, was very angry at the Germans making such a show of themselves.

It would be a mistake to conclude that Prince Frederick's education had been neglected, for only a few days beforehand, though he had also been drinking, I was quite surprised at the many stories of the Old Testament he narrated without quoting the sacred text; he even applied some of them very ingenuously to his own situation. Certainly there can be nothing surpassing a careful education, provided the Holy Spirit guides the young man when he becomes responsible for his own acts; that is what we ought to pray for to the Almighty.

As for the consequences of drunkenness, that inexhaustible fount of many sins, the Duke von Liegnitz was a terrible example of them. One night when he could no longer find some one in the humour to "keep up with him," he came to my door, trying to beguile me out of my bed. I finally told him that to sit drinking at such an hour was beyond my strength, and that I humbly begged his Serene Highness to husband both our healths. He resigned himself, though reluctantly, to take "no" for an answer. I took good care not to open.

After a fortnight's stay, the emperor left Nuremberg. Duke Frederick was so matutinal on the day of departure that on arriving about six o'clock at the Imperial residence, he was told the emperor had been gone for at least two hours. Not daring to follow the sovereign, he merely sent two counsellors to Augsburg.

I had bought at Nuremberg a handsome rapier which I wore with a Spanish belt. One morning after breakfast, being alone, I fell asleep in my chair. When I awoke I found that a skilful thief had cleverly unfastened it and carried it away. I bought another weapon, and when I had settled my bill, saddled my horse and made for Augsburg, where I landed three days before the emperor.

Prince Frederick went back to his own country with his suite; he never improved. Two students were returning to their homes; *en route* they breakfast at Liegnitz, and feeling jovial and gay they started singing. The duke, who was in his cups, was annoyed at the noise, had them apprehended, conducted outside the town, and beheaded. Next morning, before recommencing his libations, he took a ride with some of his counsellors in the direction of the place of execution. At the sight of the blood he begins to ask questions, and is informed that the executed men are the two students he sentenced the previous day. "What had they done?" he asked in the greatest surprise.

At the end of one of his orgies he ordered his counsellors to lock him up in prison on bread and water. If they disobeyed him they would answer with their heads. The dungeon already held several occupants. His Highness was taken to it, and the gaoler received the strictest instructions. When the fumes of his wine had vanished, the duke, in a livelier mood, conversed for a while with the other prisoners; then he shouted to the warder to let him out. "I am too strictly forbidden to do so," was the answer. He, nevertheless, went to inform the counsellors; the latter delayed for three days, during which time the prince left not a moment respite to the turnkeys. Finally, the counsellors came themselves; they heard his shouting and his supplications, but they remembered his threat to have their heads off, and they knew that on that subject he did not jest. He had to reassure them over and over again before he was allowed to go free.

Three years later the same prince journeyed to Stettin for no other purpose than to have a drinking bout with some of the courtiers. At the news of his coming, Duke Barnim went away with everybody except the women. At his arrival the visitor found neither the duke nor any gentlemen of the least standing, and at the castle they sent him into the town to a house assigned to him as his quarters. An old man lay dying there, and they naturally expected that this would shorten Liegnitz's visit. The very opposite happened. The prince comfortably settled himself at the dying man's bedside, recited passages from the Scriptures to him until his last moment, and closed his eyes when the breath was out of him. The collector Valentin presenting himself, poor box in hand, the duke dropped a few crowns into it; after this, he sent for mourning cloth for two cloaks, one for himself, one for Valentin, with whom, he said, he wished to accompany the corpse to the cemetery. The duchess, however, would not hear of this. He was therefore quartered in the castle, just above the chancellerie, and opposite the women's quarters, so that they could converse from one window to another. I had been to the kitchen. As I was crossing the courtyard, the duke, passing his head out of the window and making a speaking trumpet of his hands, shouted with all his might to me: "Hi-there!" I knew him from Nuremberg, and was consequently familiar with the manner of treating him, so I answered: "Hello!" at which he was delighted. "What a nice fellow," he cried. "For heaven's sake, come up; we'll keep each other company, and try to enliven each other." I thanked him humbly and continued my way.

Duke Barnim's absence being somewhat prolonged, his guest Liegnitz had eventually to think about going. The princely presents of the duchess made him comfortable for some time. Health, welfare, country, were all ruined by his roystering conduct. When drink had killed him, his wife, a Duchess of Mecklenburg, saw herself and her children reduced to the direst privation. She had to inform not only her equals, but the magistrates of Stralsund of her distress, and to declare herself unable to bring up her son according to his rank. She merely asked for slight help, scarcely more than alms. The council of Stralsund sent her a few crowns by one of the messengers she dispatched in all directions.

THE DIET OF AUGSBURG.
From an old Engraving.

CHAPTER II

On July 27, 1547, I dismounted at an inn in the wine market at Augsburg. The host was a person of consideration, and endowed with good sense; he was a master of one of the corporations. The latter had administered the city's affairs for more than a century. During a similar number of years the corporations of Nuremberg had ceded their power in that respect to the patricians. The Augsburg corporations, being Evangelicals, had sided against the emperor; consequently His Imperial Majesty proposed to exclude them at the forthcoming Diet from the government, in favour of the aristocracy, which had remained faithful to the ancient faith.

I took two rooms (each with an alcove, or sleeping closet, attached to it), of which the host had no need for his travelling patrons. The ambassadors settled in one; the other was set apart for their administration, which was composed of Jacob Citzewitz, chancellor; two secretaries of Duke Barnim, and myself. I sold my horse with its equipment, which was not worth much. I took what I could get for it; fodder was very dear, and the animal was no longer of the least use to me.

The emperor and his army arrived at the end of July. The landgrave remained behind at Donauwerth, under the guard of a Spanish detachment, while the elector, brought to Augsburg, took up his quarters with the Welsers, two houses away from the Imperial residence, and on the other side of a kind of alley by the side of my inn. A passage made between these two houses by means of a bridge thrown over the alley provided communication between the apartments of his Imperial Majesty and those of the elector. The captive prince had his own kitchens. His chancellor, Von Monkwitz, was always near him; he was served by his own attendants, so that the Spaniards had no pretext to enter his room or his sleeping closet. The Duke of Alva and other gentlemen of the Imperial suite constantly kept him company; the time was spent in pleasant conversations and equally agreeable recreations. They had arranged a list for the jousts in the courtyard of the dwelling, which was as superb a mansion as any royal one. The elector went out on horseback to the beautiful sites and spots of the town, namely, the various gardens, cultivated with much art. He had been very fond from his youth of swordplay, and while he remained well and active he indulged in all kinds of martial exercise. They therefore left him to superintend the assaults at arms, but he did not stir without an escort of Spanish soldiers. He was left free to read what he pleased, except in the latter days, namely, after his refusal to accept the Interim.

At Donauwerth, on the other hand, the landgrave had a guard even in his own apartment. If he looked out of the window two Spaniards craned their necks by his side. Drums and fifes told him of the guard coming on duty and of the guard that was being relieved. Armed sentries watched in the prisoner's room; they were relieved once during the night, and when those coming on duty entered the room, the others, when the shrill music had ceased, drew the curtains of the bed aside, saying: "We commit him to your care. Keep a good watch." The emperor's words to the landgrave, "I'll teach you to laugh," were not an empty threat.

Before retiring to rest, his Imperial Majesty, to the terror of many, had a gibbet erected in front of the town hall; by the side of the gibbet, the strapado, and, facing it, a scaffold at about an ordinary man's height from the ground. This was intended to hold the rack, and the beheading, the strangulating, the quartering, and kindred operations were to be carried out on it.

The emperor had sent to Spain for his secretary, a grandee, it will be seen directly, who stood high in his favour. As the said secretary sailed down the Elbe, coming from Torgau, a faithful subject of the captive elector hid himself in a wood on the bank of the stream. He was a skilful arquebusier, and when the craft was well within range, he fired a shot. They brought the emperor a corpse. The mortal remains of the secretary were taken to Spain in a handsome coffin; the murderer fled across Hungary in the direction of Turkey, but active pursuit resulted in his capture, and he was dispatched to Augsburg. He was driven in an open cart from St. Ulrich to the town hall, by way of the wine market. Hence, the elector had the extreme annoyance of seeing him pass under his windows. The condemned man had between his knees a pole, to which his right hand was tied as high as possible. In the midst of the drive, the sword severed the wrist from the arm; hemorrhage was prevented by dressing the wound, and the hand was nailed to a post put up in the street for the purpose. In front of the town hall the poor wretch was taken from the cart and was put on the rack.

The landsknechten quartered at Augsburg had not received their pay for several months. It was to come out of the fines imposed upon the landgrave and the towns. The rumour ran that the fines had been paid, but that the Duke of Alva had lost the money gaming with the elector, so that the troops were still waiting.

In the thick of all this, a number of soldiers made their way into the rooms of the ensigns, carrying off three standards, unfurling them, and marching in battle array to the wine market. Near the spot where the arquebusier had had his hand severed from his wrist, a proud Spaniard, impelled by the mad hope of securing the Imperial favour by rendering his name for ever glorious, flung himself into the advancing ranks and tried to get hold of a standard; behind it, however, marched three men with big swords, and one of these split the intruder in two just as he would have split a turnip. "*Qui amat periculum, peribit in eo.*" Thus it is written.

Roused to great excitement by the coming of the column, the Spanish soldiers promptly occupied the streets adjoining the market. The elector was transferred to the Imperial quarters, lest he should be carried off. The population were getting afraid of being pillaged in case the idea of paying themselves should present itself to the landsknechten. The tradesmen were more uneasy than the rest, for in expectation of the coming Diet their shops were crammed with precious wares, rich silk stuffs, golden and silvern objects, diamonds and pearls. There was an indescribable tumult to the accompaniment of cries and people foregathering in knots, though most of them barricaded themselves in their houses and armed themselves with pikes, muskets, or anything they could lay hands on. In short, as Sleidan expresses it, "the day bade fair to be spent in armed alarm."

The emperor sent to ask the mercenaries what they wanted. "Money or blood," replied the arquebusiers, their weapons reposing on the left arm, the lighted match in their right hands, and dangerously near the vent-hole. His Imperial Majesty promised them their arrears within twenty-four hours, but before dispersing they claimed impunity for what they had done, which demand the emperor granted. Next day they received their pay and were disbanded at the same time.

Now for the end of the adventure. Secret orders were given to accompany the ringleaders on their road, and at the first offensive remark on their part with regard to the emperor to call in armed assistance, and to bring them back to Augsburg. As a consequence, at the end of two or three days, some of the firebrands, having their wallets well-lined and sitting round frequently re-filled flagons at the inn, began to hold forth without more reserve than if they were on the territory of Prester John. The last thought in their minds was about informers being among them. "We'll give him soldiers for nothing--this Charles of Ghent![48] May the quartan fever get hold of him. We'll teach him how to behave. May the lightning blast him," and so forth. Not for long though. The words had scarcely left their lips than they were seized, taken to Augsburg, and hanged in front of the town hall, each with a little flag fluttering from the tab of their small clothes.

Two Spaniards, probably guilty of robbery, as was their custom, were strung up at the same gibbet. Towards night the hangman came with his cart, cut the ropes and took the bodies of the seditious men outside the town. After which there appeared a gang of Spaniards who, with more ceremony, detached their countrymen, and placed them in a bier covered with a kind of white linen. Then they spread the funeral cloth over them, and the procession started. Young scholars dressed in white cloaks marched at its head, intoning psalms; the rest, in handsome dresses and carrying lighted tapers, followed two by two. They proceeded in that manner to the church given up to the Spaniards for their worship, where the two bodies were buried. It is difficult to withhold solemn funerals from thieves when you yourself are an incorrigible thief.

The Italian and Spanish troops were distributed in the towns of the Algau and Swabia. Memmingen and Kempten compounded their liability to quarter them respectively for thirty thousand and twenty thousand florins. Thereupon a certain Imperial commissioner hit upon the idea of presenting himself in various towns as having been instructed to quarter a couple of hundred Spaniards for the winter. The terror-stricken burghers implored him to spare them such a scourge, and considered themselves only too happy to present the commissioner with a little gratification of two, three, and four hundred crowns, paid on the nail. Thanks to that ingenious system, the commissioner managed to pocket some important sums. But the rumour of the thing having reached the emperor's ears, the cheat was arrested, sentenced to death, and executed in front of the town hall at Augsburg. The work of the hangman began by strangulation. The patient (?) was placed on a wooden seat against the rail of the scaffold, his forehead tightly bound in case of convulsions, his arms bound behind his back, and fastened to the balustrade. The hangman, after having flung a rather short rope round his neck, slipped a thick stick down his nape, and began to twist it round in the manner they press bales of wares. When the wretch was strangled, he was undressed except his shirt, laid out on a board, the hangman lifted the shirt, cut away the sexual parts, ripped open the body from bottom to top, removed the intestines, and threw them into a pail under the board, and finally cut the body into four quarters.

George von Wedel stayed at my hotel. He invited the Duke of Brunswick and his steward to dinner, and chose me as the third guest. The repast consisted of six courses; the first was soup with a capon in it. I know that our landlady paid a crown for the bird, and that she charged Wedel a crown per head. I did not forget to mention to my host and my fellow guests that at Rome I had seen the hanging of the Spaniard, his servants, and the two Jews. The duke was delighted at my recollecting this, and he himself reminded us that the banquet had been given in his honour. His account of the story was, however, much longer than mine.

While awaiting the arrival of the Pomeranian delegates, I borrowed two hundred crowns of the captive Elector of Saxony, for my functions at the Diet necessitated a decent appearance, considering that I was called upon to confer with grand personages, such as the Vice-Chancellor Seld, the Bishop of Arras and Dr. Johannes Marquardt, Imperial counsellor. Besides, everything was horribly dear at Augsburg; there was no possibility of getting along without money. Our ambassadors arrived on St. Matthew's Day (September 21). I immediately refunded the two hundred crowns.

Since we left Wittenberg I had never missed an opportunity of speaking to the Imperial counsellors and advisers, sometimes to one, then to another. More than once, for instance, I happened to be riding by the side of the Bishop of Arras, *intimus consiliarius imperatoris*. I solicited his intervention for a safe-conduct for our princes, in order that they might come and plead their cause in person, or be represented by some high dignitaries. The kindly tone of his answers afforded me much hope, although he abstained from all positive promises.

One evening between Nuremberg and Augsburg chance made me alight at the hostelry where Lazarus von Schwendi was putting up.[49] At that time he was a beardless young man. We supped together, and he declared quite spontaneously that, having been sent by the emperor to the Brandenburg march as far as the Pomeranian frontiers to get information about the attitude of the dukes during the late war, he had not been able to find the slightest charge against them. He further stated that he had written to that effect to the emperor, and he announced his intention of repeating it to him by word of mouth.

In spite of this evidence, when I saw the Bishop of Arras, his father, Messire de Granvelle, the most trusty adviser of his Imperial Majesty, Dr. Seld and Dr. Marquardt at Augsburg, they seemed to vie with each other at looking askance at me, and at formulating a refusal in hard, haughty terms and entirely unexpected by me; such as: "*Bannus decernetur contra principes tuos.*"[50]

Our dukes sent their principal advisers. To do them justice, they spared neither time nor trouble, but it was all in vain, for the Bishop of Arras went as far as to growl at them: "To suppose the emperor capable of punishing innocent people as your princes pretend to be; that alone already constitutes the crime of treason against the sovereign, and deserves chastisement." His Imperial Majesty closed his ears to the truth; he was determined to act against the Dukes of Pomerania. At Wittenberg Dr. Seld had said to me: "We are going to examine the challenge of Ingoldstadt and will note for reference its instances of audacity, its offensive expressions, and its provocations. His Imperial Majesty means to show to the whole of the empire that he is neither deficient in German blood nor in power to chastize as he thinks fit no matter whom." This was an allusion to the following passage of the document defying him: "And we inform Charles that we consider him a traitor to his duty to God, a perjurer towards us, and the German nation, and deserving the Divine punishment, and also as too devoid of noble and German blood to carry out his threats."

Our ambassadors paid daily visits to the important ecclesiastical personages. They went in couples, save Chancellor Citzewitz, who considered himself, not unjustly, capable of dispensing with assistance. He laboured, however, under the disadvantage of "repeating himself," and of wearying his listeners. The chancellor of the Elector of Cologne, to whom Citzewitz paid a visit one night, said the next day to two of our ambassadors: "What is your chancellor thinking of? He constantly repeats the same things. Does he credit me with so short a memory as to forget in three or four days the *status causae vestrorum principum*, or does he imagine that our affairs leave me sufficient leisure to listen to his never ending litanies. He reminds me of a hen about to lay. At first she flutters to the top of the open barn door, clucking, 'An egg, an egg.' Then she gets a little higher up to the hay-loft: 'An egg, an egg; I want to lay an egg.' From there she goes up to the rafters: 'Look out, friends, look out. I am going to lay an egg.' Finally, when she has cackled to her heart's content, she goes back to her nest and produces the tiniest imaginable egg. I prefer the goose who squats silently on the dung-heap and lays an egg as big as a child's head."

The Archbishop of Cologne would not forgive our princes for having secularized the monastery of Neu-Camp, a branch of the parent institution of Alt-Camp, in the diocese of Cologne. Besides, the clergy of Pomerania had become suspect to him ever since its choice for the See of Cammin had fallen upon the pious, able and learned chancellor Bartholomew Schwabe. Hence, the terms in which the emperor forbade our princes to recognize the new dignitary as such were the reverse of courteous, and he moreover summoned the chapters to Augsburg to take the oath of fidelity and do homage, pending his own selection of a chief for them. The princes, the chapters, the landed gentry, and the towns, with the exception of Colberg, appealed; the Pomeranian mission was entrusted with the negotiations; the States also delegated Martin Weyer, canon of Cammin, who subsequently became a bishop.

Nor was the Elector of Brandenburg in the emperor's good books. Where then could we find somebody successfully to intercede for us?

All my supplications were in vain, for at courts and in large towns *causae perduntur quae paupertate reguntur*. Finally, Dr. Marquardt hinted discreetly that a well trained small horse would be very useful to him to proceed to the council, according to Imperial etiquette. I immediately wrote to Pomerania, whence they sent me a pretty animal, with instructions to buy an equipment to match. The present, supplemented by three "Portuguese,"[51] seemed to please the doctor mightily, and he accepted everything without much persuasion.

The melting of double ducats and Rhenish florins gave us some excellent gold of crown standard, which served to make two cups, each weighing seven marks. Citzewitz took them several times to Messire de Granvelle without finding the opportunity of offering them to him. These were indeed untimely scruples. That present, or even one of double its value, would no more have been refused then than it was later on at Brussels. In fact, in return for his friendly offices with the emperor, Granvelle willingly submitted to be presented with gold, silver, and precious objects, so that at his departure there were several vans and numerous mules laden with them. When he was asked what were the contents of that long convoy, he answered: "*Peccata Germaniae!*"

After many fruitless efforts our ambassadors found themselves reduced to inactivity, and compelled as a pastime to read two Latin pamphlets they received. The one dealt with the personality and acts of "*Carolus Quintus*"; the title of the other was, "*De horum temporum statu,*" with Pasquin and Marforio as interlocutors in Roman fashion.

There were ten flag-companies of landsknechten quartered at Augsburg, besides the Spaniards and Germans accompanying the emperor, while the outskirts held Spanish and Italian fighting men. Six hundred horsemen from the Low Countries and more than twelve flag-companies of Spaniards, who had been quartered during the winter at Biberach, were posted on the shores of Lake Constance; seven hundred Neapolitan horsemen, who had wintered at Wissemburg, lay in the Nordgau. The days, therefore, were truly spent in "armed alarm," but there was also extraordinary splendour, pomp, and magnificence.

Augsburg, in fact, had the honour of having within its walls his Imperial Majesty, his Royal Majesty, all the electors in person, with imposing suites; the Elector of Brandenburg with his wife; the Cardinal of Trent, Duke Heindrich of Brunswick and his two sons, Charles Victor and Philip; Margrave Albert; Duke Wolfgang, count palatine; Duke Augustus; Duke Albert of Bavaria; the Duke of Cleves; Herr Wolfgang, grand master of the Teutonic Order; the Bishop of Eichstedt; his Grace of Naumberg, Julius

Pflug; Abbé Weingarten; Madame Marie, the sister of the emperor, who was accompanied by her niece, the Dowager of Lorraine; the wife of the margrave; the Duchess of Bavaria, and the envoys of the foreign potentates. The King of Denmark was represented by a learned and prudent man, who had given proof of his wisdom in many a mission, namely, Petrus Suavenius, the same who had accompanied Luther to Worms and had returned with him. The King of Poland was represented by Stanislas Lasky, a magnificent, experienced, learned, eloquent and elegant, amiable, great magnate, and most charming *in familiari colloquio*.

It is almost impossible to enumerate the crowd of vicars, counts and other personages of note, but I must not forget the Jew Michael, who aped the great lord, and showed himself off on horseback in gorgeous clothes, golden chains round his neck, and escorted by ten or a dozen servants, all Jews, but who might have fairly passed muster as horse troopers. Michael himself had an excellent appearance; he was said to be the son of one of the counts of Rheinfeld. The old hereditary Marshal von Pappenheim, who had grown very short-sighted, came up with him one day, and, not content with taking off his hat, made him a low bow, as to a superior. When he discovered his mistake, he vented his anger very loudly: "May the lightning blast you, you big scoundrel of a Jew," he bellowed. The presence of so many princesses, countesses and other noble dames, handsome, and attired in a way that baffles my powers of description, afforded daily opportunities for banquets, Welch and German dances. King Ferdinand was rarely without guests. He gave magnificent receptions, splendid ballets, and beautiful concerts by a numerous and well trained band of vocal and instrumental performers. Behind the king's chair there stood a chattering jester; his master had frequent "wit combats" with him. The king kept up the conversation at table, and his tongue was never still for a moment. One evening I saw at his reception, a Spanish gentleman, with a cloak reaching to his heels, dancing an "algarda" or "passionesa" (I do not know the meaning of either word) with a young damsel. They both jumped very high, advancing and retreating, without ceasing to face each other. It was most charming. After that another couple performed a Welch dance.

The emperor, on the contrary, far from giving the smallest banquet, kept nobody near him; neither his sister, nor his brother, nor his nieces, nor the Duchess of Bavaria, nor the electors, nor any of the princes. After church, when he reached his apartments, he dismissed his courtiers, giving his hand to everybody. He had his meals by himself, without speaking a word to his attendants. One day, returning from church, he noticed the absence of Carlowitz. "*Ubi est noster Carlovitius?*" he asked of Duke Maurice. "Most gracious emperor," replied the latter, "he feels somewhat feeble."

Immediately the emperor turned to his physician. "Vesalius, gy zult naar Carlowitz gaan, die zal iets wat ziek zyn, ziet dat gy hem helpt." (Anglicé, "You had better go and see Carlowitz. He is not well; you may be able to do something for him.")

I have often been present (at Spires, at Worms, at Augsburg, and at Brussels) at the emperor's dinner. He never invited his brother, the king. Young princes and counts served the repast. There were invariably four courses, consisting altogether of six dishes. After having placed the dishes on the table, these pages took the covers off. The emperor shook his head when he did not care for the particular dish; he bowed his head when it suited, and then drew it towards him. Enormous pasties, large pieces of game, and the most succulent dishes were carried away, while his Majesty ate a piece of roast, a slice of a calf's head, or something analogous. He had no one to carve for him; in fact, he made but a sparing use of the knife. He began by cutting his bread in pieces large enough for one mouthful, then attacked his dish. He stuck his knife anywhere, and often used his fingers while he held the plate under his chin with the other hand. He ate so naturally, and at the same time so cleanly, that it was a pleasure to watch him. When he felt thirsty, he only drank three draughts; he made a sign to the *doctores medicinae* standing by the table; thereupon they went to the sideboard for two silver flagons, and filled a crystal goblet which held about a measure and a half. The emperor drained it to the last drop, practically at one draught, though he took breath two or three times. He did, however, not utter a syllable, albeit that the jesters behind him were amusing. Now and again there was a faint smile at some more than ordinarily clever passage between them. He paid not the slightest attention to the crowd that came to watch the monarch eat. The numerous singers and musicians he kept performed in church, and never in his apartment. The dinner lasted less than an hour, at the termination of which, tables, seats, and everything else were removed, there remaining nothing but the four walls hung with magnificent tapestry. After grace they handed the emperor the quills of feathers wherewith to clean his teeth. He washed his hands and took his seat in one of the window recesses. There, everybody could go up and speak to him, or hand a petition, and argue a question. The emperor decided there and then. The future emperor Maximilian was more assiduously by the side of the emperor than by that of his father.

Duke Maurice soon made acquaintance with the Bavarian ladies, and at his own quarters melancholy found no place, for he lodged with a doctor of medicine who was the father of a girl named Jacqueline, a handsome creature if ever there was one. She and the duke bathed together and played cards every day with Margrave Albrecht.[52] One day, the latter, thinking he was going to have the best of the game, ventured several crowns. "Very well," answered the damsel; "equal stakes. Mine against yours." "Put down your money," retorted the margrave, "and the better player wins." All this in plain and good German, while Jacqueline gave him her most charming smile. Such was their daily mode of life. The town gossiped about it, but the devil himself was bursting with pleasure.

Clerics or laymen, every one among those notable personages did as he pleased. I myself have seen young Margrave Albrecht, as well as other young princes, drinking and playing "truc" with certain bishops of their own age, but of inferior birth.[53] At such moments they made very light of titles. The margrave cried abruptly; "Your turn, priest. I'll wager your stroke isn't worth a jot." The bishop was often still more coarse, inviting his opponent to accompany him outside to perform a natural want. The young princes squatted down by the side of the noblest dames on the floor itself, for there were neither forms nor chairs; merely a magnificent carpet in the middle of the room, exceedingly comfortable to stretch one's self at full length upon. One may easily imagine the kissing and cuddling that was going on.[54]

Both princes and princesses spent their incomes in banquets of unparalleled splendour. They arrived with their money caskets full to overflowing, but in a little while they were compelled to take many a humiliating step in order to obtain loans; the rates were ruinous, but anything, rather than leave Augsburg defeated and humbled in their love of display. Several sovereigns, among others the Duke of Bavaria, had received from their subjects thousands of dollars as "play money." They lost every penny of it.

Our ambassadors lived very retired. They neither invited nor were invited; nevertheless, when a visitor came, they were bound to offer a collation, and to amuse their guests. One day they entertained Jacob Sturm of Strasburg.[55] During dinner the conversation turned on Cammin. Sturm gave us the history of that bishopric, of its foundation, of its expansion. Then he told us of the ancient prerogatives of the Dukes of Pomerania; of the negotiations set on foot seven years before at the diet of Ratisbon. In short, it was as lucid, as complete, and as accurate a summary of the subject as if he had just finished studying it. Our counsellors greatly admired his wonderful memory. Verily, he was a superior, experienced, eloquent, and prudent man, who had had his share in many memorable days from an Imperial as well as from a provincial view; for, in spite of his heresy, the emperor had at various times entrusted him with important missions. Without him, Sleidan could have never written his History. He avows it frankly, and renders homage to Sturm in many passages of his *Commentaries*.

Nobody throughout the empire realized to the same degree as he the motto: *"Usus me genuit, mater me peperit memoria."* A person of note having asked him if the towns of the League of Schmalkalden were all at peace with the emperor, he answered: *"Constantia tantum desideratur."*[56] It would be impossible better to express both the isolation of Constance and the mistake to which the Protestants owed their reverses. Should my children have a desire to know what Sturm was like facially, they will only have to look at my portrait, which bears such a remarkable resemblance to him as to have baffled Apelles to improve upon it.[57] Our ambassadors also received the visits of Musculus and Lepusculus, but each came by himself. The moment for serious debate had struck, for the Interim was being gradually drawn up. The time for jesting had gone by; the only thing to do was to get at the root of matters.[58]

I sometimes brought my countryman, friend, and co-temporary Valerius Krakow home with me. He was secretary to Carlowitz, and, excluded as they were from all negotiations, our counsellors were glad to learn from his lips what was being plotted. During the campaign he had not stirred from the side of Carlowitz, who, in reward for his services, had got him into the chancellerie of Prince Maurice. Another countryman of mine who came to see us was the traban Simon Plate, one of my old acquaintances, for we had pursued our studies together more or less usefully at Greifswald, under George Normann. The counsellors did not care for him, for he was of no earthly use to them. The trabans had some respectable, honest, well set-up and plucky fellows in their ranks, and enjoyed a certain amount of consideration. The emperor was particular about their dress; they wore black velvet doublets, cloaks with large bands of velvet, and the Spanish head-dress of the same material.

Plate was never tired of praising his fellow-soldier sleeping next to him, and the ambassadors gave him leave to bring his friend. He wore a most beautiful golden chain. Plate had not exaggerated. Finally he even took umbrage at the favour shown to the new comer, so that one day he exclaimed: "No doubt he is very upright and honest. He has shown his courage, consequently he pleases the emperor. It is a pity, though, that he is not a gentleman by birth." The remark, I am bound to say, displeased our ambassadors greatly, and above all Chancellor Citzewitz; but let my children look to it. I have heard many Pomeranian nobles hold the same language. According to them, intelligence, sound judgment and ability were the exclusive appanage of birth.

Plate showed himself in a better light on another occasion. Our counsellors had received several visits, and some flagons had been joyously emptied. When our guests were gone, Moritz Damis, captain of Ukermünde, a rollicking, lively creature, suddenly took a fancy to go to the court ball which was taking place that evening, not in the apartments of the emperor, but in those of his sister and niece, who likewise occupied the Fugger mansion in the wine market. His colleagues, who had not forgotten the emperor's threat to the landgrave, "I'll teach you to laugh," were afraid of a scandal, and pointed out that our princes were in disgrace; but Damitz got angry. "Our princes will give me money, but they cannot give me health," he exclaimed. "What am I doing here? Why should I deny myself the sight of such rejoicings? How am I to keep alive? I may as well make up my mind never to cast eyes on Pomerania again." Saying which, he rushed down the stairs; a counsellor tried to hold him back by his golden chain, the links of which, however, broke, and our captain ran to the ball.

Simon Plate had remained perfectly cool, and they asked him to follow the madcap. There was no difficulty for Plate to get inside the ball-room, and the first person of note of whom he caught sight was the puissant and renowned warrior-chief, Johannes Walther von Hirnheim,[59] moodily walking to and fro at the lower end of the room. Damitz had noticed standing close by the dancers a handsome woman gorgeously dressed and glittering with jewels, and in less time than it takes to tell he had addressed her: "Charming creature," he said, "are you not going to dance?" "Oh no, sir," was the answer; "dancing is only fit for young people, and I am an old woman." "What, are you married?" asked the captain. "I could have sworn that you were only a girl, and if I were told to choose with the most beautiful woman here, my choice would fall upon you." "Ah, sir, you are merely jesting." "And what is your husband's name?" the captain went on unabashed. "Johannes Walther von Hirnheim." "Johannes Walther? Oh, I know him well." The husband, somewhat curious with regard to the captain's conversation, had drawn near, though still continuing to walk up and down in silence. Damitz, though, taking no notice of either him or Simon Plate, continued his interrogatory. "Have you any children?" "No; God has ordained it otherwise." "Ah, if I had such a wife, I know what I am. God would soon grant us children." This incursion of the captain into the physical domain induced Simon Plate to interfere, to turn the conversation, and to take Damitz back to his domicile.

In December our ambassadors decided to send one of their body to Pomerania, and Heindrich Normann was selected for the journey. It was bitterly cold, and Normann endeavoured to provide against it. He put on a linen nightcap, over that a fur one, and a second of cloth, with a big muffler fastened behind and in front (just as the peasantry still wear it), and finally a thick hat, embroidered in silk. On his hands white thread gloves, chamois leather ones lined with fur; over these, and over the latter again thicker gloves of wolf's skin. His body was encased in a linen shirt, a knitted tightly-fitting garment in the Italian fashion; over that a vest of red English cloth, a doublet wadded with cotton, another lined jacket, a long coat of wool trimmed with wolf's skin, covering the whole; finally, on his feet, linen socks, Louvain gaiters reaching above the knee, cloth hose, stockings lined with sheep's skin, and high boots. When everybody had done giving special commissions, the servants hoisted him into the saddle, for he could have never got into it without their help. He went as far as Donauwerth; when he got there, his equipment decidedly seemed to him too uncomfortable. As, however, he had no desire to be frozen to death, he turned his horse's head and made for the good city of Augsburg.

Inasmuch as the narrative of Sleidan is very incomplete, I am going to write the story of Sebastian Vogelsberg. Having been an eye-witness, I made it my business to note down his last speeches. Vogelsberg was tall and of imposing appearance, his width being in proportion to his height; in short, a handsome, well-proportioned man with a head as round as a ball, a beard reaching to his waist, and an open face. No painter could have found a better model for a manly man. He had a certain amount of education. According to some people, he had been a schoolmaster in Italy. Count Wilhelm von Fürstenberg, who entered the "paid" service of the belligerent monarchs as a colonel, took him as a semi-secretary, semi-accountant. Vogelsberg, having been promoted to an ensignship, rendered distinguished service in the field; Ambitious, glib of tongue, not to say eloquent and rarely at a loss what to do, he quickly attained the grade of captain, and high and mighty potentates soon preferred him to Fürstenberg. The latter felt most annoyed at this, belonging as he did to a class of men to whom merit is inseparable from birth. He constantly inveighed against Vogelsberg, who, in his turn, did not spare his rival. Pamphlets were printed on both sides. The count appears to have begun; he appealed to his peers, their honour seemed to him at stake. The Protestant States sided with Vogelsberg, their co-religionist, while the popish camp swore mortal hatred to him.

Weary of fruitless polemics, and knowing full well that it would have been folly to take the law into his own hands, Vogelsberg decided upon bringing an action before the Imperial Chamber for damages for defamation of character. I was at the time clerk to his procurator, Dr. Engelhardt; consequently, I knew every particular of the affair. After protracted debates, the court finding for Vogelsberg, condemned Count Wilhelm to a fine of four hundred florins, a sentence which caused Wilhelm's brother, Frederick von Fürstenberg, and everybody who bore the title of count to consider themselves the injured parties.

Three *causae proægoumenae*, to use the language of the dialecticians, may be plainly discerned in this drama; namely, religion, the soldierly qualities of Vogelsberg, and the hostility of the nobles and papists. We may add two *causae procatarcticae*: the first, mentioned by Sleidan, to the effect that a twelvemonth previously Vogelsberg had taken a regiment of landsknechten to the King of France; the second, which I saw with my own eyes at Wissenburg on the Rhine, that Vogelsberg had built himself in that Imperial town a beautiful mansion of hewn stone with the arms of France, three big *fleurs de lis* artistically sculptured over the door. The papists, feeling confident that in the probable event of a new war of religion, the valiant captain would give them a great deal of trouble, and thirsting as they did for his blood, like a deer in summer pants for cooling streams, they took time by the forelock. Their skill in exploiting with his Imperial Majesty the *causae irritatrices* stood them in good stead. They were instrumental in getting two doctors of their following appointed as judges. The one was German, and the other Welch, but both promptly pronounced a sentence of death which was immediately carried out.

On February 7, 1548, shortly after eight in the morning, an ensign-corps of soldiers from the outskirts of "Our Lady," and two other ensign-corps from the outskirts of "St. Jacob," took up their position in the square of the Town Hall. Sleidan says the scaffold was erected for the purpose of executing Vogelsberg. This is an error on Sleidan's part. The scaffold had been there for six months, and had served many times. An officer from the Welch, whom they call *magister de campo* was detached from the troops with about thirty men to fetch the condemned man from the Peilach tower. The latter was brought back to the sound of drums and fifes.

Vogelsberg wore a black velvet dress and a Welch hat embroidered with silk. At his entrance into the circle surrounding the scaffold he caught sight of Count Reinhard von Solms, whose nose was half-eaten away by disease, and Ritter Conrad von Boineburg. Without taking any notice of the count, a relentless papist, who detested him on account of Fürstenberg, he asked of the ritter: "Herr Conrad, is there any hope?" "Dear Bastian," replied Boineburg, "May God help you." "Certainly, He will help me," was Vogelsberg's rejoinder. And with his firmest step, his head erect, and his usual assurance, he climbed the steps to the scaffold.

He looked for a long while at the crowd. All the windows were occupied by members of the nobility. At those of the Town Hall there were serried rows of electors, princes of the Church and of the empire, barons, counts, and knights. In a manly voice and as steady a tone as if he were at the head of his troops, Vogelsberg began to speak: "Your serenissime highnesses, highnesses, excellencies, noble, puissant, valiant seigneurs and friends. As I am this day ..." At that moment the *magister de campo* (quarter-master-general) told the executioner to proceed with his duty, but the latter, addressing the condemned man, said: "Gracious sir, I shall not hurry you. Speak as long as you please." Thereupon Vogelsberg went on: "I am to lose my life by order of the emperor, our very merciful and gracious master, and I now will tell you the cause of my death-warrant. It is for having raised ten ensign-companies last summer for the coronation of the praiseworthy King of France. No felonious act can be imputed to me during the ten years I served the emperor. As I am innocent, I beseech of you to keep me in kind memory, and to pity my undeserved misfortunes. Watch over my kindred, so that they may not come to grief on account of all this, and may benefit by the fruit of my services, for the whole of my life was that of an honest man. I am being sacrificed to the implacable resentment of that infamous Lazarus Schwendi." The latter was at the window facing the scaffold, and suddenly disappeared, but Vogelsberg did not interrupt his speech. "He came to me to Wissemburg to tell me that he was in disgrace in consequence of the murder of a Spanish gentleman in the suite of his Imperial Majesty, and that the Spaniards were also looking for me. He proposed to me to fly to France together, and borrowed two hundred crowns of me. I even gave him a horse as a present for his advice. Well, the traitor took me straight to the Spaniards. While I was in prison I asked him, for my personal need, for some of the crowns I had lent him, but he turned a deaf ear to all my requests. I beg of you to be on your guard against that skunk of a thief who bears the name of Lazarus Schwendi. No one ought to have any dealings with him. He has even dared to denounce to his Imperial Majesty his Serenissimo Highness the Elector Palatine as having entered into a league with the King of France. It is an infamous slander. If I had another life to stake, I should stake it on that. I have been refused the last assistance of a minister, of a confessor--a refusal which has no precedent. I nevertheless die innocent and redeemed by the blood of Jesus Christ." After this he walked round the circle, though above it, asking everybody to forgive him as he forgave everybody. Then he seated himself. The executioner divided his long beard into two and knotted the two ends together on the skull. Having craved his pardon, and invited him to say a Pater and the Credo, he performed his office. The head rolled like a ball from the scaffold to the ground; the executioner caught it by the beard and placed it between the legs of the body, spreading a cloak over the whole, except the feet which showed from under it.

After that the officer and his thirty arquebusiers went to fetch Jacob Mantel and Wolf Thomas, of Heilbron, who had been brought to Augsburg at the same time as Vogelsberg. Thomas was left at the foot of the scaffold. Mantel walked round the platform and said a few words, which many people could not hear. As his stiff leg made it difficult for him to kneel down, the executioner slipped a footstool under the paralyzed limb. He failed to sever the head at the first stroke, and had to finish the operation below; then he once more covered up the body.

There only remained Wolf Thomas. To judge by his dress and bearing he was not an ordinary man. He stared fixedly at the feet of Vogelsberg, showing from under the cloak; then he took his eyes off, and told those around that he had been a loyal and faithful soldier for twenty-seven years, and that he died absolutely innocent, his sole crime consisted in having served the King of France during three months, as many an honest noble and squire had done before him without incurring the least punishment. He asked those around to forgive him as he forgave them, and to pray for him as he would intercede in their favour, he being firmly assured of a place near the Almighty. He asked those who promised to say a Pater and the *Credo* for him to hold up their hands. After that he was beheaded.

At the termination of the triple execution the executioner cried in a loud voice from the scaffold: "In the name of his Imperial Majesty it is expressly forbidden to any one to serve the King of France on the penalty of sharing the fate of these three men."

The death of Vogelsberg caused universal regret. The unanimous opinion was that a soldier of such mettle was worth his weight in gold to a warlike monarch. Sleidan alleges erroneously that the two judges exculpated Lazarus von Schwendi. It was the emperor who caused to be printed and distributed everywhere a small proclamation of half a sheet, declaring Schwendi free from all blame, inasmuch as he strictly carried out the Imperial orders, and that the speech of Vogelsberg was obviously dictated by the desire to escape the most fully deserved punishment.

The King of France, it was said, was so displeased at the cry of the executioner from the scaffold that by his orders the Marquis de Saluces, on his return from Germany, was arrested and beheaded. This was the nobleman who at Wittenberg had disadvised the execution of the Elector of Saxony.

In April, Augsburg witnessed the arrival of Muleg-Hassan, King of Tunis. Thirteen years previously he had been driven forth by Barbarossa; subsequently he was re-established on his throne by the emperor, but his eldest son had ousted him and put his eyes out. A fugitive and wretched, he came to place himself under the protection of the emperor, and was soon joined in his exile by one of his sons. I often met these two on horseback, in company of Lasky, the Polish ambassador, who spoke their language.

As the pope opposed, against all expectation, the holding at Trent of a Christian, free and impartial council, and experience having taught people besides that the learned men of both parties would never come to an agreement, the States of the empire proposed to his Imperial Majesty to confide to a restricted number of learned and God-fearing men the task of drawing up a document for the furtherance of the reign of God and the preservation of the public peace.

In pursuance of this the emperor delegated personally the Bishop of Mayence, Dr. George Sigismund Seld, and Dr. Heindrich Hase.

The King of the Romans selected Messire Gandenz von Madrutz. The Elector of Mayence chose his Bishop Suffragan; the Elector of Treves, Johannes von Leyen, canon of Treves and of Wurzburg; the Elector of Cologne, his provincial; the Elector Palatine, Ritter Wolf von Affenstein; the Elector of Saxony, Dr. Fachs; the Elector of Brandenburg, Eustacius von Schlieben.

The princes selected the Bishop of Augsburg, Dr. Heinrichmann; the Duke of Bavaria, Dr. Eck.

The prelates selected the Abbé von Weingarten; the counts, Count Hugo de Montfort; the towns: Strasburg, Jacob Sturm; Ulm, George Besserer.

These personages met on Friday, February 11, 1548, but they failed to agree, which might have easily been foreseen. The ecclesiastical members of the Diet took advantage of the opportunity to have the book of the Interim composed respectively by the Bishop of Naumburg, Johannes Pflug; by the Bishop Suffragan of Mayence, appointed a little later on to the See of Meiseburg, and by the court preacher to the Elector of Brandenburg, Johannes Agricola, otherwise Eisleben, who coveted the bishopric of Cammin. The Imperial assent to this had to be obtained; they set to work in the following manner.

The Elector of Brandenburg and his wife lived on a sumptuous footing at Augsburg. The elector was fond of display; the electress, the daughter of a king of Poland, was even more lavish than her spouse. The dearth of everything and the frequency and the profusion of the entertainments had already for a long time reduced the finances of his Serene Highness to a critical state. Seven years previously, at the gathering of Ratisbon, Dr. Conrad Holde had already lent the prince close upon six thousand crowns. Their repayment had been constantly, but unsuccessfully demanded. Finally, at Augsburg, in default of ready money, he received the written promise of repayment in four instalments at the dates of the Frankfurt fairs. It was duly signed and sealed. Nothing was wanting to its perfect legality; the most suspicious would have been satisfied. Nevertheless, the payments were not made when due, and the creditor instituted proceedings before the Imperial Chamber. The elector did not know which way to turn; there was not a purse open to him. He was absolutely at a loss how to get his wife and his numerous suite decently away from Augsburg when the Bishop of Salzburg made an end of his embarrassments by advancing him sixteen thousand Hungarian florins on the duly executed promise of their being repaid in a short time. But the principal condition of the loan was that the Elector of Brandenburg should present to his Imperial Majesty the work of the three above-named personages, and bind himself and his subjects to submit to its provisions.

The Elector of Saxony instructed Christopher Carlowitz to send a copy of the "Interim" to Philip Melanchthon.[60] The latter's reply was singularly devoid of courage. It was supposed to be inspired by the theologians of Wittenberg and Leipzig, who in that way sounded the first notes of "Adiaphorism." Carlowitz promptly communicated this epistle everywhere. It aroused general surprise, as well as the most opposed feelings; grief and consternation among the adherents to the Augsburg confession, matchless jubilation among the Catholics. And the Lord alone knows how they bellowed it about in the four corners of Germany, how they availed themselves of it to proclaim their victory.

The ecclesiastical electors sent Melanchthon's letter, together with the book, to the pope, and what with backslidings and plotting the pear was very soon ripe. The publication of the "Interim" took place on May 14, at four o'clock in the afternoon, in presence of the States assembled. The emperor had it printed in Latin and in German. In the first proofs handed to the emperor the passage from St. Paul, "*Justificati fide pacem habemus*," was altogether changed by the suppression of the word *fide*; the confessionists protested energetically, and confounded the would-be authors of the fraud.

The stern tone of the act of promulgation stopped neither speeches nor scathing writings. Sterling refutations were published even outside Germany; the two best known are the Latin treatise of Calvin, which spread all over the empire--in Italy, in France, in Poland, etc.; and a piece of writing in German, which was more to the taste of everybody, and one of whose authors was Æpinus, superintendent of Hamburg.

Seigneur de Granvelle and his son, the Bishop of Arras, strongly persuaded the Elector of Saxony to adhere to the "Interim," in order to regain his freedom, but the prince remained faithful to the Confession of Augsburg. Thereupon they took away his books; there was no meat on his table on fast days, and his chaplain, whom he had kept with him with the consent of the emperor, had to fly in disguise. The landgrave, on the other hand, who did not care to profess greater wisdom than the fathers of the Church, consented to recommend the book to his subjects, and begged to be pardoned for the sake of Christ and all His saints.

At the closure of the Diet, I took, like his Imperial Majesty, the road to the Low Countries. The stay of the emperor at Ulm brought about the dismissal of the council, which was replaced by more devoted creatures. The six ministers were bidden to accept the "Interim." Four of them were not to be shaken, and they were led away captive in the suite of the emperor; the other two, in spite of their apostasy, had to leave wives and children, and scant consideration was shown to them. At Spires, the prior of the barefooted Carmelites was, like all the brothers of his monastery, a good evangelical, though all had preserved the dress of their order. During four years I had seen him going to and fro in the town, dressed in his monk's frock; each Sunday he went into the pulpit and the church was crowded to the very porch. Never did he breathe a word about the pope or about Luther, but he was a master of pure doctrine, and at the approach of the emperor he fled in a layman's dress. Worms and the whole of the country lost their preachers. Landau possessed a select group of learned and distinguished ministers, because the town offered many advantages; a delightful situation, excellent fare, and a splendid vineyard at the very gates of the town; but the ministers had to abandon the place to the popish priests, scamps without experience, without instruction, without piety, and without decency.

I often had occasion afterwards to go to Landau, where the advocate of my father, Dr. Engelhardt, resided. One Sunday, at the termination of the mass, I heard a young and impudent good-for-nothing hold forth from the pulpit in the following strain: "The Lutherans are opposed to the worship of Mary and the saints. Now, my friends, be good enough to listen to this. The soul of a man who had just died got to the door of heaven, and Peter shut it in his face. Luckily, the Mother of God was taking a stroll outside with her sweet son. The deceased addresses her, and reminds her of the Paters and the Aves he has recited to her glory, the candles he has burned before her images. Thereupon Mary says to Jesus, 'It's the honest truth, my son.' The Lord, however, objected, and addressed the supplicant: 'Hast thou never read that I am the way and the door to everlasting life?' He asks. 'If thou art the door, I am the window,' replies Mary, taking the 'soul' by the hair and flinging it into heaven through the open casement. And now I ask you, is it not the same whether you enter Paradise by the door or by the window? And those abominable Lutherans dare to maintain that one must not invoke the Virgin Mary." That was the kind of scandalous irreligion exhibited in the places where formerly the healthy evangelical doctrine was preached.

The landgrave's submission to the "Interim" only brought him into contempt. His wife, who had hastened to Spires to beseech the emperor, was allowed to remain day and night with the prisoner during his week's stay there. At the departure for Worms I saw the landgrave pass at eight in the morning, with his escort of Spaniards with long arquebuses. They hemmed him in in front, behind, and at the sides, while he himself was bestriding a broken-down nag with empty and open holsters, and the hilt of his sword securely tied to its sheath. A serried crowd of strangers and inhabitants, women and servants, old and young, were pressing around his escort, as if there had been an order given to that effect. They cried: "Here goes the wretched rebel, the felon, the scoundrel that he is." They said worse things which, from certain scruples, I abstain from repeating. It looked like the procession of a vulgar malefactor who was being taken to the scaffold.

Pure chance made me an eye-witness of a diverting scene at Augsburg. I have already said that Duke Maurice had ingratiated himself very much with the Bavarian court ladies. One Sunday, in December, when the weather was fine, he was ready to go out in a sleigh. I happened to be at the door with several others, who also heard the following dialogue. Carlowitz came down the stairs of the chancellerie in hot haste, exclaiming: "Whither is your Highness going?" "To Munich," was the answer. "But your Highness has an audience to-morrow with the emperor." "I am going to Munich," repeated the duke. Thereupon Carlowitz: "If, thanks to me, the electoral dignity is practically yours, it is nevertheless true that your frivolity causes you to be despised of their Majesties and of all honourable people." Maurice merely laid the whip on his horses, which started off at a gallop, Carlowitz shouting at the top of his voice: "Very well, then; go to the devil, and may heaven blast you and your sledge." When the prince returned, Carlowitz announced his intention of going to Leipzig. "If I miss the New Year's fair," he said, "I shall lose several thousand crowns." The elector had only one means to make him stay, namely, to count out the sum to him.

As the restoration of the Imperial Chamber necessitated my return to Spires to watch my father's lawsuit, I wrote to Pomerania to be dispensed from following the emperor. This is the answer from our princes.

"Greetings to our loyal and well-beloved. Our counsellors have informed us of thy request, which we should willingly grant thee if it were not prejudicial to our interests and those of the country, and which thou hast up to the present administered. We therefore invite thee to exercise some patience, and to serve us with zeal and fidelity as heretofore; inclined as we are to recall thee after the Diet to give thee unquestionable proofs of our great satisfaction, as well as the means satisfactorily to bring to an end the paternal affairs. We rely on thy obedience, and bind ourselves to confirm all our promises as above. Given under our hand at Stettin-the-Old, Sunday after St. James, in the year 1548."

I had lived uninterruptedly for a twelvemonth at Augsburg, save for one ride to Munich, a city well worth seeing. The Diet being about to dissolve, I bought a horse, an acquisition which that big dreamer of a Normann deferred from day to day. Of course, the inevitable happened. The moment the emperor had announced his forthcoming departure everybody wanted horses, and he who had ordered himself a handsome dress, sold it at half-price in order to get a roadster. Normann, who, in spite of my warnings, had waited till the eleventh hour, unable to find a suitable mount, took mine, which had been well fed and looked after in anticipation of the long journey. I by no means relished this unceremonious proceeding, but I could not help myself, and was compelled to put up with a seat on a big fourgon, in which I placed the golden cups intended for Granvelle. At Ulm, Martin Weyer decided that Normann should give me back my horse when we reached Spires, and that he should go the rest of the way by the Rhine. When we got to Spires, Normann was not to be found there, and we finally learnt that he had gone to the baths of Zell with the chimerical hope of getting rid of his pimples which disfigured him.

I confided the two pieces of goldsmith's work to Dr. Louis Zigler, the procurator to our princes, then went by coach to Oppenheim, and by water to Mayence. On 10 September our ship reached Cologne, and next morning I went in search of a good horse to pursue my route in company of friends, when, whom should I meet in the street but Normann. As a consequence, I was obliged to change my inn, and to part with my company. Normann was in treaty for a horse, which he finally bought. In that way we were both provided for, but without a servant, each man taking care of his own horse; however, the ostlers were excellent, and there was no need to watch; one had only to command.

We started for the Low Countries on September 12, the emperor going down the Rhine in a boat. Next day, at the branching off of the high road, we hesitated. On inquiring at the nearest inn we were told that one road led to Maestricht, and the other to Aix-la-Chapelle. The first-named was the shorter by six miles; on the other hand, Aix-la-Chapelle is the famous city founded by Charlemagne. It contains the royal throne, it is the city where the emperor is crowned after his election at Frankfurt. After we had discussed the "for" and "against" at some length, we hit upon the idea of giving our horses their heads, and leaving the bridles on their necks. By some subtle and mysterious intuition the animals chose, according to our secret desire, the road to Aix-la-Chapelle.

The city itself is large and in ancient style. The country around is barren, the soil consisting of coal, stone and slate. Previous to the foundation of the city it was simply a wilderness. There are some excellent mineral springs; the bath, constructed in beautiful hewn stone, is square, and about fourteen feet long; three steps enable one to sit down with the water up to the throat, or to be immersed at a small depth. Except the baths of the landgravate of Baden, I know of no other arrangement equally comfortable. At the town hall, castle, and arsenal of Charlemagne there are hundreds of thousands of sharp iron arrows stowed away in closed chests. On entering the church one immediately notices an ivory and gold armchair, fastened with exceeding great art. At the lower end of the nave, to the west, a huge crown of at least twelve feet diameter is suspended. I do not know the nature of the material, but it is gilt and painted in colours. In the way of relics there are the hose of Joseph. They are only shown at stated times, but whoever has the privilege of seeing them has a great many of his sins remitted.

On September 24 we reached Brussels in Brabant, and there I received the order to go back to my country, the functions of solicitor to the Imperial Chamber having been conferred upon me. Hence, on St. Denis' Day, I began this journey of more than a hundred miles, alone and across unknown countries, with abominable roads, above all in Westphalia. I was often obliged to stay the night at places which were more than suspect, and when only half-way my horse came to grief in consequence of Normann's former rough usage. I had to swop it, paying a sum of money besides, and was unfortunate enough to have come across a veritable crock which I was obliged to keep, there being no help for it. Finally, through good and evil I reached Wolgast on All Saints' Day.

CHAPTER III

As soon as my nomination was drawn up, I was dispatched with it to Chancellor Citzewitz, at his estate of Muttrin, near Dantzig. The principal personages of the land had come to consult him, and he kept me for more than ten days with him in excellent company, making me share their favourite recreation, and the thing that bored me most, namely, the chase, to which the country admirably lends itself. I returned with the chancellor to Stettin, where my warrant of appointment was duly signed and sealed.

At Wolgast Duke Philip interrogated me at length in his own study, and with no one else present, on the condition of affairs at Augsburg and Brussels. He was much surprised at my boldness in having given him such a plain and straightforward account of the doings of the court. "If only one of your letters had been intercepted, they would have strung you up at the nearest tree," he said. This was no exaggeration on his part; and supposing such a catastrophe had happened, he would, in spite of everything, have remained a prince of the empire, while there would have been an end of me. Of course, my behaviour gave him the measure of my devotion to him. He promised me a good horse; besides this, the ducal kitchen provided all that was necessary for a farewell banquet, and, in fact, at supper some pages brought us two hares from the prince's larder. I received a hundred crowns for my loyal services, and an appointment of one hundred and forty per annum; the cost of copying and dispatch of messengers being charged to their Highnesses.

I went to say good-bye to my parents at Stralsund. My mother had ordered for my sister chains and clasps which the goldsmith had as yet not delivered. I paid for them, and, moreover, left thirty crowns at home. "Use them, if there be any need. I'll manage to make both ends meet with what remains." Duke Philip had given me a strong and lively hunter. Behind the saddle I had a small saddle-bag, like the court messengers. My brother Christian accompanied me as far as Leipzig, where we wished to be for the fair.

Our journey was an uneventful one, except that one day in Mesnia, having lost our way, we came at the end of a big forest upon a small tenement which was the residence of a poor gentleman. The fast gathering darkness compelled us to knock at the noble's dwelling, which was inhabited by a young widow of only a few weeks' standing with her mother-in-law. The bad-tempered old woman roughly refused us shelter. "Go wherever you like," she snarled. Her daughter-in-law, on the other hand, said; "We did not expect any one, and we do not keep an inn, but it is getting darker and darker, and you would have to go a long way before finding one. If you will be content with our humble accommodation, you may remain for the night." At these words the other one storms and raves. "May the devil take you and them. You have found some youngsters who are to your taste, and you have already forgotten my son." I tried to appease her. "We have never before been in this country," I said to her; "at daybreak we'll be able to find our way. You need not be afraid of our using unsuitable language or doing aught that is not right, and we'll be satisfied with whatever accommodation you can give us, as long as our horses have some fodder and some straw. For all this we'll willingly pay." The virago, however, turned a deaf ear to this. If we were not the lovers of her daughter-in-law why should we have come at this late hour in the neighbourhood where no stranger ever came? The young woman was very patient throughout. After having provided us with hay and straw for our horses, she took us to a lofty room of very modest appearance. There was no man or woman servant to be seen; our supper, though, was none the worse for it. After she had set all our provisions before us, our hostess sat down and told us the sad existence she was leading. The bed was moderately comfortable, and the sheets were clean. We paid more than was asked.

At Leipzig I stopped two days to rest my horse. I gave my brother the wherewithal for his return journey, and continued my way alone. The country as far as Frankfurt was known to me. From Butzbach I went by Niederweisel and the Hundfruck, a route I had often pursued with my former master, the commander of St. John. It is more direct than by Friburg, but it swarms with highway robbers. As I was walking my horse up the slope of the forest I caught sight of two horsemen who were evidently bent on waiting for me, as they posted themselves, the one to the left and the other to the right of the road, and when I was between them they began interpellating me in a gruff voice. "From what country?" "From Pomerania." "What hast thou got in thy valise?" "Letters." "Whither art thou going?" "To Spires." "To whom dost thou belong?" "To the Dukes of Pomerania. Here is my safe-conduct." Thereupon one of them became more friendly. "And how is his Highness Duke Philip, that excellent prince? I knew him very well at Heidelberg." And on my recommendation for them to go their way and to let me go mine, they looked at me very hard for a few moments, but did not follow me. I sold my horse and equipment at Frankfurt, and went down the Main as far as Mayence, whence, going up the Rhine, I got to Oppenheim, and by the coach to Worms and Spires.

I reached the latter town on January 21, 1549. I hired a room with a dressing closet at a clothshearer's, who was also a councillor. I also boarded with him, like many young doctors of law and other notable persons detained at Spires by their functions or by their wish to get practical experience.

Dr. Simeon Engelhardt, who, by the express act of a formal decision of his Imperial Majesty, had not been reinstated in his office of procurator any more than his brother-in-law, the licentiate Bernard Mey and Johannes Helfmann had transferred his household goods to Landau. At his recommendation, Dr. Johannes Portius, for procurator, and I brought him so many clients that he would accept no fees from me. Engelhardt remained my advocate, notwithstanding the inconvenience of the distance between us. How often have I walked the four miles between Spires and Landau! By starting at the closing of the gates, I reached Landau for the hour fixed for their opening; the morning sufficed to transact my business with the doctor, and my return journey was accomplished in the afternoon. Nor did Engelhardt claim any fees, but I remember having taken to him a client who for a single act paid him twenty crowns without his asking. The correspondence, thanks to the Pomeranian couriers always at my disposal, was equally cheap.

The Lloytz of Stettin chose me as their solicitor.[61] Martin Weyer, in the "Cammin" affair, did the same. There were others, and all, except Weyer, paid me handsomely. I was getting well known among the procurators, and I finally acted *pro principale vel adjuncto notario*. I earned, then, sufficient to live comfortably without having recourse to the paternal purse. I even could put aside the whole of my appointments, and something over. The chief benefit, however, lay in the acquisition of experience, the fruits of which have extended to the whole of my family, because my pen has always been the sole means of livelihood. If that business be well learnt and well carried out, it leaves no one to starve. Folks may mention the word scribe with as much contempt as they please; the fact remains that I have had many a choice morsel, and drunk delicious draughts through being a scribe.

From Spires I wrote to Sebastian Münster that their Highnesses were particularly anxious not to hurry the printing of his excellent *Cosmographie*, because a special messenger was to bring him a description of Pomerania the moment it was finished, and that it would prove not the least valuable ornament of his work. He sent word that it was impossible for him to delay; his step-son was so deeply engaged in the undertaking that he would be ruined if he missed the next Lent fair at Frankfurt. I transmitted the reply to Pomerania; the same messenger brought back a big bundle of notes, unfortunately incomplete, as they pointed out to me. I promptly sent them to Sebastian Münster, promising to let him have the rest the moment I received them. He kindly sent me an autograph letter, which my children will find joined to that of Dr. Martin Luther.[62]

It struck me that an interview with Sebastian Münster would enable me to inform our princes accurately. The Imperial Chamber had its vacation. It was an excellent opportunity to see Alsace, flowing with corn and wine, so many handsome towns, the seat of the Margrave of Baden, bishops and courts, and, above all, the city of Basle. Hence, I undertook the journey on foot, an affair of about sixty miles there and back. At Strasburg I lodged at my friend's, Daniel Capito, a poor home, but we took our meals at the tavern of the *Ammeister*.[63]

In the church at Basle I saw the stone statue of Desiderius Erasmus, of Rotterdam. I invited Herr Lepusculus, the fugitive of Augsburg, to dinner, and we talked of many interesting things. I also became well acquainted with Sebastian Münster, who gave me a most hearty welcome. A huge room of his house contained a quantity of plates, either cast, engraved on wood or on copper. They had come from Germany, Italy or France; they were geographical, astronomical, or mathematical drawings, representing pieces of engineering work for the use of miners, and views of cities, countries, castles, or convents, that were to figure in his *Cosmographie*. He was most anxious for me to stay with him, so that he might show me the objects of interest connected with the town; unfortunately, my time was too short. After having taken leave of Münster and Lepusculus, I went back to Spires on foot.

I was just in time for a message from Pomerania relative to the lawsuit between Duke Barnim and the town of Stolpe. The latter, on the pretext of an attempt against its privileges, had deputed Simon Wolder to attend upon the emperor. Wolder was a young jackanapes without education, but pushing and cunning, and by dint of intriguing he obtained the confirmation of the said privileges, and for himself the Imperial safeguard. The people of Stolpe had their triumph, and to judge by their swaggering one would have concluded they had no longer anything in common with their prince and lord. Duke Barnim, though, having entered the town amidst his soldiers, summoned the council and the burghers to the Town Hall, and when he got them there, he forbade those who had had a hand in the intriguing to stir, while the others should stand aside. The majority of those present changed their positions; the rest, and notably the Burgomaster Schwabe, a near relation to the Bishop of Cammin, were imprisoned at Stettin, at Greiffenberg, and at Treptow, while Simon Wolder fled to the emperor, who was fighting the white Moors (?) in Africa. He succeeded in obtaining from the emperor the categorical order for releasing the prisoners, on the express penalty of being put "under the ban"; but that injunction arrived too late. The friends of the prisoners humbly interceded for them, and each liberation was bought at a heavy fine and after a long detention. As for Wolder, far from resting on his oars, he pursued his intrigues at the Imperial court, ingratiating himself with the princes, the nobles, and the cities. He enjoyed great favour; he dressed magnificently. Where did the money for all this display come from? In short, at the restoration of the Imperial Chamber, an action was begun.

The dukes of Pomerania had unquestionably cause for anxiety, for their relations with the emperor were already very strained, and the latter's victory made him very disinclined to exercise much consideration to the partisans of the Augsburg confession. Simon Wolder was jubilant; he looked upon the business as good as won; judges and assessors were papists, and their Highnesses under a cloud of Imperial disgrace. We devoted the most serious attention at Spires to the suit; procurator Ziegler and advocate Johannes Kalte amply did their duty; if need had been, I was there to spur them on. At Stettin, on the contrary, Martin Weyer and Dr. Schwallenberger, to whom the affair was entrusted, were mere sluggards whose conduct was disgraceful. We shall meet with Schwallenberger again.

In May our counsellors wrote to me to take the two golden cups to Brussels to them. The rumour ran, in fact, that the emperor's son was coming from Spain in great pomp; and our envoys hoped to secure, through the influence of certain important personages, his intercession with the emperor. I started immediately, going down the Rhine as far as the Meuse, and pursuing my journey by land by way of s'Hertogenbosch (Bois le Due) and Louvain.

When I had delivered my precious deposit, the wish to see something of Flanders impelled me to Ghent. It is a big city, formerly endowed with important privileges. For instance, the emperor could impose no taxes in Flanders or demand anything without the assent of the said city. Charles V has deprived it of its privileges. He has razed a convent and several houses to the ground, and on their site built a castle with huge, deep moats filled with water, besides other remarkable outworks, so that the city is at his mercy. In the centre of Ghent there rises a high steeple. I climbed to the top, and it is from there that the emperor and his brother Ferdinand chose the spot whereon to build their fortress; they traced there, *propriis manibus*, their symbolum in red chalk.

The castle where Charles V saw the light is a decrepit, unsightly kind of tenement, surrounded by water, and accessible only by a drawbridge. At the head of the bridge, on the parapet, there are two bronze statues; one is kneeling, and behind it there is the second with uplifted sword. Tradition has it that they represent two men condemned to death, father and son, for whom no executioner could be found. They then promised the father a full pardon if he would behead his son. At his refusal the offer was made to the son, who accepted it with joy and gratitude, and severed his father's head from the trunk.

In Antwerp I met with Herr Heinrich Buchow, the future counsellor of Stralsund. We had both heard much about the house of Gaspard Duitz, about a good mile distant from the city. People compared it to the castle of Trent, some even said that it was handsomer. We obtained a letter from the owner to his steward, who showed us everything, and really rumour had not been guilty of exaggeration. Though there were a great number of them, each room was differently decorated; each contained a bed and a table. The hangings were of the same colour as the bed-curtains, and the cloth on the table which was either of velvet or damask, black, red or violet, as the case might be. Musical instruments everywhere, but varying in every room. Here a kettledrum; there Polish viols, elsewhere lutes, harps, zithers, hautboys, bassoons, Swiss fifes, etc. The girl who showed us over the place quite correctly played the kettledrum, the viol and the lute. In front of the house a beautiful garden cultivated with art, and enhanced by many exotics. Further on a zoological collection. The ground floor has one hall of such magnificence that one day Madame Marie entertained her brother there. The emperor, having looked and appreciated everything, asked: "To whom, sister mine, belongs this house?" "To our treasurer." "Well," rejoined the emperor, "our treasurer evidently knows the science of profit-making."

This Gaspard Duitz, an Italian by birth, a shrewd and even cunning merchant, had exercised commerce on a large scale at Antwerp, and failed twice if not three times. When he had thousands upon thousands of crowns in hand, he asked his creditors for five years' delay. Madame Marie, for instance, gave him such letters of respite. Of course, those rogueries made him very wealthy, and when Madame Marie was in need of money, her treasurer came to her aid. A house in Antwerp, which had cost him thousands of florins, not having realized his expectations--the drawbacks of a structure becoming only apparent after it is finished--he had it razed to the ground and rebuilt according to his taste.

The Count Maximilian van Buren (the same who, in the Schmalkalden campaign, took the Dutch horsemen to the emperor), having heard of Duitz's famous country seat, "invited himself" to it. Master Gaspard treated his visitor magnificently, showed him everything, and when taking leave inquired if perchance the count had noticed some fault or shortcoming in the decorations or general disposition of the whole; for, if such were the case, he would alter it, even if he had to send for artists from Venice or Rome. "No," replied the count; "the only thing wanting is a high gallows at the entrance, with Gaspard Duitz securely swinging from it." That was the count's acknowledgment of his host's hospitality, and he might have added: "With a crown on his head, as an arch-thief."[64]

From Antwerp I went to Malines. What an admirable country! Louvain, Brussels and Antwerp, three big and handsome cities, are at an equal distance from each other, and Malines, which one always has to cross to get to either, stands in the centre. Along the route there are magnificent castles and lordly dwellings. Malines is a pretty city, though the smallest of the four; the water is brought there *labore et industriâ hominum*, and enables one to reach Antwerp by boat. I saw the damage caused by the lightning of August 7, 1546, when it fell on a powder magazine, which was entirely destroyed, together with the outer wall; huge quarters were hurled on the roofs of houses. There was a great loss of life and property.

At Malines I went to see Vogel Heine, who, in the days of Maximilian I, the great-great-grandfather of the present emperor, went in advance to prepare the night quarters. The emperor had left him sufficient to live upon; the woman who took care of him had her lodging and firing. Heine was so old and so decrepit as to be unable to stir from a room that was constantly heated. People gave the woman a small tip to see her charge, and in that way she made for herself a small income instead of wages.

From Louvain I took the most direct and shortest road to Juliers and Cologne; at the latter place I put up at *The Angel*. The host had a raven that spoke, and even understood what was said to it. If, in the evening, there was a knock at the door, the bird asked: "Is anybody knocking?" "Yes," replied the new-comer. But as the travellers' room happened to be at the back of the house, overlooking the Rhine, nobody stirred, and the knocking was repeated, the bird, on its part, repeating the same question. "Can't you hear?" said the claimant for admission, out of patience, and knocking much louder, so that they could hear it from the travellers' room. Naturally, the servant came to open the door, and endeavoured to mollify the would-be guest's anger by saying that they had heard no knocking. Thereupon the other called him a liar, or at any rate treated him as such; thereupon the cage with the bird in it was pointed out as evidence, and everything was well. The bird, upon the whole, was most remarkable, and many great personages made the most tempting offers for it, which were always refused. Six or seven years later, when I visited Cologne again, I inquired what had become of the bird, and its owner told me that he was then at law with a gentleman who, coming in drunk, had drawn his sword and cut the bird's head off. The host assured me that he would sooner have lost three hundred crowns.

After having gone up the Rhine as far as Mayence, I took the coach to Spires.

In June 1549 King Philip, the emperor's son, came to Spires with a numerous suite. His father had appointed the cardinal of Trent, a Seigneur de Madrutz, as his marshal. The king was then about twenty-two years of age, my junior by seven. His far from intellectual face gave little hope of his equalling his father one day. The Elector of Heidelberg, the other counts palatine, the ecclesiastical electors, all of them in their state carriages, attended on him when he went to church. Well, I often saw his father under similar circumstances. When he came out of his apartments and mounted his horse in the courtyard, where princes and electors already in the saddle awaited him, he was the first to take his hat off. If it happened to rain, so much the worse. He remained bare-headed, and was not the less affable either in speech or gesture. He held out his hand to everybody, and did the same when he came back. When, at the foot of the staircase, he turned out, faced his escort, took off his hat, and bade them farewell in a gracious manner.

King Philip, on the contrary, was most exacting with the electors and the princes, though many of them were old men. While the latter dismounted at the door of the church, Philip went in without troubling about them, making signs behind his back with his hands for them to march by his side, but they merely followed him. After the service they accompanied the king back to the palace. He jumped down, and went up the stairs without a look or a word of farewell. His marshal had, nevertheless, told him that there was a great difference between Spanish and German princes. As a proof of this, he quoted to him the paternal example, as typified by the consideration shown to the German nobles by the emperor, but Philip answered: "Between myself and my father, the difference is as great, for he is only the son of a king; I am the son of an emperor." After having officially made their appearance, the princes promptly left for their own States. Philip spent a few more days hunting and going about, his suite being reduced to fourteen or twelve horses, and then the Duke of Aarschot came for him, by order of the emperor, to take him with a magnificent escort to Brussels.

Notwithstanding my constant reminders to them of the mortal danger of delay, the Stettin authorities were terribly slow in sending me the most indispensable documents for the serious lawsuit against the town of Stolpe. As some people, moreover, were attempting to discredit me with Duke Barnim, I wrote to Chancellor Falck, who answered me: "You do not deserve the slightest reproach. All the neglect is on this side; but, in truth, the whole of your letter is so much Arabic to me, because I have not the faintest idea of the lawsuit itself." That is how things are managed at courts.

On the banks of the Rhine it is the custom to organize at twelfth night a complete court--king, marshal, steward, cup-bearer, etc. As a matter of course, the court fool is indispensable. The charges are drawn for by lot; each pays part of the expenses; alone the fool is exempt. In 1550 there gathered round our table a young baron from the Low Countries, a bright young fellow, with considerable experience of the world, also several persons of consideration who were detained at Spires by their law business. It fell to my lot to be king, with the baron for my marshal. As for the fool, chance had picked out our host, the priest, and nature seemed really to have created him for the part. In my capacity of king I had a many-coloured hooded cloak of English linen made for him. When we had visitors, and, thanks to the gay baron, this happened frequently, our host put on his cloak and took our guests to task. We shook with laughter, but he himself fared very well by it, for his buffoonery brought him many silver and even gold pieces. He bought himself silver bells for his cap, and his cloak became spangled with gold and silver coins.

This went on until "kingdom" time, which is celebrated one Sunday evening between twelfth night and Shrovetide. There are three or four kingdoms each Sunday, and the masked people of both sexes go from one gathering to another in fancy dress and accompanied by musicians. They have the right of three dances with those who give the entertainments. All this afforded capital opportunities for every kind of dissipation and debauch. One evening, for instance, it happened that a husband and his wife, after having danced together, divided for the second dance and came together for the third, without, however, recognizing each other. Side by side they went to another house, and having understood each other's desires by the pressure of their hands, they indulged their sudden fancy on their way in the penumbra of a clothworker's shop in the market place, and never did the hallowed joys of matrimony taste like the forbidden fruit of infidelity; at any rate, so each imagined. Being anxious to know who was his partner, the swain cut a snippet from her dress and, moreover, made her a present of a gold piece, then both joined the rest of the company. The husband was a chamois-leather dresser, and next morning some one came to buy a skin, and tendered a large coin. As he had no change himself, he took his wife's satchel and found the golden piece, which he recognized at once. When the customer was gone, the dame had to show the gown she wore on the previous evening, the husband confronted her with the abstracted piece of stuff. Denial was impossible, but the one happened to be as guilty as the other.

We gave our fool ample opportunity to adorn his dress. At the carnival he made himself conspicuous by many pleasant quips and pranks; the marshal also did wonders, standing erect before his Majesty, and zealously attending upon him by bringing up the dishes, carving the viands, and cleaning the table with many genuflections and kissing of hands. The king paid very dearly for his three or four hours' reign.

Our host was a careless, irresponsible creature, more fit for the life of camps or of courts than for the priesthood; a gambler, a rogue, a boaster, a drunkard, a brawler, and an adept at jesting and practical joking. He did not care whether his boarders were papists or evangelicals. He was one of the three who celebrated early mass at the cathedral. His young boarders, the graduates, were fond of cards, and clever gamblers. They thought that a seasoned gamester like their host must necessarily be a valuable adviser, so they spent their night round the board. About three in the morning their landlord cried: "Brothers, don't you move; I am going to say mass. But it will be short and sweet; just long enough to blow the dust off the altar, and I'll be back." And he was as good as his word.

It was a custom to place, during the night of Good Friday, a crucifix in one of the lateral chapels, and the three priests who said early mass were deputed to watch over it. Long files of matrons prostrated themselves, face downward, and deposited their offerings. On one occasion, towards three in the morning, the reverend guardians who no longer expected contributors, divided the receipts and began to gamble. Thanks to his long practice, our host won every penny to the annoyance of his colleagues. A quarrel ensued at the foot of the cross, followed by blows; our man being the strongest, the victory and the money remained with him.

In "Rogation Week" the clergy in their richest vestments, and carrying crosses, banners, and relics, perambulate the fields, followed by crowds of men and women. A young priest, thinking this a propitious time for an assignation, left the procession, and disappeared among the standing corn, whither a young damsel went after him. Two workmen, though, had noticed the manoeuvre; they watched for the opportune moment, surprised the couple, and only left the "black beetle" after having stripped him of his gown and surplice, both which "proofs positive" they brought to the dean of the chapter.

I have not the least doubt that the King of Spain interceded in favour of our princes. Assiduous solicitations, but above all the goldsmiths' work and the gratifications so much prized at courts and in large cities, mollified the influential counsellers, the Seigneur de Granvelle, his son, the Bishop of Arras, and others. The emperor finally consented to an arrangement, one of the conditions of which was the payment of a fine of ninety thousand florins. The Imperial chancellerie demanded three thousand florins for engrossing the act of reconciliation, which I could have done as elegantly in one day. The Bishop of Arras, to whom reverted half the chancellery fees, abandoned them in our favour, but he lost nothing by his generosity. In sum, this little matter cost two hundred thousand florins.

One of the conditions imposed upon our princes was the acceptance of the "Interim." The Pomeranian clergy unanimously rejected this work of Satan. The council of Stralsund summoned the ministers before it to forbid them pronouncing the word "Interim" from the pulpit, and, above all, to add any ill-sounding expression to it on the penalty of being deposed from their sacred office. As for the doctrines themselves, they were at liberty to weigh and to refute them by the Holy Scriptures. But superintendent Johannes Freder, an obstinate and narrow-minded man, replied that as a good shepherd he neither could nor would deliver his flock to the rage of devouring wolves, for to do this would be to imperil his own body and soul. He furthermore said that if he were dismissed God would provide, and that, moreover, men of education were not liked at Stralsund. The council adjourned the meeting, and two of its members intimated his dismissal to Freder.

The next day the ministers presented a petition signed by all except Johannes Niemann. They claimed their liberty of conscience and their right to serve the cause of truth by denouncing from the pulpit the damnable abominations of the "Interim." "One must obey God rather than men," they said. The impetuous Alexis Grosse and Johannes Berckmann were conspicuous by their anger. They hurled the most offensive accusations against honest Niemann, and tried to carry things with such a high hand that the council, greatly irritated, decided there and then upon the dismissal of Grosse, after payment of the arrears due to him. The other preachers expected the same fate, but matters went no farther, so Niemann would have risked nothing by adding his signature to that of his colleagues. Besides, the Interim was assailed from every direction; the attacks were made in German, in Latin, in Italian, in French, and in Spanish. Every line was weighed and refuted in the name of the Holy Word. The pope, for very shame, did not know where to hide his face.

Let my children bear in mind the high degree of fortune attained by the emperor. At the summit of that prosperity, when everything seemed to proceed according to his desires, he imagined that unhindered he could break his promise to undertake nothing against the Augsburg confession.

For love of the pope, he contemplated ruining the unshakable stronghold of Luther. From that moment the emperor's star waned; all his enterprises failed. Instead of being razed to the ground, Luther's stronghold was, on the contrary, furnished with solid ramparts, and to-day it counts powerful defenders in Germany, such as the Duke of Prussia, the Margrave of Baden, the Margrave Ernest von Pforzheim, and others, while among other nations the number of champions inspired by the blood of the martyrs is constantly on the increase. That stronghold shall set its enemies at defiance for evermore.

At Stettin they went on blackening my character so effectually that Dr. Schwallenberg succeeded in getting himself sent on a mission to repair the effects of my supposed neglect. On my side, I had made up my mind to resign the functions of solicitor, and to leave Spires in December. I wrote to that effect to Chancellor Citzewitz, giving him the motives for my decision.

At his arrival Dr. Schwallenberg took up his quarters at a canon's of his acquaintance--an easy method of being boarded and lodged for nothing; he had retrenched in that way all along the route, though taking care to put down his expense in the usual manner. When I presented myself at his summons, he was at table; he did not ask me to sit down, adopted a haughty tone, and even wished me to serve him. I, however, protested energetically. "This is not part of my duty. If there was an attempt to impose it upon me, I should refuse it; in that respect I have finished my apprenticeship. On the other hand, the advocate and I are very anxious to have your views on the affairs of our princes which have entailed so much writing upon me, at present without any result. Will you please name your own time?" "I'll see the advocate by himself," replied Schwallenberg. And, in fact, he went to the lawyer, but instead of entering upon the discussion of the urgent questions, he insinuated that I was a fifth wheel on the coach. "Get him dismissed, and his emoluments will increase your modest fees," he remarked. The advocate was an honourable man. He replied that I was being slandered, and that he did not care about earning money by means of a cabal. Thereupon Dr. Schwallenberg went for a trip to Strasburg.

At his return the arguments of the case were ready, but he refused to read them, alleging that they had to be submitted to the dukes. I dispatched a messenger, who also carried a missive from Schwallenberg. The latter then departed for the Diet of Ratisbon. In due time came the princes' answer, and feeling certain that it related to the lawsuit, I opened it and read as follows:

"Very learned, dear and faithful! We are pleased to express to thee our particular satisfaction at thy diligence at re-establishing our affairs, so greatly compromised by our solicitor that without thy arrival on the spot they would have entirely lapsed. As for the arguments thou hast elaborated with the advocate, we have ordered them to be returned to thee the moment our counsellors shall have examined and according to need amended them. We also authorize thee to go to the Diet of Ratisbon at our cost, etc."

It would be difficult to conceive blacker treachery. For at least a twelvemonth I had despatched messenger after messenger for instructions. In spite of that, all the delay had been imputed to me. A rogue presented as his work arguments not one word of which belonged to him; he had not even taken the trouble to read the documents. And while the princes tendered him their thanks, my disgrace was complete.

I had no longer anything to expect from my fellow-men; the Almighty, however, chose that moment to make my innocence patent to every one, and to confound my enemies. Thus was Mordecai laden with honours after the ignominious fall of Haman. Yes, even before the arguments were sent back from Pomerania, the Chamber delivered the following judgment: "In the matter of the town of Stolpe and of Simon Wolder against his Grace Barnim, Duke of Pomerania, etc., we decide and declare that the said duke is acquitted of all the charges and obligations advanced against him by the plaintiffs." What hast thou to say against that, infamous libeller? Hide thy head with shame, vile hypocrite! The feelings with which I despatched a special messenger to the duke may easily be imagined. It may be equally taken for granted that I did not mince matters in pointing out the merits of Dr. Schwallenberg. And although his diabolical machinations had filled my heart with sadness, they turned to my profit and my salvation, so true it is that the Lord converts evil into good. I was, however, strengthened in my decision to abandon the office of solicitor, and, above all, the princes' service, and that notwithstanding Citzewitz's offer, both verbal and in writing, of a profitable position at the chancellerie of Wolgast. I had become disgusted with the life at courts. A new career was open to me in a town where, though the devil and his acolytes have not quite given up the game, there is nevertheless a means of enjoying one's self and to live and die according to God's precepts. My sister, who was married to Peter Frubose, burgomaster of Greifswald, proposed to me to marry her sister-in-law. As I expected to be at Greifswald on New Year's Day, I wrote to her to arrange the wedding before the carnival. A cabinet messenger, who was going home for good, sold me a young grey trotting horse, with its bridle and saddle.

Everything being wound up and settled with the advocates and procurators, etc., and having taken regular leave of them, I bade farewell to Spires on December 3, 1550, so disgusted with the Imperial Chamber as to have made up my mind never to return to it during my life. I had remained in foreign parts for five years in the interests of my father's lawsuit, in addition to the two years I had spent in behalf of the dukes of Pomerania. These years were not altogether without result. In fact, both in the chancelleries of Margrave Ernest and of the Commander of St. John, as well as at the secretary's office of our dukes and at the diets, I furthered my own affairs and amassed more money than many a doctor. It had all been done by my talent as a law writer, an art which is neither taught in Bartolus nor in Baldus, but which requires much application, memory, readiness to oblige and constant practice. Truly, I had worked day and night, and, as this narrative shows, incurred many dangers. Many folk after me, dazzled by my success, tried in their turn to become law writers, but they very soon succumbed to the monotony of the business, to the incessant labour, to the protracted vigils, to hunger, thirst, cares and dangers. Barely one in a hundred succeeds.

I reached Stettin on December 21, and, all things considered, there was nothing to grumble at in the welcome I received. The counsellors, among whom were Schwallenberg's confederates, heard my explanations at length as they said on behalf of the prince. I was warned that they had agreed upon baulking me of an audience. The next day they informed me that the duke was as pleased with the energy I had shown as with the tenour of my report, and that I was authorized to bring a plaint against Schwallenberg. As for the prince's promise of a gratification, he had not forgotten it, and he asked me to exercise patience for a few days. He evidently wished to consult with the court of Wolgast. I answered as follows:

"Great is my joy to learn that my lord and master appreciates my devotion and acknowledges how undeserved was my disgrace. I should be grieved to have to attack Dr. Schwallenberger on the eve of my marriage. The evidence, however, is conclusive; the duke is more interested than I in the punishment of the rogue. What, after all, have I to gain by a lawsuit now that the prince, heaven be praised, thanks me by word of mouth and in writing? Nor is it possible for me to wait here for the promised recompense. I prefer to come back after the wedding."

When they became aware of my determination to abandon the court for the city, all the counsellors intoned a "hallelujah." There was an instantaneous change of language and behaviour to me. They were lavish with offers of service, but the first sentence of Chancellor Citzewitz at our meeting was: "A plague upon the bird that will not wait for the stroke of fortune." Here ends the story of my life previous to my marriage.

PART III

CHAPTER I

I reached Greifswald on January 1, 1551, at nightfall. I was thirty years old. After I had written to Stralsund for my parents' consent, and had conferred with my Greifswald relatives and those of my future wife, the invitations for the betrothal were sent out on both sides. On January 5, in the chapel of the Grey Friars, at eight in the morning, Master Matthew Frubose made a solemn promise to give me his daughter, in the presence of the burgomasters, councillors, and a large number of notable burghers. Burgomaster Bunsow gave me a loan of two hundred florins.

The worshipful council had been obliged to suppress the dances at weddings, because the manner in which the men whirled the matrons and damsels round and round had become indecent. Those who infringed the order, no matter what was their condition, were cited before the minor court. It so happened that a week after our betrothal my intended and I were invited to a wedding at one of the principal families. When the wedding banquet was over, my betrothed came back to me, and, being ignorant of the council's orders, I danced with her, but most quietly, and a very short time. Notwithstanding this, an officer of the court came the next morning and summoned me to appear. At the first blush I could scarcely credit such an instance of incivility. Moreover, it boded ill, and I could not help foreseeing struggles, animosities, and persecution in this manner of bidding me welcome by a satellite of the hangman after an absence of eight years. Does not the poet say, *Omina principiis semper inesse solent*? I was very indignant, and ran to the eldest of the burgomasters. He pointed out to me that urgent and severe proceedings were necessary against the coarse licence of the students and others, but my case being entirely different, he promised to stay all proceedings.

I had not said a word about the dowry, and least of all had I inquired as to its amount; but my sister told me that my father-in-law gave his daughter two hundred florins. I made no answer. My chief concern was to get a wife.

According to my brother's calculations, one hundred marks yearly would suffice to keep the house. Experience told me a different story.

I went to Stralsund for my wedding clothes and other necessary things. My father gave me some sable furs he had had for many years. I bought the cloth for the coat as well as the rest of my marriage outfit. My father had put in pledge the things I intended offering to my bride. I was obliged to redeem them. Among several other objects there was a piece of velvet for collarettes for my betrothed and my sister. At Frankfurt-on-the-Main I had bought a dagger ornamented with silver. Those various purchases exhausted my stock of money.

Although I had invited my numerous Stralsund relatives on both sides in good time, only Johannes Gottschalk, my old schoolfellow and colleague at the chancellerie of Wolgast, came to my wedding. He made me a present of a golden florin of Lubeck.

My marriage took place at Greifswald on February 2, 1551. As I was one of the last to "mount the stone," it may be interesting to give an account of that old custom. At three in the afternoon, and just before the celebration of the marriage service, the bridegroom was conducted to the market place between two burgomasters, or, in default of these, between the two most prominent wedding guests. At one of the angles of the place there was a square block of stone, on which the bridegroom took up his position, the guests ranging themselves in good order about fifty paces away. The pipers gave him a morning greeting lasting about five or six minutes, after which he resumed his place in the wedding procession. The purpose of the ceremony, according to tradition, was to give everybody an opportunity of addressing some useful remark to the bridegroom at that critical moment. These remarks were often more forcible and outspoken than flattering, and were not always distinguished by their strict adherence to the truth.

Johannes Bunsow, the son of the burgomaster, had been a suitor for my wife's hand; the preliminary arrangements to the marriage were as good as completed, and the invitations to the betrothal festivities were about to be sent out when everything was broken off, in consequence of the exacting demands of the proud wife of the burgomaster from the parents of the girl. The burgomaster's wife was considerably upset about all this. It so happened that on the wedding-day at the breakfast my wife was seated between the dames Bunsow and Gruwel. My father, who was her cavalier, sat opposite. All at once, the burgomaster's wife said to the bride, "Eat, my girl, eat, for this is the happiest day of thy life. I had made other plans for thy happiness, but thou didst not fall in with them. The culprit is either thy brother or his wife. Keep thy husband at a distance, for if thou givest him an inch he will take an ell; therefore, be 'stand-offish' with him in the beginning." At these words Dame Gruwel exclaimed: "Good heaven, what sad advice! Make thy mind easy, child; there are many happy days in store for thee."

Eighteen months later, as we were standing talking in the street, Peter and Matthew Schwarte and I, Dame Bunsow who went by, spoke to us. With the admirable volubility that distinguishes the women of Greifswald, she had a word for all of us. "Dear cousins," she said to the Schwartes, "how do you do? how are your wives? and how are your children?" Then, turning to me, "And how are you, cousin? How is your wife? I need not ask you about the children. You are having a good year of it. In these hard days one may as well save the bread." "That's farthest from our thoughts," I answered, "but that's because my wife is not 'stand-offish' enough with me." She knew what I was driving at, turned crimson, and went away without saying another word.

A week after my marriage, on the Sunday, I returned to Stettin, as had been agreed upon. It was a fatiguing, not to say dangerous journey, because of the inundations. From the moment of my marriage the devil seemed to have declared war against me. It was, I suppose, his revenge for my having disappointed him by leaving the court, where I might have proved of great service. On the other hand, his Master, our Lord and Saviour, took me under His protection. A very heavy snowfall had been succeeded by a sudden thaw, the effect of a warm and continuous rain. As a consequence, the overflowing of banks everywhere, the mill-stream near Ukermünde had swept away the roadway at several spots. On the very day of my departure, a van laden, among other things, with a case of sealed letters, registers, documents and parchments, had passed that way, coming from Wolgast. Our travellers, knowing that they were on the high road, went ahead. Suddenly the horses fell into a deep rut; the cart was overturned, and only by a mighty effort did beasts and men escape drowning. They had to spend the night at Ukermünde to dry the letters.

I came to the spot of the accident in the afternoon. I was gaily trotting along, for I was following the highway and the fresh traces of the vehicle from Wolgast. My good fortune befriended me in the shape of a miller's lad who was standing by the water. He called out and showed me a little lower down, to the right, the way to a small burgh, having passed which I should find a long road and a bridge, the only available passage left. Though night was gathering fast, I ventured into the sodden road, beaten by big muddy waves. My horse was soon breast deep in the water, the force of the current threatening at every moment to sweep it off its legs. The poor beast was perfectly conscious of its danger, and reared whenever it felt the ground slipping away. Finally, the journey was accomplished without serious mishap, though it was completely dark when I got to the inn at Ukermünde, where the travellers from Wolgast and the host himself could scarcely believe their eyes.

I felt confident of having faithfully served Duke Barnim; I was, therefore, justified in my expectation of a princely remuneration. Heaven forbid that I should impute unfairness to this excellent gentleman, but part of the counsellors connected by birth with the people of Stolpe, were dissatisfied with the issue of the lawsuit, while others, such as Martin Weyer, had disgraced themselves by assisting Schwallenberg in his intrigues. In short, they discussed me so well that the prince only allowed me five and twenty florins as a gratification, while Duke Philip, whose business had not given me a hundredth part of the worry, presented me with five and twenty crowns. The court at Wolgast had waited to see what Stettin should do. Later on it employed me in a great many cases yielding large fees and spreading my name throughout the country. From Wolgast they sent me for my wedding a wild boar and four deer; at Stettin, the marshal told me that they intended to do likewise, but no one had paid any further attention to the matter.

On returning from Stettin night overtook me on the heath. It was infested with wolves, boars, and other dangerous animals; moreover, strange apparitions and terrible noises were often seen and heard there. I saw nothing; I heard nothing; and, besides, felt not in the least afraid.

I have already mentioned that the discussion with regard to the bishopric of Cammin had been brought before the Imperial Diet.[65] Canon Martin Weyer, the delegate of the chapter, was on most friendly terms with the Bishop of Arras; they had studied together at Bologna. In the course of their discussions on the subject, they put themselves this question: If the deposition of the bishop is to be persisted in, where can we find a candidate agreeable to the emperor, and not too antipathetic to the dukes of Pomerania? Thereupon his Grace of Arras conceived the idea of proposing Weyer himself. At first, the latter opposed the project altogether, objecting that he was not of the popish religion. His interlocutor assured him, however, that there was a means of arranging with the legate to obtain a dispensation. Briefly, when restored to favour, the dukes of Pomerania asked the emperor to accept as Bishop of Cammin Martin Weyer, their faithful subject, servitor and counsellor, and besides, a saintly man, almost an angel. He soon laid bare the bottom of his heart, *honores enim mutant mores et magistratus virum docet*. At the manifest instigation of the legate and of the Bishop of Arras, the new prelate sent his secretary to Rome to render homage to the pope, who afterwards granted the bulls *in optimâ formâ*.

I fancied the time had come for Martin Weyer largely to remunerate the services I had rendered him as his solicitor at the Imperial Chamber during two years, but to my written requests he answered with very bad grace when he answered at all. I must admit that having been for a twelvemonth or so Weyer's companion at Augsburg, and during the journey to the Low Countries, I did, perhaps, not treat him with sufficient ceremony according to his taste. I deemed it sufficient to address him as "Your Grace," without the "serenissime," and that vexed him. Besides, he failed to digest the defeat of Schwallenberg and his gang, not the least accessory to which he had been.

I have seen at the chancellerie of Wolgast a missive from Weyer to Duke Philip couched in the following terms: "From the authentic copy herewith of the papal bulls, your Grace" (he did not add "serenissime") "will perceive that his Holiness, yielding to his inclination for my person even more than to your Grace's recommendation, has entrusted me with the spiritual government of Cammin." The affair ended in a convocation of one day at Cammin, where Weyer was assisted by Dr. Tauber, of Wittenberg, invested with the title of chancellor. It was positively stated that he had promised him fifteen hundred golden florins. I went to the convocation with the delegates of Greifswald to try to drag something from the new bishop, and finally, Canon von Wolde succeeded in getting thirty crowns for me. I had therefore an opportunity of witnessing a sitting of the diet.

Two tables covered with black velvet cloths had been placed in the hall fifteen paces apart. At the one sat Duke Bogislaw, acting for himself and in the name of his brothers, at that time absent from the country. Standing before him were the Marshal Ulrich Schwerin, the Chancellor Citzewitz, and several counsellors and delegates of the States. The bishop occupied the other table, Tauber standing by his side; and in front the episcopal counsellors and the delegates of the chapter. Each party exposed at length the rights with which it was invested. Citzewitz having said, "The princes are lords of the chapter," Dr. Tauber replied, "Yes, *sed secundum quid*? His Grace," turning towards the bishop, "is in plenary possession of the right of administration of the chapter." Ulrich Schwerin, who was not well versed in letters, asked the meaning of *secundum quid*. "It's a term of contempt," said Citzewitz; "it's tantamount to saying that the dukes are princes like those on the playing cards." Schwerin's angry face was worth watching. "A plague upon the scoundrel for treating our princes like playing card personages." From that time Tauber was known throughout the land as the doctor *secundum quid*.

After a most lengthy disputation, each party presented its formula for the convocation of the bishop to the diets and sittings. That of the princes was as follows:

"To our venerable chief prelate, counsellor, dear and faithful Seignor Martin, Bishop of Cammin. Our greetings, dear, venerable and beloved! The welfare of our countries and of the common fatherland forbidding us from further delay in the convocation of a diet, we have decided to hold it on the ... in our city of Stettin, where we graciously request you to be present on the said day, to hear our intentions."

As for the bishop, his formula was indited somewhat differently:

"To the high and venerable in God, the Seignor Martin, Bishop of Cammin, our signal friend. Our friendly greeting, high and venerable in God, and signal friend. The welfare of our countries and of our common fatherland forbidding us from further delay in the convocation of a diet, we have decided to hold it on the ... in our city of Stettin, where we amicably request you to be present on the said day."

I never knew the issue of the debate, and took no trouble to find out, as at the conclusion of the first sitting I embraced an opportunity of returning home by carriage. I am disposed to think that the chapter had better remain under the authority of the House of Pomerania. Princely titles are best suited to born princes; people of mediocre condition do not know how to bear them. They carry their heads too high, and their would-be magnificence exceeds all bounds.

CHAPTER II

I trust my children may be enabled to read the following attentively and remember the same as my justification. They will learn that I devoted every moment to my work, and avoided all useless expense, that I kept away from the tavern, went but rarely to weddings or banquets, and only entertained guests when not to do so would have been unbecoming, as, for instance, on occasions of family feasts or of civic repasts. It is--thanks to that retired life, scarcely diversified by the rare indulgence of a favourite dish washed down by a copious libation--that I have been enabled to amass a sufficient competence to make the devil and his acolytes burst with envy. Their jealousy goes as far as to accuse me of having arrived very poor at Stralsund, and to have ransomed the city, magnified my travelling expenses, and abused the custody of the seals. This third part of the story of my life will explain the origin of my fortune. Stralsund has never been instrumental in making my position, and I have never proved false to my oath.

My monetary provision after my wedding consisted of Gottschalk's golden florin, hence, two florins of current coin; my savings and the gratifications were nothing more than a memory. I had nothing to expect from my father. We were in a bare and cold tenement we had rented; in default of a boiler my wife did the washing in an earthen jar. Without money and without a livelihood, I did not dare to ask my father-in-law for the promised two hundred florins, for he had warned me that it was my father's duty to begin paying up. I was obliged to listen to the humiliating words, "To get married without anything to live upon." My wife herself was getting fretful; a loaf of fine flour on our table set her grumbling as a luxury beyond our means. She said to her mother, "You did not advise me; you simply handed me over." A friend of her childhood, a burgomaster's daughter, had married a wealthy old man. Wallowing in luxury, the owner of two houses (I was his tenant), she overwhelmed us with jokes, and asked my wife what she intended to do with her swallow's tail, alluding to the sword I continued to wear.

What a deplorable beginning! God's help has, nevertheless, enabled me to provide during the space of forty-six years for my wants and those of my family. It was not a small affair, considering that the maintenance and starting in life of my children cost more than nine thousand florins, and my household, one year with another, three hundred florins. I, moreover, own a well appointed house, and am enabled to live *ex fructibus pecuniae salvo capitali*, and for the last forty-six years could truthfully say: "I am better off to-day than yesterday." And I have accomplished all this with my pen. Thanks be to the Lord.

The people of the city asked me to be their scribe. The richest grain merchant, a personage without merit save that of his money, dictated a long petition to me, intended for the sovereign. He was pleased with my editing and writing of it, and he asked me how much he owed me. As I did not care to accept any remuneration, he flung two schellings of Lubeck on the table, exclaiming, "Don't be an ass. Have you not got your paunch to fill?" From the lips of any one else this would have savoured of sarcasm, but that man meant no harm.

The public and private courses of the *artistae, philosophi et jurisperiti* of Greifswald could only be profitable to a scribe and notary; hence, I spent every available moment attending them. I hired a room in the priory building, and was there from morn till night, only going home to dine, and coming back immediately afterwards. My first clerk was the son of Master Peter Schwarz, but I could do nothing with him; then I took Martin Speckin, who by now is a rich young fellow. His Greifswald people brought him to me; part of his duty was to keep my room at the priory sufficiently heated, and to precede me with the lantern when I went out. He was a zealous servitor.

Meanwhile, I incurred everybody's criticism, and my wife showed her displeasure pretty openly. People, she said, thought it disgraceful for me to return to school once more. My maternal grandmother asked me if as yet I had not learnt to keep a family. The remarks did not affect me in the least. I continued attending the lectures of Joachim Moritz, and day by day it appeared to me I got a better understanding of the practice of law. My interest in useful literature also increased day by day. *Crescit amor studii quantum ipsa scientia crescit.* Not less true did the other proverb begin to appear: *Crescit amor nummi quantum ipsa pecunia crescit.* I also followed the public courses of Balthazar Rau, to-day Dr. Rau of the *Libellus de anima* of Philip Melanchthon. Nor was I ashamed to join his *discipuli privati*, to whom he expounded at his house the *Dialectica* of the same author. I felt very satisfied with myself for doing all this, and on February 19, 1552, the Imperial Chamber inscribed my name on the roll of its notaries, on the presentation of Duke Philip.

My eldest son saw the light on August 29 of the same year. The confinement was a most critical one, and through the midwife's blundering, he had a stiff neck for his life.[66] On September 1 he was christened, and received the name of Johannes. His two godfathers were the burgomasters Gaspard Bunsow and Peter Gruwel, and his great-grandmother stood as his godmother. My eldest daughter, Catherine, was born on December 6, 1553, and christened the next day.[67]

The wife of V. Prien, a daughter of the House of Maltzan, had taken possession of the fief of Schorsow, in virtue of the privilege accorded to noble damsels by the laws of Mecklenburg. When she died, and even before she was buried, the Maltzans of Mecklenburg violently invaded the fief. Joachim Maltzan, of Osten and of Nerung, who had helped his cousins by sending them reinforcements, was cited before the Imperial Chamber, in *poenam fractae pacis*. As he was most uneasy about the issue of the suit, Dr. B. vom Walde and Chancellor Citzewitz advised him to send me to Spires provided with counsel's opinion of Joachim Moritz. I complied with their wish, though the journey was exceedingly inconvenient to me. Joachim Maltzan provided me with two completely equipped horses, and the necessary funds; the chancellor and the doctor promised me a handsome gratification at my return. Instead of a servant, I took my brother Christian, and we started on the Sunday of Quasimodo (the Sunday after Easter). At Spires I fully instructed both procurator and advocate. The document drawn up by Moritz elicited their praise. They had no idea of the existence on the shores of the Baltic of a lawyer of that merit. They soon considered their client as being out of his difficulties, and, my mind at rest, I set out for my return journey to Pomerania.

I got there at Whitsuntide. When sending back the horses to Maltzan, I added my report, which put an end to his anxiety, and at the same time forwarded an account of my expenses day by day, the price of each meal, etc., leaving him to decide the amount of my honorarium. Well, the moment he felt reassured, Maltzan did not show the least inclination to settle with me; on the contrary, he accused me of having been too lavish. "Look at the fellow, and then consider the copious meals he took. May all the evils of Job befall thee." That was his favourite objurgation. In vain did I call to my aid the two counsellors who, as it were, had forced my hand. Maltzan turned a deaf ear to all my requests. At the beginning he would have given hundreds to get over his difficulties, but now he sang out, "I have broken the rope, and I do not care."

He was very rich, but very mean and coarse beyond description. One night at Wolgast, I saw him send his hose at bedtime to be repaired. When early next morning the tailor brought the garment back, he asked a florin for his work. Maltzan refused to give more than a schelling, and overwhelmed the poor wretch with curses. The latter had, however, to take what he could get. Maltzan, who could neither write nor read, was obliged to have a secretary, but in consequence of his avarice, he had to be content with mediocre individuals. Dr. Gentzkow found him one who was satisfied with earning his food and a small salary. After a couple of years, during which his master had dragged him about with him to Rostock and elsewhere, everybody knew him as Maltzan's servant. He knew all Maltzan's investments, as well as the dates of his revenues being due; it was he who stored away the money in linen bags. "Put a hundred crowns into each bag, and place them in a line," said Maltzan. "In that way, I can see at a glance where I am; ten bags make a thousand crowns." One fine morning the secretary stamped a blank sheet of paper with the seal of his employer, departed for Rostock, took on credit at the ordinary tradesman's as much velvet, satin and damask as he could conveniently carry away, filled in the blank sheet in his master's name, then returned and took from each bag only ten crowns in order to dissimulate his theft. After that he went collecting the outstanding debts, farmers' and tenants' rents, etc., and disappeared with a sum sufficient to remunerate a good secretary for a decade of years or more. Maltzan himself had the annoyance of having to make good the merchant's losses. He had never been married, and his property, amounting to a hundred thousand golden florins, fell to two cousins, who spent it in feasting, swilling, and riotous living. One died burdened with debt; the other is alive, but in a similar position. Ill-gotten goods do not last.

The only means of bringing Maltzan to book seemed to me to inform the Spires procurator of everything, and to ask him to write to Maltzan that he was going to lose his case in default of some documents that had remained in my possession. Duke Philip immediately recommended me to hand them over on the penalty of being held responsible for all the damages that might accrue. I promptly replied that I would bring them into court, where I should have the honour of presenting my respects to Signor Maltzan, and to claim at the same time the salary due to me. This had the effect of making the generous gentleman swear like a devil incarnate, to the vast joy and diversion of the prince and the counsellors, who took great pleasure in pouring oil upon the flames. Maltzan was obliged to count out to me there and then a hundred crowns, which was much more than I had originally asked, and he received, besides, a severe reprimand. My energy in the matter was fully acknowledged, and they added: "If ever we should ask you a similar service, you may refuse to render it without the fear of displeasing us."

The sacristan of Müggenwald committed homicide. The lord of the manor, who wished to get him out of the trouble, entrusted the case to me. A relative of the victim had retained Dr. Nicholas Gentzkow and Christian Smiterlow for the prosecution. I obtained a verdict for the accused.

Dr. Johannes Knipstrow having announced from the pulpit, in the name and by order of the prince, that Master J. Runge was going to succeed him in the office of superintendent, the Greifswald council considered the nomination as an infringement of its rights. Its *syndicus* at Stralsund, Dr. Gentzkow, formulated before me, a public notary convened for the purpose, both a verbal and written protest, of the latter of which I delivered a duly executed duplicate to the council of Greifswald, the legitimate charge for the same being three crowns.

Bartholomew, of Greifswald, a most intelligent, but also an exceedingly depraved goldsmith, had established himself at Stralsund with his son-in-law, Nicholas Schladenteuffel. As their expenditure exceeded their income, Bartholomew made counterfeit coin, Lubeck, Rostock, Wismar and Stralsund currency. The schellings supposed to issue from the latter city's mint contained nothing but copper. By means of some tartaric composition he made them look so wonderfully like silver as to deceive everybody. In a very short time both the city and the country were inundated with this spurious coin, for Nicholas made large purchases of cattle for the slaughter-houses. Finally, in September 1552, when the farmers and peasantry came to pay their rent, the suspicions of the ducal land-steward were aroused, and the fraud discovered. The witnesses' depositions pointing unanimously to a cattle-dealer of Stralsund, the prince wrote to the council, asking it if they struck money of that description. At that very time Schladenteuffel was going his business rounds. Warning was given, and one morning, when he came back to the city with some cattle, he was apprehended and taken to prison, where his wife and five accomplices promptly joined him. Among the latter there was one of the vicious sedition-mongers mentioned in the first part of my recollections, namely, Nicholas Knigge. He was, in reality, the leader of the gang; he furnished both the copper and the silver, and he found an outlet in Sweden for sham silver, spoons, goblets, jugs, etc. Dr. Gentzkow, whose daughter he had married, had his sentence changed to one of lifelong banishment. Bartholomew, although the people who came to arrest him were close upon his heels, managed to escape.

In the Semmlow Strasse there lived a very rich merchant named C. Middleburgh. His sordid avarice kept him away from church. On the other hand, he carried on an extensive and harmful traffic. He exported Bogislaw schillings and other good coin; he also got hold of gold and silver pieces, and clipped those that appeared to him to be overweight. In spite of this, he did not benefit by his wealth. One day he took the Rostock coach, but instead of coming down at midday to dine with the other travellers, he had a sleep. When the company returned and while the ostler put in the horses, he asked the price of the meal. He was told it was two schellings. "Very well," he said; "I have earned two schellings by going to sleep." He was always ready to lend money on silver plate--of course at high interest. He lived and scraped money for many, many years. His widow continued his trafficking; she was, however, less cautious, and fell into the hands of scoundrels, who reduced her to beggary.

To come back to Middelburg. On October 28, 1552, at two in the afternoon, he found himself in possession of a big cask containing twelve barrels of gunpowder of twenty-four pounds each; hence in all weighing two hundred and eighty-eight pounds. Close to the cask there sat a young servant weaving some kind of woollen lace, and, as it was very cold, she had a small stove filled with charcoal under her feet. At that moment there appeared upon the scene old Tacke and made a payment of a hundred Bogislaw schellings, which, having been carefully counted by Middelburg, were left on the table while he went to the stable for a moment. During his short absence, the servant stirs the incandescent charcoal, a spark of which falls on the floor and ignites the grains of powder; the house and the next to it are blown up; walls, beams, rafters come crashing down with a horrible noise. The city imagines that the end of the world has arrived. Of the young girl herself they found a foot here, an arm there, a leg elsewhere, and fragments of flesh pretty well everywhere. It was never known what had become of the hundred schellings that were lying on the table or of the furniture. One servant-girl was dug out from the ruins without a hurt; she was more fortunate than the brother-in-law of the burgomaster of Riga. They managed to drag him out by sawing some rafters beneath which he was buried, but he died of his wounds on the third day. Two children, though stark dead when picked up, still held a slice of bread and butter in their tiny hands. Three persons from the country, a mother and daughter and the latter's intended husband, who had stopped before the house to make some purchases for their new home, were killed outright on the spot. There were in all seven people killed. The neighbours brought an action against Middelburg which he had to settle. Even as far as the Passen-strasse my father had the window of his entrance hall broken; the stove in one of the upper rooms cracked and could never be used again; a hook used for hanging the salmon to be smoked, and belonging to Middelburg, was found in the gutter on our roof.

The advice of some well-meaning people, and ever growing necessity caused me to make up my mind to practise as procurator at the Aulic Court of Wolgast, though Counsellor Joachim Moritz, who boarded with my uncle, tried to dissuade me. As a professor of law at Greifswald, a jurisconsult of the court, and an assessor of the tribunal, he had had some close experience of the idiocy, the ignorance, and the underhand methods of my future colleagues. "*Procuratorum officium vilissimum est,*" he said to me. In fact, with the exception of Dr. Picht, the procurators were but little versed *in grammaticâ vel jure*. When their dean, who was a judge at Brandenburg, and a Mecklenburg counsellor, came up for his degree of *licenctiâ juris* at Rostock, he referred to an insolvent litigant, "*Non est solvendus,*" which provoked the repartee of the promoter: "*Recte dicit dominus licentiandus, quia non est ligatus.*"

One day at Rostock we happened to take our dinner at the same table with this procurator and the burgomaster of Brandenburg who, however, was fairly well versed in the *grammatica*. The conversation turned on a witch who was in prison at Brandenburg, and who professed to be pregnant by the devil. The burgomaster having put the question, "*Quod diabolus cum muliere rem habere et impregnare eam posset?*" Our licentiate replied without wincing: "*Imo possibile est, nam diabolus furat semen a viribus et perfert ad mulieribus.*"

Simon Telchow, another procurator, for a long while master auditor at Eldenow, and who was married to a damsel of noble birth, after having set up as a brewer at Greifswald, had "to shut up" shop and come back to his pen. Having contracted at court a taste for drink, he never went to bed without being "muddled." As a matter of course, he was not very matutinal. He, moreover, only practised *pro nudo procuratore*, and his clients had to provide themselves with an advocate. *In causis mandatorum*, when the *mandatarii* eluded execution, Telchow asked for an *arctiorem mandatum*. Sworn procurators there were none in those days, and as the procedure in general was oral, any one endowed with the "gift of the gab" could present himself at the bar. Since then things have changed to the glory of the prince and the advantage of litigants.

The experience I had gained at Spires was most useful to me in my new career. The judges, the chancellor, and the litigants themselves seemed to listen to me with pleasure; nay, this or that party who had not entrusted me with his cause, made me, nevertheless, accept his money, because he wished to retain my services, if the occasion required, or, at any rate, deprive his opponent of them. People came to fetch me from the country with chariot and horses to mediate between them. I was brought back in the same manner, and each time, besides the hard cash I received, I was laden with all kinds of provisions, hares, shoulders of mutton, haunches of venison or of wild boar, magnificent hams, quarters of bacon, butter, cheese, and eggs by the dozen, bundles upon bundles of flax. My reception at home may be easily imagined. There was no longer any risk of hearing the sad complaint, "Mother, you did not advise me; you simply handed me over."

Peter Thun, of Schleminn, a violent-tempered man, and but too prompt to fire a shot or to draw the sword, was at constant loggerheads with his neighbour Ber. They were joint owners of a nice pond. Ber claimed the exclusive enjoyment of the half adjoining his estate, and which also happened to be the better stocked with fish. Thun, on the other hand, maintained that the whole of the pond was joint property. Ber having planted hemp along the common road, Thun sent his cattle to graze there, and went himself on horseback so that his mount might trample the plant down. Finally, a lot of peasants went under the personal command of Thun to Ber's windmill, and promptly sapped its foundations, so that it came down with a crash. Naturally, the law is set in motion. Thun is condemned to indemnify Ber *constrictibus*; then comes an appeal to the Imperial Chamber, which upholds the first verdict with *executoriales cum refusione expensarum*; the total amounting to about nine hundred florins.

Puffed up with his success and purse-proud besides, Ber applauded each scurvy trick his people played his enemy. Thun, on the other hand, was not a man to be played with. One of Ber's servants (in fact, his illegitimate son, a young, brazen and robust fellow), finally assailed Thun. The latter stood his ground valiantly, but his affrighted wife seized his arm; the bastard's sword went right through him. Thun's only heir was his nephew, a minor, the succession was most involved, and its liquidation cost me a great deal of trouble and a number of fatiguing journeys. My honorarium was fixed at twenty florins per annum. I only took ten from the minor, because I never returned from Schleminn empty-handed. Later on, his guardians made it up to me in presents of money and in kind; they provided for my building operations splendid oaks, which made magnificent joists. In sum, this affair yielded a good three hundred crowns to me.

H. Smeker, of Wüstenfeld, was a character who ruined himself in litigation and in building. He left this or that structure which was ready to be roofed in to be spoilt by the rain or the snow, after which he had it completely razed to the ground. A Mecklenburger named Negendanck was, it would appear, one of his important creditors. To get his claim settled he employed a means rather common in his country. One night he arrived at Wüstenfeld at the head of a troop of armed horsemen. Smeker was asleep in his room, and his wife, who had just been brought to bed, lay in an adjoining closet. Lievetzow, her brother, a handsome young fellow, had been accommodated with a room near the drawbridge. Negendanck, swearing and bellowing, orders the bridge to be lowered. Lievetzow, in his shirt, issues from his room and tries to appease him by informing him of the condition of his sister. Negendanck replies with a shot which kills the defenceless and scantily-dressed stripling on the spot. Then, taking the passage by storm, he gets as far as the invalid's room, lays his hand upon everything, shatters the silver chest, which he knew where to find, takes whatever he likes, and finally drags the body of her brother to the foot of the sister's bed. Smeker, who had been awakened by the noise, had taken flight in his nightgown. Knowing the moat to be fordable, he had crossed it with the water shoulders high, and after making for the stables, had taken refuge in a kind of bog inaccessible to the horsemen. Negendanck took all the horses and cattle away with him.

Naturally, the Imperial Chamber was finally called upon to try the affair. A rule having been granted to prove his allegations, Smeker came to Greifswald to enlist my services. He was an old man with a grey head and short beard; a fluffy white gown with large pleats and black girdle reached to his feet. In short, the feathers pretty well indicated the nature of the bird. I had so often heard them call out at Spires, "Smoker *contra* Negendanck," "the Duke Heindrich of Mecklenburg *contra* Heindrich Smoker," as to make the name familiar to me. To my question if he was the identical Smoker, he replied in a surly tone, "My name is Smeker, not Smoker."

He produced a host of witnesses, many of whom lived in outlying regions of Pomerania or Mecklenburg; their hearing involved constant travelling. Smeker would have never got out of the difficulty by himself, in consequence of his want of ready money. The moment he found himself in possession of some, he got hold of the horse of one of his peasantry as if to ride to the nearest village, and never drew rein until he got to Spires. If, during his journey, the money ran short, he borrowed from people who all knew him and were sure of being repaid by his son Mathias. Not only did he pay nothing to his procurator, Dr. Schwartzenberg, but the latter had to feed him, to advance the chancellery fees, and to look to his return journey. Mathias, on the other hand, was most open-handed. His secretary, who came to Greifswald in order to watch the proceedings, lavished claret wine and tarts on the commissaries, and even sent some to my wife. Each session was worth from between fifty to seventy crowns to me. That secretary appreciated my trouble like a true expert. Said inquiry brought me about two hundred and fifty crowns.

On the occasion of a suit before the Imperial Chamber, and in which little Heindrich gained the day against big Heindrich--that was the designation of Smeker respectively of himself and his adversary--the Duke of Mecklenburg, the latter carried off all Smeker's sheep. Among the flock there was an old ram, accustomed to get a bit of bread at meal times from his master's hands. The animals either escaped, or perhaps the duke had them driven back to Wüstenfeld. At any rate, the ram appeared at the head of the flock, its appetite sharpened by the march, and, moreover, fond of bread, ran towards the table. No sooner did Smiterlow catch sight of it than he got up, doffed his hat, and bade it welcome. "What an agreeable surprise!" he exclaimed. "*Bene veneritis!* The soup of princes is not to thy taste, it appears, inasmuch as thou comest back already." But Smeker caught at the chance of another lawsuit at Spires which brought me twenty crowns.

His son and his son-in-law, who did their best to save the considerable paternal fortune, hit upon the idea to credit the suzerain, Duke Heindrich, with the intention of retiring the fiefs. Starting from that gratuitous supposition, they pointed out to the old man that the journeys to Spires became more and more difficult to him; that, moreover, he incurred the risk of being dispossessed, and that, in such a case, his son would have the greatest possible trouble to be reinstated. What, on the other hand, could be more simple than the averting of the blow by a pretended renunciation in favour of Mathias? He, the father, would take up his quarters for some time in a house close by, which he liked very much; he should always come and take his meals with his sons, or merely eat and drink there when he liked; they would give him a young, nice and bright peasant girl to take care of him, for in spite of his age he refused to dispense with female company. Heindrich Smeker, having been prevailed upon, signed an act duly engrossed on vellum, which the principal county gentlemen of Mecklenburg attested with their seals, and to which Duke Heindrich promptly affixed his ratification.

When the old man's eyes opened to the deception it was too late. He was furious, and accused his son of having enacted the traitor to him, calling him all kind of names. Then he begged of me to bring the affair before the Imperial Chamber, but I had an excellent excuse for refusing, as I was only a notary. His robust constitution enabled him to make another journey to Spires--on a cart-horse as usual. Having been politely bowed out by Dr. Schwartzenberg, he simply wasted his breath with the other procurators--all of whom knew him. Finally, Schwartzenberg gave him the money to go home. Like a dutiful son, Mathias loyally kept his promise and showed his father every attention and consideration. He invited his father to his table or had his meals taken to him. He sent him beer and wine, and there was always a capital bed at his disposal when the fancy took him to lay at his former domicile. It was the sweetest existence imaginable, but the administration of his property was denied to him.

The worshipful council of Rostock having been cited before the Imperial Chamber by the kindred of an individual named Von der Lühe, who had been beheaded for highway robbery, the commissaries entrusted with the case took me as their notary in the inquiry made at Rostock, and as delegate notary in the inquiry set on foot by the plaintiffs. The *attestationes* and the *sententia definitiva* conclusively proved my assiduity in the matter; hence my honorarium amounted to four hundred crowns, *plus* a present in silver worth fifty crowns.

The counsellor Anthony Drache, a most pious gentleman, had only one brother who was drowned and left no issue. Drache pretended to reduce the widow's share, in accordance with the feudal laws of Pomerania; but besides his fiefs or hereditary tenures of land, the deceased possessed considerable property, the dividing of which was to be effected according to the urban or local statutes. Duke Philip, of blessed memory, having carried the affair into court, the trustee of the widow confided the case to me. I worked it up very conscientiously, assisted as I was by my particular studies, by the courses I had followed of Joachim Moritz and other professors at Greifswald, and finally by my private consultations with Moritz, who was good enough to give me his directions *in specie*. I had a verdict on all counts, though Dr. Gentzkow was on the other side, which, moreover, could count on the sympathy of the judges and even of the prince. This success had the effect of spreading my name throughout the land, and it prompted Dr. Gentzkow to propose my appointment as secretary to the council of Stralsund. My client gave me twenty crowns, a quantity of butter and a flitch of bacon.

Chancellor Citzewitz took me with him to Stettin, and afterwards to Stargardt to assist him in a personal lawsuit. There was no question of honorarium, for we were both of opinion that his kindness to me warranted such gratuitous service.

In 1553 the Owstin family had a lengthy lawsuit with reference to a village which Citzewitz finally took away from them. In my capacity of notary to the Owstins, I received forty crowns for my work. When Valentin von Eichstadt, the new chancellor, married his daughter to an Owstin, he bore his predecessor a grudge for his success in the matter. Meanwhile, the grand marshal of the court of Wolgast, Ulrich Schwerin, became involved in litigation with Dr. B. vom Walde; the latter and Citzewitz took sides against Schwerin and Eichstadt, and each tried to harm the other as much as possible. Duke Ernest Louis intervened. The report of his displeasure was maliciously exaggerated. In a fit of despair Citzewitz stabbed himself to death.

J. vom Kalen, at that time high bailiff of Rügen (although he could neither read nor write), had sentenced an individual for having caught a small fish in the stream flowing past his garden. The angler appealed against the sentence, probably at the instigation of expert people, wishing to do the bailiff a good turn. The latter had entrusted the affair to me, merely saying that when I got to Wolgast I should get to know what it was "all about"; but when I presented myself and obtained communication of the documents, I declined to move in the matter. I nevertheless considered myself entitled to the three crowns I had received as a deposit; besides, they were not claimed.

The city of Pasewalk had to stand the brunt of a man named Fürstenberg, who, because matters did not always proceed according to his wishes, had renounced his citizenship. Not satisfied with that, he one night nailed to the post before the city gates a placard threatening to set fire to the place. He was almost as good as his word, for he set fire to several barns outside the walls. He was arrested at Lebus, and confined in the tower of the castle. The duke chose me to assist the two counsellors entrusted with the prosecution by the authorities of Pasewalk. The prisoner was put to the rack in our presence, judged the next day, and beheaded by the sword. To our great surprise the council allowed us to depart without offering the smallest present. On the other hand, the duke sent to my home two measures of rye, worth at that time about ten florins.

Holste, the governor of the convent of Puddegla, an eccentric and even dangerous young man, came to Greifswald to entrust me with his law affairs. He promised to remunerate me largely, and as an earnest gave me ten crowns. Shortly afterwards he had a difference with the duke, who had him confined to his quarters, but I succeeded in settling the affair to the satisfaction of both. My client was short of money for the time being, but the convent of Puddegla is situated on the banks of a beautiful lake teeming with fish (as a rule monks are not in the habit of choosing the worst spots). There was an abundance of enormous cray-fish, of various kinds of perch, of breams an ell long, of fat eels, of carp as black as soot and having only one eye, the fat and flesh having closed the other; they were indeed fit for a king's table. Holste filled my conveyance with victuals of that description, and I was glad to cry quits with him for some time to come.

It was well I felt so disposed, for in a short time he got another affair on his hands. At first he thought that the advice of his maternal uncle George vom Kalen, and three captains from Rügen would be sufficient to settle matters, and as a matter of course he invited them to his small property at Wusterhausen, where he filled them with food and drink night and day. It was all in vain; their brain refused to suggest a way out of the difficulty except that he should send for me, which recommendation he followed. I drew up a humble petition to the duke. As I intended to leave early the next morning, Holste gave me six crowns, for the liquor that was in him already rendered him more generous than usual and than there was any occasion, considering the state of his revenues.

The gentlemen caroused till deep into the night, for long after I had retired I was awakened by George vom Kalen steadying himself by grasping my pillow. He came to propose to me to transact his law business for the future. As I was by no means anxious for that practice, I declined, though in most guarded terms. Notwithstanding this refusal, my interlocutor drew three crowns from his wallet, and slipped them into my purse, which he took from under my pillow. His two companions follow his example, and present me each with two crowns. In vain do I point out to them that I cannot accept what I have not earned, and I take the seven coins from my purse to hand them back. Thereupon George vom Kalen tells me plainly that if I persist in refusing this money, he will flay me alive as I am lying there. Knowing the people with whom I had to deal, I deemed it more prudent to listen no longer to my scruples. The company resumed their drinking, and by the time I was back at Greifswald with my thirteen crowns in my pocket, they were probably still snoring stretched under the table.

A small farmer had got his step-daughter with child. When the truth leaked out, the girl's mother moved heaven and earth to shield her husband from the death penalty by flight. As for her daughter, her only child, to fling her upon the world in that condition was exposing her to disgrace, to starvation, and perhaps to everlasting punishment. At the request of some friends, I personally went to Wolgast and presented a petition to be handed immediately to the prince. After considerable waiting, I saw him come out of his apartment. "Why does this woman speak of her daughter and not of her husband?" he asked. "Because he has taken flight," I answered; "besides, considering the heinousness of the crime, she is afraid that to mention him will not avail much." "You lawyers," retorted his Highness, "you have a way of presenting things, of polishing and whitening the most atrocious and blackest horrors. It really requires some experience to determine whether your petitions are compatible either with law, equity, or religion. I am bound to remember that God has entrusted me with the punishment of gross and impious excesses. I shall not decide upon this case to-day, but think it over." These are the words of a just, but nevertheless merciful prince, and the petitioner had the proof of it.

Michael Hovisch, the son of poor peasants, had been brought up from his earliest years in town, put to school, and then into a business establishment. He succeeded in gaining the confidence of his employers, who sent him to Sweden and Denmark. Gradually he began to operate on his own account. Modest in behaviour, neat, and even elegant in appearance, he could aspire to a good match. Meanwhile Captain Dechow took it into his head to claim him for gratuitous and enforced seignorial labour. An old ducal farm had to be rebuilt. In vain did Hovisch offer a considerable sum instead.

Dechow resolved to constrain him by imprisonment. He was a relentless despot, who tried to make himself conspicuous by oppressing the peasantry and, wherever it could be done, also the urban populations. Hovisch was compelled to take flight. At the request of some personages whom I was anxious to oblige, and being moreover strongly interested in the young fellow himself, I personally presented to Duke Philip a petition in which the vexatious proceedings of the captain were set forth at length. I defy people to guess the prince's reply. Here it is: "That my subjects load thee with butter, eggs, cheese, poultry, geese, sheep and the rest, is all very well, nay, perfect in its way," he said. "Take my word for it, though," he went on, "that I can manage to govern them rightly enough with the assistance of my captain without your meddling." I told Citzewitz plainly that if the oppressed were thus deprived of their right of humble petition there was "no saying" how things would end. "Dechow," remarked Citzewitz, "is an arbitrary, hasty brute, but he has managed to ingratiate himself with the duke. Fortunately, his Highness has been warned. I'll recur to the subject when I get an opportunity; there must be a change." Dechow left Wolgast for Lubeck, where the people soon got tired of him. Michael Hovisch was never again heard of. It was the last time I took it into my head to present a petition, and especially to wait for its answer.

To sum up, in the space of two years, the occupation of procurator, and, above all, of notary, brought me eleven hundred and four and twenty crowns in hard cash.

Magister J. Schoenefeld acted as notary in four cases before the court presided over by Dr. von Walde. Duke Philip was the plaintiff. As it happened, Schoenefeld was too old to proceed energetically; the going from "pillar to post" frightened him; besides, people had become more exacting. He therefore decided upon handing his documents over to me, and they contained several interesting items. The prince, for instance, summoned Lutke Maltzan to prove his right to the fiefs of Sarow, Gantzkendorf, and Carin. Maltzan declined, pleading prescription in virtue of thirty years' possession. The fiefs in question had belonged to Jacob Voss, nephew and ward of Berendt Maltzan, surnamed "the Bad." (Berckmann and other historians amply explain the reasons for the sobriquet.) The uncle having advanced two hundred or three hundred florins on the lands of his nephew, persuaded the latter to go to the war with a couple or so of horses. He made sure of never beholding him again. Jacob Voss, a model of honour and courage, distinguished himself in many a campaign, and the esteem in which he was held by all enabled him to borrow the necessary sum to redeem the paternal property. He gave notice to Berendt Maltzan of his intention to refund the money at the new year, and at the appointed time he arrived at his uncle's--a fortified domicile, most appropriate to his brigandage, rapine and exactions. For several days Maltzan loaded him with kindness, they drank together, played cards and diced; in short, honest Jacob Voss, instead of redeeming his lands, lost the borrowed money.

His despair and his thirst for vengeance prompted him to extreme measures, and with a servant expressly engaged for the purpose, he several times set fire to his former possessions. Thereupon his uncle enjoined his tenants to proceed to his nephew's capture. One Sunday Voss and his companion having fallen asleep in the wood near Gantzkendorf, which they intended to burn down that night, were discovered by a little dog of some peasants gathering nuts; and not later than the Monday following Berendt Maltzan had the son of his sister "racked" alive. During the journey Jacob Voss apostrophized the tenants at labour by their names. "Johannes, Peter, Nicholas," he exclaimed, "can you understand this horrible and ignominious death for claiming my own property?"

To come back to the suit of the prince against Maltzan. The judge sent the document to the faculty of law at Leipzig, which asked an honorarium of forty crowns. Its decision, the seal of which was broken in the presence of the parties as represented by their counsel and read there and then, concluded in favour of Maltzan, to the great vexation of the ducal advisers, Chancellor Citzewitz severely reprimanding Dr. von Walde for not having opened the reply in order to amend it. An appeal was entered at the Imperial Chamber, and the case only ended several years after my establishment at Stralsund. The parties paid me more than one thousand crowns.

Towards 1542 a Dane said to Christopher von der Lanckin, of Rügen, that the willow bow-nets for the catching of fish in the Danish fashion would be more profitable to him than two big houses he had at Stralsund. In fact from the time two of those contrivances arrived, Christopher, who had been very hampered in money matters, settled his debts very quickly. Struck with the result, two notable burghers of Stralsund, namely councillor Conrad Oseborn and Olof Lorbeer, the son of the burgomaster, went into partnership with some of their kindred, and promptly exploited the invention. The new nets, though, in consequence of their size, obstructed the entrance to the streams; the fish no longer passed, and it meant ruin to the inhabitants of the interior. There were protests on all sides. Duke Philip wrote to Stralsund; the council replied ironically that fish not being taken by hand, everybody was free to ply for it as he liked. An inquiry was set on foot, the prince prohibited the big bow-nets, and had those belonging to Lorbeer seized. Thereupon the whole gang began to shout that the liberties of the city were in peril, a galley was fitted out to guard the nets, and finally, Stralsund resorted to law.

If, in taking the succession of Schoenefeld, I had suspected my countrymen of being so unreasonable as they were in this instance, I should certainly have declined the brief, albeit that my presence counterbalanced the hostility of the inquiring magistrate. In his examination C. von der Lanckin stated loyally that from his point of view, the Danish bow-nets were excellent, inasmuch as they had enabled him to pay his debts, but that on his faith and honour of a gentleman the new contrivance would ruin the country. The deposition of the fishermen was very clear: "Whosoever will rid us of those nets will no longer need to go to church or to say Paters. We ask for nothing else from heaven from morn till night."

In spite of everything, Stralsund persisted in its wrong. Finally, on the opinion of counsel and the verdict of September 28, 1554, the duke gained his cause, and the city was condemned in costs. On the spur of the moment the council wanted to lodge an appeal, but it thought the better of it. The suit had lasted twelve years, and had bred between the two parties a feeling of misunderstanding which only vanished with the death of the prince. As there had been two hundred and fifty witnesses, the six hundred crowns I received in fees was, I take it, not an excessive remuneration.

CHAPTER III

The Greifswald magistrates, who had the opportunity of seeing me daily at work, gradually arrived at the conclusion that I could not be altogether devoid of merit, considering that highly placed personages and even the prince himself entrusted me with important affairs. Schoenefeld, being no longer up to the standard required, they offered me his charge on the condition of my completely relinquishing my practice as procurator. In consequence of this, on December 29, 1554, I was appointed secretary to the city of Greifswald.

The first burgomaster of Stralsund, Christopher Lorbeer, had two sons, who spent their time in the chase, in the taverns, and at the brilliant receptions of the nobility and of the opulent burgher class. They took it for granted that they might do anything they liked, and operated with dogs and nets on Greifswald territory. It so happened, though, that several young nobles and rich burghers of the latter town had excellent packs of hounds, and were, in consequence, often invited by the prince. As a matter of course, they objected to this poaching on the part of the Lorbeers. One day the two parties came face to face, and the attitude of the Greifswald people caused the others to face about and to abandon their nets. As a balm to their wounded pride, the Lorbeers, lying in ambush at the inn at Testenhagen, assailed pistol in hand a carter from Greifswald, maltreated him, and finally carried off his best horse. The Greifswald council wrote to Stralsund in the most measured terms, as ought to be done among neighbours. The reply was supercilious, and couched in most intemperate terms. I was, therefore, instructed to draw up an appeal to the duke. The moment was unquestionably exceedingly well chosen, considering the behaviour of Stralsund in the matter of the bow-nets. And although the reports of that lawsuit were as yet not published, I was familiar with them, and had no difficulty in conceiving the irritation of the prince against the Lorbeers. I nevertheless disadvised having recourse to his intervention; I deemed it more prudent to go to Stralsund and discuss the matter.

The moment I had presented my credentials the Stralsund council met in solemn assembly. One of them received me most graciously, and introduced me. Burgomaster Lorbeer's polite anxiety to make room for me on the bench of the council showed to me his secret hope of seeing me betray the interests of my clients, and of metaphorically falling at his feet. After the usual civilities, I pointed out to the meeting the seriousness of the case, going fully into the facts in a firm and perhaps somewhat plain language, reminding them of the Imperial "orders" with regard to the preservation of the public peace. Nor did I scruple to represent, as a good neighbour ought to have done, the danger of obstinacy, above all with a prince who was already more or less displeased.

I could read the exoneration for this bold speech on many a countenance, but Christopher Lorbeer and his staunch adherents, who were not accustomed to hear the truth to their faces, turned colour; their hitherto affable looks changed into scowls, and the burgomaster, beside himself with anger, rose and said: "Thou art too eager to break thy first lance. I beg to submit that this man be strictly watched." "And clapped into gaol if necessary," I retorted. Thereupon Lorbeer walked out, and I was dismissed without being reconducted as I had been introduced. In a little while, word was sent that the affair requiring further examination, the answer would be communicated later on. A couple of hours afterwards Dr. Gentzkow, the syndic, sent for me to come to the St. Nicholas' Church. "I am obliged to admit," he said, "that your language was justified in law as in fact, but Master Christopher has taken mortal offence at it, inasmuch as he is not accustomed to have people adopt this tone with him, or to hear himself and his sons taxed with disturbing the public peace. He can do you a great deal of good or a great deal of harm. His influence, both in the city and in the country, is immense. In short, if the council have rightly interpreted your message, the Greifswald folk desire to terminate this affair in a friendly manner; very well, let us appoint a day at Reinberg to arrange matters as good neighbours should. I am asking you for your best endeavours to bring this about."

The Stralsund people made their preparations for the day in question by slaughtering a great many birds and game, by roasting and boiling the same, and by broaching casks upon casks of beer and wine. Besides the principal burghers of the city related to them by blood and in thorough sympathy, the Lorbeers invited their friends from the neighbourhood, and their young boon companions, who appeared armed with pistols, arquebuses and spikes, so that the gathering looked more like a call to arms than like a friendly meeting. Consequently, some of the councillors and citizens of Stralsund secretly warned the people of Greifswald to send no one to the spot, and my father was particularly cautioned not to let me go, for that I should surely be killed. The Greifswald magistrates remained coy, and did not reply a word to the invitation; then, at the very hour of the invasion of Reinberg by the Lorbeer band, they wrote that if the horse were returned to them in three days they would return the nets sequestrated in just reprisal. If this were not done, the prince would be requested to dispense justice. At the news of Greifswald's abstention from the quasi-festivities the Lorbeer camp broke into an avalanche of imprecations and threats. Wound up with drink, they swore that they would murder everybody. Nevertheless, before the three days had expired, a stable-man brought back the horse, receiving in return the nets; and so there was an end of that disagreement.

There was a time when "milord" burgomaster Christopher Lorbeer did pretty well as he liked with everybody without meeting with any resistance, and as a matter of course, his wife and children followed suit. Odd to relate, my mission was coincident with the heyday of his fortune, and it was really owing to a few simple words from my lips that his star suddenly waned. He did not mind being treated as ungodly, and as a soul likely to incur eternal punishment, and when I say this I am speaking on the authority of his eldest son, but he objected to being accused of endangering the public peace, or, in other words, to forfeiting his honour; it is that which put him beside himself. His annoyance at having failed in his contemplated revenge against Greifswald and against me seriously undermined his health. A most painful illness confined him to his bed for six months, during which no one was allowed to see him. It seemed a terrible retribution which profoundly moved both the city and the country. The burgomaster's victims raised their voices, and the exactions by which he had hitherto kept up his grand style of living were at an end. When his wife attempted to revictual the establishment as of old, she met with refusals. A grain dealer to whom she had sent her pigs to fatten brought them back to her, pretending "hard times." She was beginning to "ride the high horse" with him, but he pointed to the room of the burgomaster, saying: "Don't forget that 'I command you' is lying there." After a protracted agony, which practically reduced him to the condition of a mere animal, Christopher Lorbeer died on October 16, 1555, and was buried in the choir of the St. Nicholas' Church, by the side of my mother and my two sisters, and under the same flagstone where my father subsequently lay. The council, greatly affected by his death, let three weeks pass before naming a successor to the deceased; after which the syndic, N. Gentzkow, and the first secretary, Anthony Lickow, were solemnly and joyously elected to the dignity.

Though as yet my emoluments were not fixed, the Greifswald council had already given me several proofs of its high confidence. At Stralsund, on the other hand, I was the constant butt of the violent enmity of the most notable citizens, who would have rent me to pieces if they had got hold of me. Stralsund being thus closed to me, no place was more suitable as a residence than Greifswald, where I was born and had many of my kindred. But the owner of the house I rented made me very uncomfortable with his mania for transforming the dwelling into a storehouse for the most lumbering material, such as wood, stone, mortar, sand, etc.; he also used the place for the weddings of his servants, without the least regard for my wife, whether she was sick or in childbed. All our objections were met with the same answer: "If you do not like it you had better move." Hence, I finally made the acquisition of a house in the Fischhandler Strasse (Fishmonger Street), belonging to Johannes Velschow, the father-in-law of Brand Hartmann. Its price was three hundred and fifty florins, payable in four quarterly instalments. Brand Hartmann was the son of that George Hartmann with whom my father had had such grave differences. He felt very wroth at seeing the house his father had built for his use pass into my possession, but the sale was effected in due legal form. I had given the deposit (God's pfenning) and put down the first hundred florins in the presence of several councillors and notable burghers.

Masons and carpenters were set to work at once. The front door had to be widened, the heavy roof to be strengthened, the rooms, stables, cellar and yard to be overhauled. My father had had a great deal of building done in his days and gained much experience. He came to superintend matters. Now and again he somewhat bullied the workmen, and even dismissed them, replacing them by others. Looking back on all this, I cannot help wondering at my audacity, for my purse was practically empty, and the workmen had to be paid on Saturdays. With God's help my practice provided the necessary money every week. My profession took me away from home a great deal; hence, there was some delay in the building operations, but for every florin I lost in that way, I earned ten and more elsewhere.

On September 25, 1555, Duke Philip, with a numerous suite stopped at Stralsund for the night and was entertained by the council. He was going to Bergen, in the island of Rügen, where he stayed until October 11, and at his return he lay once more at Stralsund, equally at the expense of the city. The aim of the journey was to check the encroachments of the Jasmund nobility, which, not content with cutting down the forest of Stubenitz for its own benefit, conceded the same rights to others--for a consideration. The prince took me with him as secretary. The aristocracy having proposed a friendly settlement, there was much parleying, during which the duke was at a loss to kill time. He was lodged in the apartments of the prior at the monastery of Bergen, and which looked out upon the courtyard, and spent hours in watching from his windows the pages and valets and their constant bickerings, quarrels and fights. He could even hear their opinions of him. One day, when standing in his usual coign of vantage while four Polish violins performed several pieces of music in the room itself, he heard a valet below saying to his fellow, "The people of Stralsund have much better musicians than their prince. What he has got is simply ridiculous. Duke Bogislaw keeps four trumpeters and a kettledrum player; they, at any rate, produce some effect. But this prince up there, with his caterwauling things, is absurd." The duke sent Prior Gottschalck to ascertain who was talking in that strain, but Gottschalck, having noticed a relative of his in the group, made them a sign to be off, and went upstairs, saying that they had been too quick for him, and that he had failed to recognize any one. The prince promptly repeated to his familiars word for word what he had heard on the art of keeping up his rank, and long afterwards he was fond of reminding them of the incident.

Another anecdote: A lot of boys were noisily playing in the courtyard, and one of the most turbulent was the illegitimate son of the bailiff (his real father having sent him to school, though he bore the name of his putative parent, Arndts, the tailor of Bergen). His Highness having given order to drive the yelling beggars away and to box their ears if necessary, the footmen executed his orders to the letter, right and left. The prince noticed, though, that they spared Arndts, and he shouted that he more than any of the others deserved correction, but the servant to whom the recommendation was addressed simply smiled and shrugged his shoulders. "Do you hear me?" cried the duke; "rub it into the little devil." "Oh, no," replied the flunkey. "Oh, yes, lay it on thickly." "Nay, nay; heaven preserve me from doing such a thing." "And why, what's to prevent you?" "What? to trounce the son of a bailiff! I should repent it afterwards." At these words the duke burst out laughing. He told the story to every one, even in the bailiff's presence. On one occasion the boy was sent for and placed by the side of his father. His eyes, his nose, his head and his legs were compared with those of his sire. The governor of Cammin, after having made the lad march up and down the room, said to the bailiff, "That's your son, right enough; he is shaped like you."

The attempt at conciliation having failed, the parties met at the monastery in a large room provided with chairs, seats and two tables, one for his Highness, the other for the *pares curiae*. I took place at the latter in my capacity of *notarius judicii*. The chancellor, in his master's name, gave a summary of the facts, after which, the prince, rising from his seat, came to the second table, and there, facing me, he made a long speech, not at all badly composed. I only give its conclusion: "In your presence, Master Notary, I maintain having been animated by most friendly intentions towards my subjects, but they rejected all attempts at settling matters. In consequence of this, and as a guarantee of my rights, I command you to state everything that has happened, including the present declaration, and to draw up a duly attested act which you shall remit to me in consideration of your lawful remuneration." The matter did not go farther that day, but the duke instructed me to pursue the inquiry jointly with the Governor of Cammin, which took us several days.

The "instrument" gave me a great deal of trouble, filling, as it did, seven of the largest skins of parchment, constituting fourteen sheets. It contained more matter than a quire of paper. There was no room to affix my signature and the *signum notariatus* at the end of the deed, according to custom, so I made an impression in wax of my seal engraved on lead, and suspended it from the string holding the sheets together. His Highness, without asking, gave me a fee of thirty crowns.

Magister Joachim Moritz, *professor juris* at Greifswald and ducal counsellor, had never been to Stralsund, and knew nobody there. At my return from Bergen he asked me to "put him up" at my father's, which I was very glad to do. Having risen early to see the city, he went shortly after seven into St. Nicholas' to hear the sermon. Zabel Lorbeer, who caught sight of him, mistook him for his former boon companion, George Steinkeller. The likeness between these two seems to have been so striking as to have deceived people generally. Many a gentleman upon beholding Moritz on the bench at Wolgast, said to his neighbour, "And where the devil did Steinkeller get his knowledge of the law from, to constitute him a judge?" Lorbeer, then, coming from behind, takes Moritz by the ears and shakes him for full a minute, the professor, altogether nonplussed, asking himself all the while who it could be giving him such an energetic welcome. He made sure it was me. Finally, he managed to turn round, and Lorbeer, perceiving his mistake, was most profuse with apologies. Moritz was fond of relating the adventure, especially in the hearing of the Stralsunders, and no one enjoyed the story more than the duke.

The Stralsund council took the opportunity of my visit (which happened during the very week of Burgomaster Lorbeer's funeral), to offer me the position of secretary. My surprise may easily be imagined. I considered myself so compromised in the eyes of the Stralsunders that, without the company of the governor of Cammin and the commission I held of the prince, I should not have deemed myself safe in the city. Those overtures, though, caused me as much pleasure as they did to my kindred; nevertheless, I felt bound not to give a definite answer until I was relieved of my engagement at Greifswald, although I had not taken the oath. Being anxious to hasten my return, the Stralsund council sent me a messenger to Greifswald with a saddle-horse.

I pointed out to my friends and to the magistrates at Greifswald that, although I had to a certain extent begun my functions, there had as yet been no positive agreement; not a syllable had been uttered, for instance, about salary. Why then should I decline the important Stralsund appointment? My uncle and godfather, Burgomaster Bertram Smiterlow, summoned the council to the chancellerie, and a fixed salary of eighty florins was allotted to me. Never had a secretary been so well paid. I asked to let the matter stand over till the next morning, so that I might consult with my family. My wife's relatives implored me to accept; my father-in-law, a centenarian, promised me, with tears in his eyes, a hundred florins if I stayed. At the instance of all these, I declared myself ready to receive the luck-penny (the earnest-money) commensurate with the dignity of the office and of the council, it being, furthermore, understood that I should be allowed to remain at the chancellerie and not be elected to the council. The *camerarii* counted me out eight crowns as earnest-money, and my predecessor, Johannes Schoenefeld, sent me word to engross my own act of appointment. More than one precedent justified me in expecting about a year's salary as earnest-money, but after some hesitation I took the eight crowns.

My father-in-law was anxiously waiting for the result of the interview. I flung the money on the table. "Just look, father," I exclaimed, "did I not sell myself at my worth? You had better get your hundred florins ready." But he had apparently recovered from his first depression, and seemed not at all touched by my obvious sacrifice, for he said tetchily, "If it suits you to go, very well, go; but you'll not have one florin as far as I am concerned." I felt hurt, although I fully intended to refuse the hundred florins, lest my brother-in-law should look askance at me.

I put the Stralsund horse up in Burgomaster Smiterlow's stable, my own not being ready. My first impulse was to send it back the same day. Then I began to reflect that it would be better to draw up my "act of appointment"; after that, the letter to the Stralsund council would not take long. In drawing up the act, I could, however, not help noticing that neither the period nor the place of payment was stated, and next morning I went to ask Schoenefeld about all this. He told me that I should receive two florins one day from this person, and half a florin the next from another, so that at the end of the year the eighty florins would be complete. I certainly did congratulate myself for having kept a back door open, for the misunderstanding was very serious, casual instalments and fixed appointments being by no means the same thing. After leaving Schoenefeld, I ran against Burgomaster Smiterlow and the *camerarii* in the market-place, and told them that if Schoenefeld's version was true, I preferred returning the wretched earnest-money. "Your conduct will surprise them," they replied. "To summon the council at such a short notice is no more possible than to take back the earnest-money without its leave." I, on the other hand, maintained that it was yet time to arrange affairs. "Should I be deserving of the magistrates' confidence if I were so incapable of conducting my own affairs? I am going to the burgomaster at once to deposit the earnest-money on his daughter's table. She'll know right enough to whom to hand it. After which I shall get into the saddle and take the road to Stralsund." Thereupon the council was summoned.

I went to tell my wife, her brother, and my sister whom he had married. My wife, not satisfied with shedding tears, declared categorically that she should not leave Greifswald. She would take a room somewhere and earn her living knitting. My sister and her husband were also much excited. "What shall you do with your nice house?" said my sister. "Why vex our parents? Stop here out of consideration for them; here where there are so many opportunities of being useful to them." An old aunt, a sensible, upright and honest matron whom my wife had called to her aid was the only one to express a contrary opinion. "Dear nephew," she said, "though I should be too pleased to keep you near me, for after God you are the prop of my old age, I'm bound to admit that there is no comparison between the post of Greifswald and that of Stralsund. If I placed an obstacle to your stroke of good fortune, my conscience would reproach me afterwards, so take my advice and carry out your plan. Do you remember how your wife mourned her mother? Does she still cry at the mention of her name? Well, she'll get just as used to living at Stralsund." My wife's tears flowed all the faster at these words.

The messenger from Stralsund went to saddle my horse. Booted and spurred I joined him almost immediately, and had the animal brought round to Burgomaster Smiterlow's door where, somewhat impatiently, I awaited on the steps his return from the Town Hall. He told me that no secretary in the past had received the appointments allotted to me, and that no secretary in the future was likely to receive them, and yet I had still found better; hence the council felt most reluctant to hamper my career and sent their best wishes for my welfare. I immediately got into the saddle and left the town, avoiding our house, on the threshold of which I could see my wife standing surrounded by her kindred. It was on November 29, 1555. My residence at Greifswald dated from January 1, 1551. During that period my earnings amounted to five thousand three hundred florins, exclusive of presents in kind, which often exceeded the strictly necessary. Here ends the third part of the story of my life.

INDEX

Berlin

Bensançon

Besserer, George

Beuter

Biberach

Bilder aus der Deutschen Kulturgeschichte

Bischof

Bitterfeld

Blumenow, Johannes

Bole, Victor

Bogislaw X., Duke
Duke Barnim
Duke George

Boineburg, Ritter Conrad von

Bois le Duc

Boldewan, Abbot

Bologna

Bolte, Nicholas

Bonus, Herrman

Bonnus

Botzen

Brabant

Brandenburg
Culmbach
Elector of
Wachim of

Brandenburg-the-Old

Brassanus, Matthias

Bremen, Christopher, Bishop of

Brenner

Brettheim

Brixen

Broecker, Jacob

Bruchsall

Brunswick, Duke Henry of
Duke Philip of

Brunswick-Luneberg

Bruser, Hermann

Bruser, Leveling

Bruser, Mrs.

Brussels

Buchow, Bartholomäi

Buchow, Heindrich

Bugenhagen, Johannes

Bukow

Bunsaw, Gaspard

Bunsow, Dame

Bunsow, Johannes

Burgrave of Mesnia

Burenius Arnoldus

Burn, Count Maximilian

Burnet, Bishop

Burtenbach, Captain Schaerthin von

Burwitz, Joachim

Buss, Valentine

Butzbach

Calvin

Camerarius

Cammin, Bishop of

Cannstadt

Capito Daniel

Carin

Carlowitz, Christopher

Carmelites

Cassel

Cassules

Castle of St. Angelo

Cellini, Benvenuto

Charlemagne

Charles V.

Citzewitz, Jacob,

Citzewitz, James

Classen, Bernard

Clerike, Jacob

Cleves, Anne of

Cleves, Duchy of
Duke of

Coburg

Colburg

Cologne
Elector of

Compestella

Constance

Copenhagen

Cosmographie, Munster's

Damitz, Captain Moritz

Danquart

Dantzig

De Anima

Dechow, Captain

Denmark, King of

Deux Fonts, Prince

Devonne

Dialectica Caesarii

Dick, Dr. Leopold

Düren

Dinnies, Laurence

Domitz, Maurice

Donat

Donauwerth

Dorpat, Bishop of

Drache, Anthony

Droege, Gerard

Duitz, Gaspard

Eck, Dr.

Eger

Eichstedt, Valentin
Bishop of

Einfriedlaw

Eisleben

Elbe

Eldenow

Emek Habakha

Engelhardt, Dr. Simeon

Engeln

Epitome Annalium Pomerania

Erasmus, Desiderius

Erckhorst, Cyriacus

Erfurt

Ernest, Margrave

Esslingen

Faber

Fachs, Dr.

Falck, Chancellor

Falcke, Dr.

Falsterbo

Farnese, Peter Aloys

Fasti, Ovid's

Ferrara

Ferdinand, King

Florence

Franconia

Frankfurt

Frederick, III., Duke

Frederick, King of Denmark

Freder, Johannes

Freedom of a Christian Man

Frese, Widow

Friesland

Fribourg

Friedrich, Johannes

Frobose, Peter

Frock, Otto

Froment

Frubose, Matthew

Furstenburg, Count Wilhelm
Frederick von

Gadebusch

Gantzkendorf

Garpenhagen

Gatzkow, Abraham

Gelhaar, Joachim

Geneva

Gentzkow, Dr. Nicholas
Burgomaster Nicholas

Ghent
Charles of

Goeslin, Margaret

Gotha

Gottschalk, Heinrich
Johannes
Prior

Grammatica Bonni

Granvelle, Cardinal
Nicholas, Perremot de

Greiffenberg

Greifswald

Grellen, Barber

Gribou

Grosse, Alexis

Gruwel, Peter

Gruyère, Count Michael de

Grynaeus, Simon

Guelderland

Gutzkow, Count

Hahn, Werner

Halle, xxii.

Hamburg

Hannemann

Hartmann, Brand, George

Hase, Dr. Heinrich

Hausen, Erasmus

Hawthorne

Heidelberg
Elector of

Heidelsheim

Heimsdorff

Heindrich, Duke

Heinrichmann, Dr.

Helfmann, Johannes

Henry II. of France

Henry VIII.

Hentzer

Heine Vogel

Hertogenbosch

Herwig, Christian

Hesiod

Hesse, Philip of

Hildebrand, Nicholas

Hirnheim, Johannes Walther von

Hochberg

Hochel, Dr. Johannes

Holde, Dr. Conrad

Holme, Johannes

Holste

Holstein, Duke Christian

Homedes, Jean de

Horns, the family of

Hose, Dr. Christopher

Hovisch, Michael

Hoyer, Dr. Gaspard

Hundfruck

Hutten, Ulrich, von

Ingoldstadt

Innspruck

Itinerarium Germanicae

Juliers, Duke of

Kalen, George von

Kalen, J. von

Kalte, Johannes

Kantzow, Thomas

Kasskow, Master

Kempe, George

Kempten

Ketelhot, Christian

King Arthur

Kirchschwarz

Kismann

Klatteville, Peter

Kloche, Johannes

Krugge, Nicholas

Knipstrow, Dr.

Koenigstein

Krahow, Valerius

Krossen, Johannes

Krou, Frau

Kruse

Kurcke, Johannes

Kussow, Michael

Labbun, Christopher

Lagebusch, Johannes

Lanckin, Christopher von der

Landau

Landshut

Lasky, Stanislas

Leipzig

Lepper, Hermann

Lepusculus

Lertmeritz

Leveling
Marie

Lezen, Johannes von

Lickow

Liegnitz
Duke Frederick von

Lievetzow

Lingensis, Heinrich

Livonia

Lloytz, The, of Stettin

Loewe, Nicholas

Loewenstein, Christopher von

Loewenhagen, Joachim

Lorbeer, Christopher
Olaff
Zabel

Loretto, xx.

Lorraine, Dowager of

Louvain

Lubeck

Lubbeke

Ludwig, Duke Ernest

Lake, Constance

Lühe Von der

Luther, Martin

Madrid

Madrutz, Gandenz von

Maestricht

Magdeburg

Malines

Manlius

Mantel, Jacob

Mantua
Duke of

Marburg

Marforio

Marie, Fräulein, of Saxony

Maries, The three

Marquardt, Johannes

Marschmann

Mattzan, Berendt
Joachim
Lutke

Maurice, Duke

Mauritz

Maximilian, Archduke

Mayence
Bishop of
Elector of

Mecklenburg

Meisisch, Leonard

Meiseburg

Memmingen

Melanchthon, Philip

Mesnia

Mense

Mey, Bernard

Meyer, Christopher

Meyer, Gerard

Meyer, Hermann

Meyer, Marx

Middleburgh, C.

Milan

Moller, Rolof

Moller, George

Monkwitz, Von

Montefiascone

Montfort, Count Hugo von

Moritz, Joachim

Mount Scarperia

Muggenwald

Muhlberg

Muleg Hassan, King of Tunis

Munich

Munster, Sebastian

Musculus

Muthrin

Nares

Naumberg
Bishop of

Naumberg, Duke of

Naves, Seigneur Jean

Negendanck

Nering, Nicholas

Nerung

New Camp

Neuenkirchen

Nicholas

Niederweisel

Niemann, Johannes

Nordgau

Nordhauser

Normann, George
Heinrich

Nuremburg

Octavius, Duke

Offices, Cicero's

Offing

Oppenheim

Ornans

Oseborn, Zabel

Osnaburgh

Osten

Ostiglia

Ovid

Palatine, Count
Elector of

Pappenheim, Marshal von

Parow, Christian

Pasewalk

Pasquin

Paul III., Pope

Petrus

Pflug, Gaspard
Johannes
Julius

Pforzheim
Ernest von

Philip, Duke

Philip I.

Philip V. of Spain

Picht, Dr.

Place Moland

Plate Simon

Plawe

Pô

Poland, King of

Pomerania
Duke of

Pomeranus

Portius, Dr. Johannes

Praecepta Grammaticae

Prestor, John

Prien, V.

Prussia, Duke of

Pritze, Joachim

Puddegla

Putkammer, Dr.

Putten

Quilow, Johannes Osten von

Ranke

Rantzau, Count Johannes

Rantzin

Rantzow, Joachim

Ratisbon
Diet of

Rau, Balthazar

Ravenna

Reiffstock, Dr. Frederick

Reinburg

Rheinfeld

Rheinhausen

Rhodes

Ribbenitz

Richter

Rhode, Nicholas

Roetteln

Roevershagen

Rode, Nicholas

Rome

Schaerlini

Schenck, Dr. Jacob

Schermer, Frau

Schladenteuffel, Nicholas

Schlackenwerth

Schlemm

Schlieben, Eustacius

Schmalkalden, League of

Schwallenberg

Schoenfeld, Johannes

Schorsow

Schwede, Bailiff

Schwabe, Bartholomew

Schwallenberger, Dr.

Schwarte, Matthew
Peter

Schwartz, Arndt
Christian

Schwartzenberg

Schwartz, Dr. Peter

Schwendi, Lazarus von

Schwendi, Lazarus

Schwenkfeld, Gaspard von

Schwerin, Marshal Ulrich

Seld, Dr. George Sigismund

Selneccerus

Senckestack, Johannes

Sickermann, Heindrich

Siena, Virgo

Sievershausen

Silesia

Sitten, Nanz von

Sixtus IV., Pope

Skramon, Admiral Peter

Sleidan

Smalkald

Smeker, H.

Smiterlow, Anna
Bartholamäi
Bertrand
Christian

Smiterlow, George
Johannes
Nicholas

Solms, Count Reinhard

Sonnenberg, Nicholas
Heinrich

Speckin, Martin

Spires

Stargurdt

Stainbruck

Steinkiller

Steinwer, Canon Hippolytus

Sterzing

Stettin

Stiten, Franz von

Storentin, Frau

Stochkolm

Stolpe

Stralsund

Stranck, Anna

Strasburg
Bishop of

Stroïentin, Dr. Valentin

Verona

Virgil

Vischer, L.

Viterbo

Vogelsberg, Sebastian

Vogt, Johannes

Voss, Jacob

Walde, Dr. B. von

Wallenstein

Walter, Anthony

Wardenburg, Zutfeld

Wedel, George von

Weingarten, Abbé von

Weinleben, Chancellor

Welch

Welfius, Heinrich

Welsers

Wessels, Franz

Westphalia

Wetteran

Wetzlar

Weitmulen, Sebastian von

Wezer, Martin

Willemberg, Castle of

Willershagen

Wismar

Wissemberg

Wittenberg

Wolde, Canon von

Wolder, Simon

Wolfenbuttel

Wolff, Frau

Wolgang

Wolgast

Worms

Wulflam, Wulf

Wullenweber, George

Wurzburg, Bishop of

Wustenfeld

Wustenhausen

Zell

Ziegesar

Ziegler

Zigler, Dr. Louis

Zittau

Zober

Zwingli

FOOTNOTES:

Footnote 1: At the beginning of the sixteenth century the monetary unit in Pomerania was the golden florin, which within a fraction was equivalent to the Rhenish florin and represented eight francs, sixty-five centimes, regard being had to the fact that the value of silver compared to that of gold was a third more than to-day. The golden florin was divided into forty-eight schellings (not shillings), sixteen of which constituted a mark; the schelling again was divided into twelve pfenning. The schelling of Hamburg and of Lubeck were worth double that of Stralsund.--Translator.

Footnote 2: House property was classified in three categories: dwelling houses (*Häuser*), shops (*Buden*), which were very light constructions set apart for trade or for accommodating strangers, and cellars (*Keller*), or places below the level of the ground floor. The scale of house-tax was for booths, stalls or shops half, for cellars a quarter of that due for dwelling-houses. A census of 1554 gives for Stralsund 559 houses, 1,133 booths or shops, and 535 cellars; of which numbers 30 dwelling houses, 39 booths and 38 cellars are not tenanted. To these figures must be added for the faubourgs or beyond the gates 239 tenements of lesser importance.

On the site of the house in Huns' Street stands or stood a few years ago the Hotel Jarmer. An inscription on its frontage recalls the birth of Jeremy Sastrow. According to a competent etymological authority, the name of the Hunnenstrasse in Greifswald has not the faintest connexion with the Huns, but is simply a Low German corruption of Hundestrasse, *Platea Canum*, like in Lubeck and in Barth. In the latter town the thoroughfare thus designated was the locale of the Prince's pack of hounds.--Translator.

Footnote 3: Nicholas Smiterlow, who was councillor in 1507 and burgomaster in 1516, enacted an important part at Stralsund at a period when the political influence of that city spread far beyond its walls. Events pleaded loudly in favour of the resolute and prudent burgomaster against his adventurous adversary, George Wullenweber. In spite of his dislike to popular agitation, Smiterlow was "one of the first and best upholders of the Reformation," if we are to believe the evidence of a chronicler of the sixteenth century. He died in July, 1539. Hailing originally from Greifswald, he had got married at Stralsund in 1498. The Smiterlows, Schmiterlows, or Smiterloews interpreted their name in the sense of "Smiters of Lions." Their arms represented a man wielding a club and a lion by his side. It was said that during the Crusades their ancestor had laid low one of those animals with the blow of a club.--Translator.

Footnote 4: It was the custom to give a present to a relative or to a friend as a contribution to the furnishing of his house.--Translator.

Footnote 5: When Sastrow became secretary of Stralsund he took care to collect, under the title of "Rubrikenbuch" all the documents relating to the privileges and property of the city; a collection which proved useful to the magistrates in office and which is of interest to-day as a contribution to the local history.--Translator.

Footnote 6: The ancient monastery of Belbuck, near Treptow on the Rega, became, under Abbot Boldewan, a nursery of learning. From thence came George von Ukermünde, who was the first to preach the reformed doctrine at Stralsund; the impassioned preacher Kurcke or Kureke; Ketelhot, born in 1492, died in 1546, whom the chronicler Berckmann calls the "Apostle of Stralsund and the founder of the holy doctrine"; Peter Suave, the pioneer of the Reformation in Denmark and Holstein; and finally, Johannes Bugenhagen, famous under the name of *Pomeranus*, born in 1485, died in 1558, pastor at Wittemberg since 1523, the author of the first historical work on Pomerania, the translator of the Bible into Low-German, and the veritable organizer of Protestantism into those northern regions. Duke Bogislaw X, displeased with the spirit that prevailed at Belbuck, suppressed that institution in 1523; the dispersion of the monks only resulted in the prompter diffusion of the new doctrines.

The chronology of the history of the Reformation at Stralsund remained uncertain up to 1859, in which year the archives of the Imperial Chamber, forgotten at Wetzlar, brought to light the documents in connexion with the lawsuit brought by Canon Hippolytus Steinwer against Stralsund, in order to despoil the city of certain revenues and privileges. The principal dates may be fixed as follows: 1522.--First conflict of the city with the Catholic clergy who refuse to be taxed; Zutfeld Wardenburg, administrator of the diocese, flies to Rome. 1523 or end of 1522.--Arrival of the first reformed monks and preachers, George Kempe, Heindrich Sichermann, George von Ukermünde. 1524.--First preachings of Ketelhot (at Easter), and of Kurcke on St. Michael's Day. 1525.--The Monday after Palm Sunday (April 10), the churches and convents are invaded; suppression of Catholic worship.

1525.--The Sunday after All Saints' (November 5), official recognition of the Reformation through the promulgation of the ecclesiastical and scholastic ordinances of Johannes Alpinus.

With regard to political events the confusion was the same. Otho Frock, the recent historian of Pomerania, made it his business to apply the remedy, and the following are the results arrived at. 1524, from May to June.-- Installation of the Forty-Eight; voluntary exile of Smiterlow. 1525, January.- -Frustrated attempt of Smiterlow to return to Stralsund with the support of the Hanseatic towns. 1525 (probably April 15).--Riotous election of Rolof Moller and Christopher Lorbeer as burgomasters, of Franz Wessel, Hermann Meyer and six other partisans of the Reformation as councillors. 1525 (at St. John).--Entry into Stralsund of Dukes George and Barnim; the rendering of homage and confirmation of privileges. 1527 (July 24?).--Rolof Moller leaves Stralsund, and on August 1 or 5 Smiterlow returns. 1529.--Return and death of Rolof Moller.--Translator.

Footnote 7: There are various versions of the origin of this famous tumult. According to some documents the servant's mistress was a widow named Frese, who lived in the old market.--Translator.

Footnote 8: The fishmonger's bench or stall of Vischer reminds one of that of the reformer Froment, preaching on the Place Molard at Geneva, just as the departure of the nuns of St. Brigitta, at Stralsund, reminds one, though not quite so seriously, of the flitting from Geneva of the Sisters of Santa Clara.--Translator.

Footnote 9: In the ducal House of Pomerania the law of succession admitted all the sons indistinctly to the throne. They reigned in common, but if an understanding was impossible, the county was divided between them. In 1478 the whole of Pomerania was united under the sceptre of Bogislaw X. At the death of this able prince, which took place in 1523, Dukes George and Barnim wielded power conjointly, in spite of their utterly opposed sentiments. George remained faithful to the old belief; Barnim, on the other hand, proceeded to the university of Wittemberg, and in 1519 had accompanied Luther to Leipzig when he was disputing with Eck. The honour accrued to Barnim in his capacity of rector, a dignity seldom conferred upon a student.

George died in 1531, leaving an only son, Philippe. The division of Pomerania long desired by Barnim occurred the following year. Barnim's chance gave him Eastern Pomerania as far as the Swine, and with Stettin as a residence. To his nephew, Philip I, fell Western Pomerania, of which Wolgast became once more the capital. That agreement, concluded for ten years, was renewed in 1541, and its effects were prolonged until 1625, at which date there was a new reunion under Bogislaw XIV, of the Stettin branch, who died in 1637, the last of the House. The franchises of Stralsund, in fact, were so extensive as to reduce the authority of the princes to a mere nominal rule. The bond between them only consisted of a kind of perfunctory rendering of homage and the payment of a small tribute, the amount of which had been fixed once for all. The suzerain only entered the city after a notice of three months. In 1525, with the political and religious crisis at its height, the rendering of homage was preceded by protracted negotiations. No safe-conduct, though delivered by the prince, was valid at Stralsund unless it was countersigned by the council. The city exercised its jurisdiction not only within its walls, but in its exterior domains. Though exempt from military obligations as far as the reigning dukes were concerned, the city imposed compulsory service both by sea and by land on its citizens. It had the power to conclude treaties and was its sole arbiter with regard to peace or war. These privileges were preserved by Stralsund during the whole of the sixteenth century, in spite of the decline of the Hanseatic bond.--Translator.

Footnote 10: Franz Wessel, born at Stralsund, September 30, 1487, died May 19, 1570, was the son of a brewer of the Lange Strasse. At a very early age--when scarcely more than twelve--he embraced a commercial career and made long stays in foreign countries, besides pilgrimages to Trèves, Aix-la-Chapelle, Einfriedlaw, and St. James of Compostella. In 1516 he was back at Stralsund, and was one of the most energetic and first promoters of the Reformation. Councillor in 1524, burgomaster in 1541, he played a scarcely less important political part. Wessel is the author of a curious piece of writing on divine worship at Stralsund at the period of papistry. The very year of his death, Gerard Droege, who had been brought up in his house, published his biography at Rostock.--Translator.

Footnote 11: Christopher Lorbeer, who was councillor in 1507, burgomaster in 1524, and who died in 1555, belonged to a much respected family of Stralsund and enjoyed great consideration there.--Translator.

Footnote 12: According to tradition King Arthur or Artus, chief of the Knights of the Round Table, lived in the sixth century. He and his companions had devoted themselves to the recovery of the Holy Grail. Arthur himself is supposed to have conquered Sweden and Norway. On the other hand, the historian Johannes Magnus, Archbishop of Upsal, who died in 1554, mentions a Swedish Arthur famed for his doughty deeds, and he adds: "Even in our days, there exist in certain towns along the Baltic, for instance at Dantzig and Stralsund, houses, *domus Arthi*, on which the term illustrious has been bestowed; it is there that the notables foregather for the relaxation of their minds, as if it were a kind of school of the highest courtesy and amenity." Hence in the trading cities of the north the magnificent structures set apart for public and private rejoicings, as well as for commercial transactions, were intimately bound up with the tradition of a legendary hero. If I am not mistaken, only one of those buildings still remains, namely, the *Artushof* of Dantzig, which does duty as an exchange, and the ancient halls of which were the scene of the interview of the German Emperor and the Czar in September, 1881. The local chroniclers assert that the *Artushof* of Stralsund was built with the ransom of Duke Eric of Saxony, taken prisoner by the city troops in 1316 The great fire of June 12, 1680, completely destroyed it. On its site stands the official residence of the military governor of the place.

When near his end Ketelhot expressed his regret at having, at that period of his scant resources, too eagerly accepted the burgher's hospitality. Johannes Knipstro (Knypstro or Knipstrow), born May 1, 1497, at Sandow in the March, was at first a Franciscan monk. He and Ketelhot are considered as the most active propagators of the Reformation at Stralsund. But for the earnings of his wife, it is said, he would have been compelled to beg his bread, his salary being too small to keep body and soul together. She was an erewhile nun, and provided for both with her needle. Knipstro became superintendent-general at Wolgast in 1535, and professor of theology at Greifswald. He died October 4, 1556.--Translator.

Footnote 13: Doctor and ducal councillor Valentin Stroïentin was the friend of Ulrich von Hutten. Bugenhagen dedicated his *Pomerania* to him. He died in 1539.

Footnote 14: Johannes Aepinus (in German Hoeck or Hoch, high), was born in 1499 at Ziegesar in the Urich, and died in 1553 superintendent at Hamburg, where he had discharged the ministry since 1529. Aepinus laboured hard at ecclesiastical and scholastic reform. Many writings, especially against the Interim, came from his pen.--Translator.

Footnote 15: Hermann Bonnus, born in 1504, near Osnaburgh; he preached the new doctrine at Greifswald, Stralsund and Copenhagen, and died on February 12, 1548, superintendent at Lubeck, a post which had been confided to him in 1531. Bonnus has written a chronicle of Lubeck.--Translator.

Footnote 16: Nicholas Gentzkow, doctor of law, born December 6, 1502, the son of a shoemaker, according to the annalist Berckmann, and deceased February 24, 1576, was elected burgomaster of Stralsund in 1555. He, nevertheless, remained syndic, that is, legal adviser to the city, just as, after his admission to the council, Sastrow continued his functions of protonotary, or first secretary. Sastrow, who had many disagreements with Gentzkow, as, in fact, with others, succeeded him in the dignity of burgomaster. Gentzkow left a diary of which Zober published extracts in 1870.--Translator.

Footnote 17: Wulf Wulflam, the head of the patricians of Stralsund, and illustrious in virtue of his warlike exploits, treated on a footing of equality with the crowned heads of the fourteenth century.--Translator.

Footnote 18: The same story is related of the Schwerin family at Lubeck.--Translator.

Footnote 19: A jocular allusion to the three Maries of Bethany, viz., the mother of James the Minor and sister of the Virgin; the mother of the Apostles James and John, and Mary of Magdala.--Translator.

Footnote 20: The dean of the Drapers had precedence of the deans of all the other corporations; in all the ceremonies he came immediately after the council.--Translator.

Footnote 21: George Wullenweber was born about 1492, probably at Hamburg. When the political and religious struggle broke out at Lubeck, he was settled there as a merchant, and he distinguished himself by being in the front rank clamouring for changes. At the end of February, 1533, he was elected councillor and afterwards burgomaster. From that moment the whole of his attempts tended in the direction of the restoration of the commercial monopoly the Hanseatic cities had so long possessed on the shores of the Baltic. The aim was to close those ports to the Dutch merchant navy, and to cause the influence of Lubeck to prevail in the three Scandinavian kingdoms.

In the spring of 1533, Lubeck made up its mind to come to close quarters with the Dutch, those detested rivals. A well-equipped fleet stood out to sea; the erewhile landsknecht, Marcus Meyer, who began by being a blacksmith at Hamburg, and had married the rich widow of a burgomaster, assumed the command of the mercenaries. The others had, however, been forewarned, and only some unimportant captures were made. Meyer, after having confiscated English merchandize found on board of the captured craft, made the mistake of landing on the English coast to revictual; he was arrested for piracy and taken to London. By a whim of Henry VIII, jealous of the power of the Netherlands and of Charles V, Marx Meyer, instead of being put to death, received a knighthood and immediately served as an intermediary between the king and Wullenweber in the more or less serious negotiations they started.

This first campaign had cost much, and its issue was not very profitable. The Dutch fleet had got some good prizes, and pillaged on the Schonen (Swedish) coast some of the factories belonging to the Hanseatic combination. The complaints of the traders themselves became general. Was the war to be pursued? A diet foregathered at Hamburg in March, 1534, in order to come to an understanding. Wullenweber was received with universal recrimination; his haughty attitude drew from the Stralsund delegate the famous and prophetic reminder recorded by Sastrow a few pages further on. The proud burgomaster left the place at the end of a few days, angry and embittered at heart; in spite of this, an armistice of four years was signed:

Naturally, Wullenweber felt it incumbent to retrieve this check. The elective throne of Denmark had become vacant through the death of Frederick I of Holstein: His son, Christian III, was unfavourably disposed towards the Hanseatic cities. Under those circumstances Wullenweber hit upon the idea of the candidature of Christian II, who had been deposed and afterwards confined to the castle of Sunderburg in the island of Alsen. A condottiere of high birth, Christopher of Oldenburg, accepted the chief command of the expedition. But the bold burgomaster, not satisfied with the restoration of Christian II., offered to Duke Albrecht of Mecklenburg the crown of Sweden at that time borne by Gustavus Wasa. That monarch had committed the blunder of not showing himself sufficiently grateful for the aid lent to him by Lubeck in days gone by.

The beginnings of the campaign were successful. Copenhagen opened even its doors to the Count of Oldenburg. Christian III, however, had secured an able captain in Count Johannes Rantzau, who, leaving the enemy to carry on his devastations in Sealand, boldly came to invest Lubeck, inflicted a bloody defeat on Marx Meyer and captured eight vessels of war. Wullenweber understood that it was time to make concessions; his partners retired from the councils, and on November 18, 1534, the very curious convention with Rantzau was concluded at Stockeldorf by which the Lubeckers were left free to continue warring in Denmark in favour of Christian II, but bound themselves to cease hostilities in Holstein.

The candidates for the Danish throne increased. Albrecht of Mecklenburg and even Count Christopher laid more and more stress upon their pretensions; Wullenweber, in order to conciliate the Emperor, put forward at the eleventh hour the name of a personage agreeable to the House of Hapsburg, namely, Count Palatine Frederick, the son-in-law of Christian II. The war went on with Christian III, whose cause Gustavus Wasa had espoused. Marx Meyer fell into the hands of the enemy; left prisoner on parole, he broke his pledge, made himself master of the very castle of Warburg that had been assigned to him as a residence, and his barbaric and cruel incursions terrified the country all round. The naval battle of Borholm on June 9, 1535, was not productive of a decisive result, a storm having dispersed the opposing fleets, but on June 11 Johannes Rantzau scored a victory on land in Denmark; and finally, on June 16, at Svendsburg, the Lubeck fleet fell without firing a shot into the hands of Admiral Peter Skramon. Added to all these catastrophes, Lubeck was threatened with being put outside the pale of the Empire; the game was evidently lost. Nevertheless peace with Christian III was only signed on February 14, 1536.

Marx Meyer, after a splendid defence, surrendered Warburg, on the condition of his retiring with the honours of war; in spite of their promise, the Danes tried and executed him together with his brother on June 17, 1536. On July 28 of the same year Copenhagen capitulated, after having sustained a twelve months' investment, aggravated by famine. Christian III gave their liberty to Duke Albrecht of Mecklenburg and to Count Christopher, although he inflicted repeated humiliations on the latter. As for the Duke, the adventure left him crestfallen for a long while.

At Lubeck the men of the old regime obtained power once more, Wullenweber having resigned towards the end of August, 1535. In the beginning of October, while crossing the territory of the Archbishop of Bremen, the brother of his enemy, Duke Heinrich the Younger, of Brunswick, he was arrested, taken to the castle of Rothenburg, and put on the rack as a traitor, an anabaptist and a malefactor. After which he was transferred to the castle of Stainbrück, between Brunswick and Hildesheim, and flung into a narrow dungeon, where to this day the following inscription records the event: "Here George Wullenweber suffered, 1536-1537." Finally, on September 24, a court of aldermen summoned at Tollenstein, near Wolfenbüttel, by Heindrich of Brunswick, sentenced the wretched man to suffer death by the sword, a sentence which was carried out immediately, the executioner quartering the body and putting it on the wheel. Such was the deplorable end of the man whose ambition had dreamt the political and commercial domination of his country in the north of Europe. According to a sailor's ditty of old, "The people of Lubeck are regretting every day the demise of Master George Wullenweber." The historian Waitz has devoted three volumes to the career of the famous burgomaster; the purely literary men and dramatic authors, Kruse and Gutzkow, have also seized upon this dramatic figure.--Translator.

Footnote 22: Under the name of Wends, the Sclavs settled on the shores of the Baltic, engaged in maritime traffic, and became the founders of the Hanseatic League. In the sixteenth century the kernel of that confederation still consisted of the group of the six Wendish cities: "Lubeck the chief one, Hamburg, Luneburg, Rostock, Stralsund and Wismar."--Translator.

Footnote 23: The Hanseatic League had established its most important factories, and above all for the herring traffic, in Schonen; enormous fairs were being held there from the beginning of July to the end of November. The centre of all this commerce was Falsterbo, at the extreme southwest of Sweden.--Translator.

Footnote 24: Valentin Eichstedt died in 1600 as Chancellor of Wolgast. He wrote the life of Duke Philip I, an *Epitome Annalium Pomerania* and *Annales Pomeraniae*. Johannes Berckmann, a former monk of the order of St. Augustine, and preacher, an eye-witness of the scenes of the Reformation at Stralsund, is the author of a chronicle of that city which was published in 1833 by Mohnike and Gober. Sastrow has now and again borrowed from him for events anterior to his personal recollections; he nevertheless rarely misses an opportunity of attacking his fellow-worker in history. This may have been due to hatred of the popular party and perhaps to professional jealousy, apart from the fact of Berckmann being more favourable to his patron Christopher Lorbeer than to Burgomaster Nicholas Smiterlow. Born about the end of the fifteenth century, Berckmann died in 1560.--Translator.

Footnote 25: Robert Barnes, chaplain to Henry VIII, and sent by the latter to Wittemberg in order to consult the theologians on the subject of Henry's divorce from Catherine of Arragon. At his return to London he showed so much zeal for the new faith that Henry sent him to the Tower. He recanted in order to recover his freedom; then overwhelmed with remorse fled to Wittemberg and stayed there several years with Bugenhagen under the name of Dr. Antonius Anglus. Henry VIII, after his rupture with the Pope, reinstated Barnes as his chaplain and entrusted him with the negotiations of his marriage with Anne of Cleves; but when the divorce took place, Barnes was brought before Parliament and was burned July 30, 1540. He wrote the lives of the Roman pontiffs from St. Peter to Alexander III.--Translator.

Footnote 26: Arnold Büren, the son of a peasant, took his name from the hamlet of Büren, in Westphalia, in the neighbourhood of which he was born, in 1484. He spent fifteen years at Wittemberg with Luther and Melanchthon. The latter recommended him to the Duke of Mecklenburg, Henry the Pacific, as a tutor to his son Magnus, who was reported to be the most learned prince of his times. To Büren belongs the credit of having restored the prestige of the University of Rostock, seriously impaired by the pest and by the troubles of the Reformation. He died on September 16, 1566. His tomb is in St. Mary's, at Rostock; among the scutcheons adorning it are the Genevese key and eagle.--Translator.

Footnote 27: The herring fishery and the brewing industry gave a great importance to the coopers' guild, which was moreover protected against foreign competition by ancient enactments.--Translator.

Footnote 28: Gaspard von Schwenkfeld, born in 1490 at the castle of Offing, in Silesia, died at Ulm in 1561. Entered into holy orders, he reproached Luther with restoring the reign of literal interpretation and with neglecting the spirit. Banished from Silesia as a fanatic, he made his way to Southern Germany, and stayed at Strasburg, Augsburg, Spires and Ulm. For some time he seemed to incline towards the Anabaptists, but soon parted from them to found a particular sect. He taught that God reveals Himself in direct communication to every man, and that regeneration is accomplished by the spiritual life and not by outward means of grace. His profound conviction and great piety gained him many adherents, notably in Swabia and Silesia. A colony of his persecuted disciples settled in Philadelphia, U.S.--Translator.

Footnote 29: At the head of the bands recruited by the Duke of Cleves and the King of Denmark, Martin van Rosse, or von Rossheim, acting in concert with the French troops, had ravaged Brabant. Not only did the Duke of Cleves retain Guelderland, on which Charles V pretended to have claims, but he continued his intrigues with France and Denmark. To put an end to these, Charles, in 1543, got together 35,000 men, Spaniards, Italians and Germans, and proceeded down the Rhine. The fortified place of Düren having been carried by assault, the Duke considered himself lucky to be able to conclude a peace which only cost him Guelderland, and Martin van Rosse took service once more with the Emperor.--Translator.

Footnote 30: Sastrow has the whole of the grant of poet laureate, with the full description of the arms conferred. In reality it was not a patent of nobility in the proper significance of the term.--Translator.

Footnote 31: Les especes enlevées, il renferma la bourse et le fou de s'écrier: "Monseigneur, appelez votre coquin de prêtre (il ne le calumnioit point) qu'on le taille à son tour. Votre Grace sait qu'il a engrossé une fille de Butzbach." On suspendit derrière le poêle les angelots cousus dans un sachet.

Footnote 32: Duke Henry of Brunswick endeavoured to hold his own against the Protestant princes, but in 1545, abandoned by the mercenaries, he was compelled to surrender to the Landgrave Philip of Hesse.--Translator.

Footnote 33: On the subject of the child Simeon, the following may be read with interest in the martyrology of the Israelites, entitled *Emek Habakha*, or *The Valley of Tears* (published by Julian Sée, 1881): "At that period (1475), a scoundrel named Enzo, of Trent, in Italy, killed a child of two years old with the name of Simeon and flung it secretly into a pond, not far from the house of the Jew Samuel without any one having seen the deed. Immediately, as usual, the Jews were accused of it. At the order of the bishop their houses were entered into; the child, of course, was not found, and everybody went back to his home. The body was found afterwards. The bishop, after having had it examined on the spot itself, ordered the arrest of all the Jews, who were harassed and tortured to such a degree as to confess to a thing which had never entered their mind. Only one among them, a very old man, named Moses, refused to avow this signal falsehood and died under his torture. May the Lord reward him according to his piety."

Two Christians, learned and versed in the law came from Padua to judge for themselves. The wrath of the inhabitants of Trent was kindled against them and they were nearly killed. The bishop condemned the Jews, heaped bitterness upon them, tortured them with red-hot pincers, finally burned them, and their guiltless souls ascended to heaven. He subsequently took possession of all their property as he had intended, and filled his cellars with spoil. The child was already reported as admitted among the saints, and was supposed to perform miracles. The bishop disseminated the announcement of it throughout all the provinces, crowds rushed to see, and they did not come empty-handed. All the people of that country began to show great hatred to the Jews in the spots where they resided, and ceased to speak peacefully to them. Meanwhile, the bishop having asked the pope to canonize the child, considering that it was among the saints, the pope sent one of his cardinals with the title of legate to examine the affair more closely, and the latter did not fail before long to discover that it was nothing but an imposture and fancy. He also wished to see the corpse; the corpse was embalmed. Thereupon the cardinal began to jeer; he declared in the presence of the people that it was nothing but sheer deception. The people, however, became furious against him; he was obliged to flee and to take refuge in a neighbouring town. When there he sent for all the documents relating to the avowals of the unfortunate Jews and the measures taken against them, had the servant of the scoundrel who killed the child arrested, and the latter declared that the crime had been committed by order of the bishop in order to ruin the Jews. The cardinal took the servant with him to Rome, gave an account of his mission to the pope, who refused to canonize the child as the bishop kept asking him. The child was only "beatified," but up to the present (1540) it has not been "canonized." Still, it was canonized in 1588, and its "day" is celebrated with great pomp at Trent on March 24.--Translator.

Footnote 34: Ascagne, Count of St. Florian and Cardinal, was the son of Constance Farnese, daughter of Pope Paul III.--Translator.

Footnote 35: Duke Octavius was the son of Peter-Aloys Farnése.--Translator.

Footnote 36: This epicure was prelate of Augsburg, Johannes Fugger, who in reality travelled for the sole purpose of getting a knowledge of the different vintages. His servant had the following words cut on his tombstone: "*Est, Est, Est et propter nimium Est; dominus meus mortuus est.*" The defunct left a legacy to empty so many bottles of wine on his grave once a year, a ceremony replaced nowadays by a distribution of bread to the poor. The wine of Montefiascone owes its name of *Est, Est, Est* to this adventure.--Translator.

Footnote 37: The famous Captain Schaertlin von Burtenbach had received the command of the Protestant forces, among which figured the contingents of Ulm and Augsburg: The successful night-surprise against the fortress of Ehrenberg-Klause marks the beginning of the war of Schmalkalden. From that moment Schaertlin, having become master of the passages of the Tyrol, could stop the reinforcements despatched from Italy to the emperor; he could descend into the plain and drive away the Council of Trent. The citizens of Augsburg, though, being anxious for the safety of their own town, pressed him to come back. "He obeyed, racked," says one of his own companions, "by the same despair that Hannibal felt when recalled from Italy by Carthage." The taking of the same fortress by Mauritz of Saxony in 1552 compelled Charles V to leave Innspruck in hot haste.--Translator.

Footnote 38: Here follows a very unsavoury passage, showing the lamentable want of cleanliness even among the educated middle classes in the sixteenth century throughout Europe, for the particulars given by Sastrow did not apply to Germany only.--Translator.

Footnote 39: It is not the final dissolution brought about by the defeat of Mühlberg. A passage from Sleidan explains the league of Schmalkalden at the end of 1546. "The embassies of the Protestants, which were not agreed, foregathered with the hope of being enabled to deliberate more efficiently. But inasmuch as the 'Allied of the Religion' gave no help, and the confederates of Luneburg and Pomerania did not assist in anything, inasmuch as the other States and towns of Saxony were most sparing with their subsidies, as there came nothing from France, and the army dwindled down day by day because the soldiers took their discharge on account of the season and other discomforts, it was proposed to adopt one of three measures: to give battle, to retire and put the soldiers into winter quarters, or to make peace. The discussion resulted in a hint to make peace. But because the emperor, who was aware of the state of things through his spies, proposed too onerous conditions, it was decided to take the whole of the army into Saxony. In consequence of all this, the war was by no means successfully conducted."--Translator.

Footnote 40: Gaspard Pflug, the chief of the Protestant party in Bohemia, must not be mistaken for Julius Pflug, Bishop of Naumburg, one of the three men who drew up "the Interim."--Translator.

Footnote 41: Sastrow gives only one specimen, but I cannot reproduce it.--Translator.

Footnote 42: After the victory of Mühlberg, the imperial army went to lay siege to Wittenberg, which finally capitulated at the advice of Johannes Friedrich of Sachsen himself.--Translator.

Footnote 43: The jurist, George Sigismund Seld, born in 1516, the son of a goldsmith at Augsburg, had become vice-chancellor at the death of Nares. His deputies were Johannes Marquardt of Baden, and Heinrich Hase, formerly counsellor to the Count Palatine and the Prince of Deux-Ponts. Seld died in 1565.--Translator.

Footnote 44: Christopher von Carlowitz, born at Heimsdorff, near Dresden, on December 7, 1507, died on January 8, 1578. He was the able counsellor of the valiant but changeable Maurice of Saxony, who, as is well known, deserted the Protestant side for that of the emperor, and was rewarded with the electoral dignity of which his kinsman and neighbour Johannes-Friedrich was deprived. A few years later, Maurice, at the head of the vanquished of Mühlberg, recommenced the struggle against the emperor, and in 1552 imposed upon that monarch the peace of Passau. In July 1553 Maurice met with a glorious death on the battlefield of Sievershausen, where the Margrave of Brandenburg suffered a defeat.--Translator.

Footnote 45: It was at Ingoldstadt that the challenge of the Protestant princes was presented to Charles V. by a young squire, accompanied by a trumpeter. The emperor simply sent word to the two messengers that he granted them a safe-conduct; as for those by whom they were sent, he should know how to deal with them. That is the modern version of Ranke. According to Sastrow there were two challenges and he gives them both. The first was brought to Landshut by a gentleman accompanied by a trumpeter. Charles refused to receive him. The second is that of Ingoldstadt, and is posterior by three weeks to the other. It was presented on September 2. "This missive," adds Sastrow, "has been the cause of all the great ills that have befallen Germany, and I verily believe that wishing to chastise the German nation for her sins, God allowed it to be written with infernal ink. Neither Sleidan nor Beuter mentions it; it seems to me that there was an attempt to garble or altogether to suppress it."--Translator.

Footnote 46: Sastrow had no easy task for his diplomatic beginnings: Charles V had gained the crushing victory of Mühlberg over the German Protestants on April 24, 1547; the League of Schmalkalden had ceased to exist; its chiefs, the Elector Johannes-Friedrich of Sachsen and the Landgrave of Hesse, Philip the Magnanimous, were both prisoners. Though they were members of that league since 1536, the Dukes of Pomerania had, it is true, observed a neutral attitude during the latter years; nevertheless, the emperor's resentment inspired them, not without reason, with great fear. Preparations for defence commenced everywhere; Greifswald and Stralsund strengthened and increased their fortifications. Finally, the dukes obtained their pardon, in consideration of humiliating excuses, the acceptance of the Interim, and the payment of a large contribution, towards which Stralsund contributed 10,000 florins.--Translator.

Footnote 47: The Duke Frederick III von Liegnitz in Silesia, born in 1520, had become reigning duke in 1547. His ill-regulated conduct caused him to be called "the Extravagant." Finally, the Emperor ordered him to be deposed. Frederick III, who died in 1570, spent the last six years of his life dependent upon private charity at the castle of Liegnitz. Heindrich XI, his son and successor, followed his example in every respect.

Far distant from Silesia, in a mountainous region of Switzerland, there lived at that period another offshoot of an illustrious princely house, namely, Count Michael de Gruyère, who, the last of his race, was soon compelled to abandon to his creditors even the manor of his ancestors By a curious coincidence the two incorrigible spendthrifts met at the French court and became, it appears intimately acquainted, for the noble Silesian paid a visit to the French noble in 1551 at his seat at Devonne, near Geneva. It would be impossible to conceive a better matched couple. Michael, finding his guest to be suffering from fever caused by a fall from his horse at Lyons, took him to the Castle of Gruyère. True to his custom, Frederick soon asked for a loan, and obtained a big sum which the count himself had borrowed.

When it came to repayment they fell out; there was a lawsuit at Friburg, and the Duke, ordered to refund, gave some jewels as security, which, after all, were not redeemed. A letter from the Countess de Gruyère says, in fact, that Count Michael, holding several precious stones of great beauty, having belonged to the Duke von Liegnitz, has pledged part of them with the lords of Lucerne and another part with various people of Friburg. An innkeeper of that town with whom the prince had lodged put a distraint on certain jewels and other objects. Frederick succeeded in leaving the country, as usual, without paying.--Translator.

Footnote 48: Those who refused to Charles V the title of Emperor Called him Charles of Ghent.--Translator.

Footnote 49: Lazarus von Schwendi was born in 1525. After a brilliant university career at Basle and Strasburg, he entered the service of Charles V, who employed him both in warfare and in diplomatic negotiations. It was he who was ordered to arrest, at Wissemburg, Sebastian Vogelsberg, who, in spite of the Emperor's prohibition, had taken service with France, and was relentlessly executed as an example to Schaerlin and other Protestant captains who had taken refuge at the court of the king. Schwendi became a member of the Imperial Council for German Affairs. He went through all the campaigns in Germany, the Low Countries and Hungary. In 1564 he was appointed general-in-chief against the Turks. He retired to Alsace, and from it in order for thee to copy it clearly, for I have my doubts about the word *'Braunfisch'* (if I have read aright), and even stronger doubts with regard to the English and Spanish. I shall feel obliged by thy writing me those names more distinctly and to send them to me at the Easter vacation by one of the many merchants from Basle who pass through Spires on their return from the fair. Meanwhile, I wish thee good health! Basle, Wednesday after *Riminiscere* (the second Sunday in Lent)." The printer of the *Cosmographie* was H. Petri. Artopaeus points out the theologian Peter Becker as the author of the description of Pomerania largely consulted by Münster.--Translator.

Footnote 63: A very ancient custom obliged the Ammeister, or first magistrate of Strasburg, regularly to take his two meals per day during his year of office at the expense of the city, at "The Lantern," unless he preferred the stewpans patronized by his own tribe. The table was open to every one willing to pay the fixed price. "*Ad istum prandium omnibus et incolis et peregrinis pro certo pretio accedere licet,*" says the *Itinerarium Germaniae* of Hentzer, who visited Strasburg in 1599. Seven years later a gentleman from the March mentions also in his journal the *Ammeisterstube* (the *Ammeister's* room), where the *Ammeister* and two *Stadmeister* take their daily meals. Everybody is free to go in and to be served by paying. Each tribe (set) has its particular stewpan. What becomes of the *Ammeister's* usual haunt when the *Ammeister* is a member of that particular tribe? Nevertheless, the establishment mostly patronized is that of the Grain Market, which is conveniently situated. Among other strictly observed formalities are the blessing and the grace, announced by the rapping with a wand, and the proceedings are always opened by a reminder of the submission due to the authorities. The custom no doubt had its origin in the provisions for public order which induced the magistrates of Geneva to close all the taverns in 1546. They were replaced by five so-called abbeys, each having at its head one of the four syndics or their lieutenant; but after a few weeks, this reform, the idea of which had been brought, perhaps, from Strasburg by Calvin had to be abandoned. The *Ammeister* for 1570 being too feeble to eat twice a day at the expense of the city, the supper was suppressed. It would appear, however, that the magistrates "forgot themselves" at table, for the Council of Fifteen made an order in 1585 obliging the *Ammeister* to be at the Town Hall at one o'clock. "The magistrates too often only appeared at the Senate and at the chancellerie between three and four o'clock," says a chronicler. Apparently the order did not remedy the evil, as in 1627 it was decided to do away with the ancient institution.--Translator.

Footnote 64: An allusion to the thief whose execution Sastrow saw in Rome.--Translator.

Footnote 65: The bishopric of Cammin had been secularized; the importance of the debate bore wholly upon the revenues.--Translator.

Footnote 66: This son, who became a doctor of law and who died in 1593 without issue, had a very hasty temper. On one occasion he drew his sword at a sitting of the Council whither his father had sent him to present a document. On another occasion he shook the hall by violently striking the magisterial bench with his fist, while his father kept saying: "Gently, Johannes, gently."--Translator.

Footnote 67: It is to his two daughters Catherine and Amnistia, and to his two sons-in-law Heinrich Gottschalk and Jacob Clerike, and to their children, that Sastrow has dedicated his *Memoirs*, his son being already dead.--Translator.